Energy Astrology

Volume 1 - Introduction to Energy Astrology

Brian Parsons

Samarpan Alchemy Publications

Energy Astrology – Volume 1: Introduction to Energy Astrology
© January 2020, Brian D. Parsons

ISBN 978-1-907167-75-1

Published by:

Samarpan Alchemy Publishing
Bradninch
Exeter
EX5 4QZ
United Kingdom

Email: info@audio-meditation.com
Web: www.audio-meditation.com
www.energy-astrology.com

To the rest of my Sun conjunct Pluto + Uranus tribe... still time to deliver the messages we all brought with us to Planet Earth to help make a difference... so keep the faith, guys. And to **Sue Keeping**, who passed over just before this book was published, but who had supported and encouraged the development of **Energy Astrology** for many years. You truly were an Earth Angel.

Medical & Psychiatric Disclaimer:

The information contained in this book is aimed at resolving emotional, mental and spiritual issues, and is not intended to directly resolve physical and/or medical complaints and illnesses.

In all such cases, individuals are strongly advised to consult with a qualified medical practitioner about their physical condition.

If an individual is suffering from severe emotional and/or mental conditions, it is also strongly advised that they consult a qualified medical practitioner or other qualified mental health specialists.

Individuals should only use the information contained in this book in accordance with the laws and regulations of their country of residence.

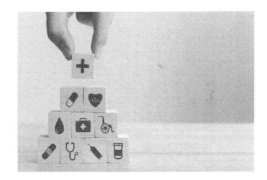

Real-Life Case Studies
& Stories:

Many of the examples, case studies and stories contained in this book are drawn from real-life.

However:

Wherever possible, permission for their inclusion has been obtained.

And personal details have always been changed to ensure that the privacy and anonymity of all those individuals is secured and maintained, without changing the meaning of the story itself.

Quotations:

*Read the book of your life which has
been given to you.*

Rumi (translated by Coleman Banks)

*Astrology cannot become a science yet... But the possibilities are
there; if people work, the possibilities are there. Because we are
linked with everything. That much in it is true, that everything is
interlinked, that existence is interdependent, that even if a leaf or
grass is destroyed then something in the stars is destroyed. It is a totally joined network. It is like a spider's web, you touch one thread
at one place and the whole web vibrates. It is just like that. But it has
to be discovered.*

Osho - LET GO!

*All gods send their gifts of love upon this earth, without which it
would cease to exist. My faith teaches me more clearly perhaps,
then yours, that life does not end with death, and therefore that love
being life's soul must endure for all eternity.*

Anana, Chief Scribe and companion to Pharoh Jentile Leti II (about
1320 BC)

From A.T. Mann - The Divine Life

Vibrations can be understood as both cause and as effect. Vibration causes movement, rotation, circulation; but on the other hand it is the rotation of the planets and the circulation of the blood which causes vibration. Thus the cause as well as the effect of all that exists is vibration... It is the same force which sets everything in motion on the physical plane, and this continues on all other planes of existence, setting them all in motion. It also explains to us that it is vibration, a certain degree of vibration which brings to the earth the things of the inner world that is perceived though not seen; and a change of vibration takes away the things that are seen into the unseen world.

* * * * *

The soul is light, the mind is light, and the body is light - light of different grades; and it is this relation which connects man with the planets and stars.

Hazrat Inayat Khan - The Sufi Message of Hazrat Inayat Khan - Volume XI - Philosophy, Psychology, Mysticism, Aphorisms

Table of Contents:

PART ONE: WHAT IS ENERGY ASTROLOGY?

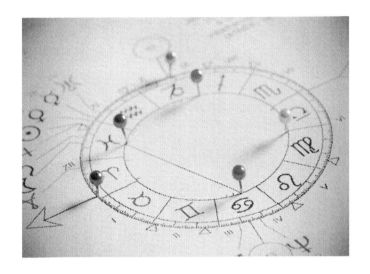

Chapter 1-1: Energy Astrology - Series Introduction

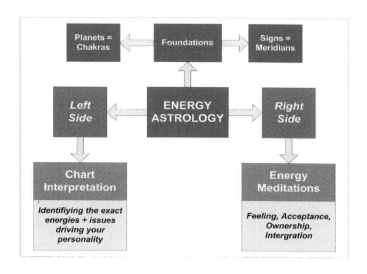

This is the first book in a series on **Energy Astrology**.

This book is an Introduction to **Energy Astrology** and outlines and explores the foundations of this unique approach to Astrology.

However, there are many sides to **Energy Astrology**... as the above image shows... and we shall be exploring that potential as well... **Energy Astrology** as a way of interpreting an Astrological Chart... and also a system of practical self-development.

Chapter 1-2: What Is Energy Astrology?

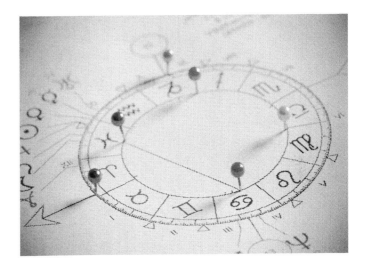

Note: This Chapter is based on a Facebook post which went viral back in 2015, and was shared across social media over 3100 times, and reached 296,000 people.

I am often asked these 3 questions:

- What is **Energy Astrology**?
- How does it work?
- What can it offer me?

Which are all pretty reasonable questions to ask when you are considering investing time and money in a new personal development course, system, and/or book.

I have found the best way to answer these 3 questions is to explain the process which initially brought **Energy Astrology** into existence, a process which has taken nearly 20 years to complete (and is probably not complete even now, but is still ongoing, there are probably lots still to learn and explore... always is).

The story starts with my original training as a crystal therapy practitioner back in the 1990s, and my subsequent research into the subtle anatomy of the Human Body – the Chakras and Nadis of the Yoga and Ayurvedic systems, and the Meridians, Vessels and Tan Tiens of the Chinese system.

What has always fascinated me is that there are two main energy systems within the Human Body, apparently separate, and yet overlapping, and in some kind of resonance with each other.

The Chakra System and the Meridian System.

(Actually, there is more than two, but that's for another time, for the moment. let's stick with these two.)

Plus, I have always had a deep feeling that the Meridian system was important, and it could do a lot more than suggested in the Meridian literature currently available in the West.

This research led me to develop a number of crystal therapy techniques which work with the different areas and components of these subtle energy anatomical structures, the Chakras and the Meridians.

The next step on from this was the realization that there was a link between the Chakras and the Astrological Planets.

Now, many spiritual and healing traditions have believed, or still believe, there is a direct relationship between the Planets and the Chakras, between *the down & in here* and *the up & out there*.

For example, in his book *Ayurvedic Astrology*, **David Frawley** explores the correspondence between the 7 main Chakras and the 7 Inner Planets within the context of Indian Astrology.[1]

Building upon this belief for there being a direct energetic relationship between the Planets and the Chakras, I worked out a list of correspondences between the 14 main Planets and point energies of the standard Astrological Chart and their Chakra equivalents, which is outlined in the following list:

- **The Sun** = Heart Chakra
- **The Moon** = Sacral Chakra
- **Mercury** = Hands / Feet Chakras
- **Venus** = Throat Chakra
- **Mars** = Solar Plexus Chakra
- **Jupiter** = Base Chakra
- **Saturn** = Elbows / Knee Chakras
- **Chiron** = Thymus Chakra
- **Uranus** = Brow Chakra
- **Neptune** = Crown Chakra
- **Pluto** = Soma Chakra
- **IC / MC** = Bottom / Top of Sushumna Nadi
- **North Mode/South Node** = Upper / Lower Connection between Ida & Pingala

Don't worry if you're not sure what some of the above are, I will explain it all later on in this book.

---

1   Ayurvedic Astrology doesn't include any of the relatively newly discovered Planets... such as **Uranus**, **Neptune**, or **Pluto**. Basically, if it wasn't mentioned in the Ayurvedic Astrology literature, several thousand years ago, then for traditional Ayurvedic Astrologers now, it just doesn't exist or isn't considered to be important.

For now, it is important to recognize that this table does not completely tally with many other spiritual and healing systems which define the correspondences between the Planets and the Chakras.

In fact, with the exception of **The Sun**, **The Moon**, and **Mars**, these other systems often do not agree among themselves on which Planet corresponds to which Chakra.

However, my experience of working with the above Planet and Chakra correspondences, and from the experience of other **Energy Astrology** students, it has been found that:

- No one system is ever going to hold the complete picture of a Chakra's energy, as the energy is too vast and multi-dimensional for that. What is important is the question "*Does this particular Planet/Chakra correspondence work for you, does it provide you with new insights and healing?*"

- Human Consciousness and potential is constantly changing and evolving over time, and as it does so, new resonances and correspondences between the Planets and the Chakras surface, and so the Planets may indeed start to be experienced and felt in different Chakras. Basically, what worked 5,000 years ago may no longer work now, because Human Consciousness is always evolving, and the Age of Aquarius is just around the corner. So the system of Energy Astrology outlined in this book is what is working *now*.

- The Nadis – the energy lines which flow between and through the Chakras and so create them through their vibrations – are of primary importance; and in **Energy Astrology** each energy transmission for a Chakra is really the energy transmission for the 12 major Nadis which create that Chakra, which creates as complete an energetic set-up for that Chakra as it is possible to achieve.[2]

- Because each Chakra is created by the Nadis which flow through it, this means that the energy flow along the Nadis, and so between the Chakras, corresponds to the various Planetary aspects found on any Astrological Chart.

It is also possible to map not just the Planetary energies on to the Human subtle anatomy, but also the various additional energy points found on an Astrological Chart, such as the **IC/MC** axis, which relates to the Sushumna channel, and the **North Node/South Node** axis, which relates to the Ida / Lunar and Pingala / Solar Nadis.

After the establishment of a table of correspondences between the Planets and Chakras, the next stage in the development of Energy Astrology was the discovery of the life work of **Reinhold Ebertin** (1901 – 1988), a German Physician and Astrologer who was very influential in the field of Medical Astrology and is considered to be the founder of modern **Cosmobiology**. In his book *The Combination of Stellar Influences*, **Ebertin** lists the following correspondences between the 12 Meridians and the 12 Astrological Signs, outlined in the list below:

- Kidney Meridian = **Aries**
- Triple Warmer Meridian = **Taurus**
- Liver Meridian = **Gemini**
- Stomach Meridian = **Cancer**
- Heart Meridian = **Leo**
- Large Intestine Meridian = **Virgo**
- Heart Protector Meridian = **Libra**
- Bladder Meridian = **Scorpio**

2   The definition of a Chakra is where 3 or more Nadis cross, thus creating a vortex of energy. There are said to be 72,000 Nadis in our energy anatomy, although some put this number higher... so that means there are many places where Nadis crossover and Chakras form.

- Spleen Meridian = **Sagittarius**
- Gallbladder Meridian = **Capricorn**
- Lung Meridian = **Aquarius**
- Small Intestine Meridian = **Pisces**

When I used **Ebertin's** list and cross-referenced the meaning of Astrological Signs against the meaning for its corresponding Meridian in the Chinese energy system, and then later in different Kinesiology systems, I found a deep and remarkable similarity and resonance between them all.

For example:

- One of the challenges for **Libra** is to find balance in relationships, so that you can be supportive for others without compromising your own sense of self, and not allow people to walk all over you. One of the functions of the **Heart Protector Meridian** in the Chinese energy system is to set appropriate boundaries between yourself and others, so that you only lower your defenses for people you want to be intimate with, but have strong boundaries around people who might want to abuse or control you.

- In the Chinese energy system, the **Gallbladder Meridian** is seen as the decision-maker and is linked to our ability to take decisive action and be courageous, which is another way of saying we follow through once a decision is made. In Astrology, **Capricorn** is often portrayed as being the most decisive and ambitious of the Astrological Signs and is known for its strong mental focus.

- The Astrological Sign of **Aries** is known as the pioneer and the adventurer and is seen as the individual who needs to face and overcome life's challenges. In the Chinese energy system, the **Kidneys** are seen as the container for the life-force of the body, and the source of our willpower, our ability for overcome life's challenges, the energy which propels us forward.

- In the Chinese energy system, the **Small Intestine Meridian**
  is linked to truth and our ability to discern truth from untruth.
  Pisces, when well balanced, is known for its ability to walk the
  fine line between reality and fantasy, which is another way of
  describing truth and untruth.

I could go on, but that is enough for now... and also, the
correspondences between the Planets and Chakras also make
similar sense... and we will be going into each Astrological Sign and
Meridian correspondence in more detail later in this book.

Basically, I have found **Ebertin's** list of correspondences between
the Astrological Signs and Meridians does indeed work and so
increases our understanding of both the Meridian system and the
Astrological system. And most importantly... *it helps people make
sense of their lives... and also gives them practical and effective
tools to help them live up to their higher nature, and to achieve
their life potential.*

The whole of Energy Astrology is built upon this insight, and
practical application.

Because as **Gautama the Buddha** used to say... *Truth is that which
works.*

There is not much point in having the most sophisticated and
elaborate theory ever... if it cannot help people.

You see.. establishing the link between the 12 Meridians and the 12
Astrological Signs meant that the crystal techniques which I had
found, and which were helpful for a particular Meridian or Chakra
could also be used when working with a problematic or loaded Sign
within an individual's natal chart.

Because there was... and is... a definite tie in... and so therefore a map to show where, and how, beneficial and supportive energies can be applied for each individual, through an understanding of their Astrological natal chart.

But there was still the question of the 12 Houses... did the 12 Houses also have an energetic equivalent in our Human subtle anatomy?

I reasoned that if the Houses did have an energetic counterpart in the Human subtle anatomy, then it would most likely lie within the Meridian system itself, for the 12 Houses are closely associated with the 12 Astrological Signs, which as we have seen above are linked to the 12 Meridians.

Well... I discovered that there is a subtle web of 144 energy lines which connect all of the 12 Meridians to each other (and which even connects a Meridian to itself).

Each of these 144 energy lines corresponds to one of the 144 possible Astrological Signs / Houses combinations which exist on a natal chart – i.e. Aries in the 1st House, or Capricorn in the 7th House, or Pisces in the 11th House.

It is interesting to note that in the Chinese system, there are often references to a fine web of energy which lies *below* the level of the Meridians, and which connects them all. I believe this is this energy web which ties the House system into an individual's subtle anatomy.

And the Angles between Planets in a natal chart, all those squares, and trines, and sextiles, inconjuncts and conjunctions, they also have a unique vibration... which can also be captured, isolated vibrationally, and replicated...

Because as Kashmiri Shivaism states... *everything is vibration.*

So, at this point in the story of the development of **Energy Astrology**, I had developed a wide range of crystal therapy techniques to help an individual work with:

- Planets
- Signs
- Houses
- Aspects
- IC/MC
- Nodal Axis

The final breakthrough moment came for **Energy Astrology** shortly after the birth of **Audio Essences** (a technology to record and transmit subtle vibrations in digital format... more about this in Chapter 1-5).

This was the moment when I realized that it was not only possible to create and capture a vibration relating to a Planet... or an Astrological Sign.

But that it was also possible to **combine** and **merge** all these various different vibrations in a single **Audio Essence**.

Creating a single vibration which captured the energy of a particular Planet in Sign.

That's when I realized that it was possible to transmit:

- Sun in Aries in 7th House
- Jupiter in Cancer in 12th House
- Mars and Saturn in any aspect
- North Node in Gemini in 7th House and South Node in Sagittarius in 1st House
- IC in Taurus and the MC in Scorpio

Or any other combination of Planet, Sign or Houses energies to be found in an individual's Astrological natal chart... or in any chart,... or any transit... past, present or future.

When I realized that, I also realized that I had accidentally stumbled upon a new way of working with an Astrological chart for personal development and inner growth, and this is what I call **Energy Astrology**.

But, as we shall explore more in Chapter 1-3... there are two sides to **Energy Astrology**:

- **One**... A different way to understand and interpret an Astrological chart
- **Two**... A way to explore an Astrological chart on a *feeling* and *energy* level

Now I know... I know... that is a huge claim to make... a monumental claim in fact.

But, first, I have to admit ... I only got here by standing on the shoulders of the Giants who came before me.

And anything I claim... just try it out for yourself... see if I am right about any of this.

Like **Gautama the Buddha** said... *Truth is that which works...*

And I have set-up this book... and the online resources which go with this book, and support it...

I have set it all up so that people can try **Energy Astrology** on for size, see if it holds any truth for them, before they decide to commit, if they want, before they decide to dive in further.

How the Planets influence people on Earth is still unclear, but from the work I have done, it would appear that the Planet, Sign and

House pattern at the moment of our birth is literally imprinted or burnt on to our subtle anatomy – through the relationship and resonance between the Chakras and certain Meridians – just in the same way as a music track can be burnt on to a blank CD.

We literally carry the moment of our birth around with us, locked into our subtle anatomy, in the way in which our Chakras and Meridians relate to one another.

For example, someone with:

- **Sun in Aries**... for that individual, there is a locked-in resonance between their Heart Chakra and Kidney Meridian.

- **Saturn in Taurus**... for that individual, there is a locked-in resonance between their Elbow-Knee Chakras and Triple Warmer Meridian.

- **Neptune in Capricorn**... for that individual, there is a locked-in resonance between their Crown Chakra and Gallbladder Merdian.

- **South Node in Pisces**... for that individual, there is a locked-in resonance between the point where the Sushumna, Ida and Pingala Nadis meet at our Base, and with our Small Intestine Meridian.

From that point onwards, after our moment of birth, it is not that we cannot experience other Planetary energies, for our Chakras, Nadis and Meridians are like antenna continually awake to the ever-changing energy broadcasts around us... from the Celestial sky above us.

But the Planets and Signs which were directly experienced at our moment of birth, and imprinted on to our Chakras and Meridians, are where we are overly sensitive, and the energy does not flow as easily through them as our other energy channels, and so our personality starts to crystallize and form around these areas.

One way to think of it... a coral reef... especially a coral reef which forms around a sunken ship.

As soon as the ship hits the bottom of the sea, fish come to live in it... finding safety and shelter... shellfish attach themselves to the hull.

And in a short while, the ship itself becomes buried under a mass of sea creatures... the ship literally comes alive.

In a funny way, our personality self is a bit like this.

We're what happens when Consciousness attaches itself to our Astrological natal chart, and then our personality starts to form around that.

Now, it is a popular belief that the Astrological natal chart, the chart calculated using the date, time and location of our birth, is the closest thing we will ever have to a User Manual for our life, our personality and our higher purpose.... a Manual written specifically for us.

Each of the Planets is said to represent a specific type of energy, and where each Planet is placed in our individual natal chart shows how and where that energy functions in our life (... or is maybe stuck). An Astrological chart can, therefore, show and guide us to a better and deeper understanding of our strengths and our weaknesses, our potential and our problem areas.

Because each Planet is in a different Sign and House, depending on the date, time and location of birth, so the energies which are expressed through each natal chart will be different for each individual.

For example, assertiveness *will* be different for each of us, the ability to nurture ourselves and feel self-worth *will* be different, the appreciation of beauty *will* be different, and the ability to get our needs met *will* also be different for each of us, all dependent on where a particular Planet lies in our Astrological Chart.

The challenge for an individual, therefore, is to identify exactly how these energies are different, and learn to appreciate this uniqueness, within themselves, so that it starts to work for them, and not against them.

And sometimes, getting a handle on the uniqueness of our own energy, can be the work of a lifetime (because the outer Planets... Jupiter, Saturn, Chiron, Uranus, Neptune and Pluto... move slowly... and so life lessons are exactly that... they take a lifetime to unfold).

And if that is your intention, to maximise your inner growth during your lifetime, then having a good map and User Manual can cut years, or even decades, off your journey time.

To understand an Astrological chart normally requires years of work and study, at the end of which a person may have a good intellectual knowledge of their Planetary energies, but lack the direct connection and experience with those individual energies which can lead to the mastery and fulfilment of their life.

Because that is one of the ironies of a subject like Astrology.

Just because someone understands their own natal chart, doesn't automatically make them a true master of its energies. A mental understanding does not always lead to a transformational breakthrough, especially not if feelings and emotions are still being suppressed and not accepted.

To do all that you need to become more conscious of yourself, you need to step into the energy pattern of your own birth moment, you need to get engaged on all levels of your Earth presence, and not just the thinking / mental level.

It's a bit like someone who has read 1000 books on sailing, considers themselves to be an expert on the subject, but who has never stepped in a boat, let alone set sail or gone to sea.

Intellectual knowledge isn't awlays a good guide to practical skills and experience and doesn't always translate well into that mysterious thing called *wisdom*.

And that is, to my mind, the true beauty of **Energy Astrology**...

Because it has two sides.

One side to help you understand your Astrological chart, in a simple and straightforward way.

And the other, to help you work with the energies of your Astrological Chart, in a simple, direct and straightforward way.

With **Energy Astrology**, it is now possible to explain... work with... even transmit to an individual the exact energies found within their individual Astrological chart, the exact transmissions for each Planet in its specific Sign and in its specific House.

It is possible to transmit the complete energies which form an Astrological House within a natal chart, and also the different energies which create a particular Planetary aspect (i.e. trines, squares, sextiles... even inconjuncts).

The benefit this brings to an individual is that they are able to directly and easily experience and *feel* for themselves how the energy of their different Planets set-up in their psyche, both the energies which they feel at ease with and also those energies which they may find harder to acknowledge and own... even the ones they are actively on the run from.

Once an individual can feel and accept a Planetary energy, this can open a space for a shift in many areas of their life – relationships, abundance, health, work, spiritual growth, and creativity.

On a practical **Energy Astrology** weekend course, an individual is able to experience these Planetary energies even if they have no previous knowledge of Astrology, for the energy transmissions in the course work on a level above and beyond the rational mind. The only real skill which is required is the ability to relax and feel the energy.

And, hopefully, the way I am planning to put **Energy Astrology** out into the online world will allow many more people... all around the world... to experience that... and so gain the many positive benefits of this unique approach to Astrology... one which is based on... energy.

* * * * * * * * *

FEELING, ACCEPTANCE, OWNERSHIP AND INTEGRATION

There is a law of the human psyche known as *projection* that states that when an individual does not acknowledge and own an energy within themselves, that energy is projected outwards and manifests in some area of their life, usually in the form of challenging situations or recurring conflict, until that person is able to acknowledge and integrate those energies within their own psyche consciously.

Basically, projection is a form of *hiding*... removing the parts of ourselves that we are afraid will make us unattractive, or unwanted, in our eyes, the eyes of other people, or our culture or society.

But, fundamentally, projection is fueled by the self-belief that there is something wrong with you, and you decide to hide it.

Dialing down our energy presence, making sure that we are not seen for all the wrong reasons.

But the thing is, we can never truly disown or escape our own energy, it just finds another way to come back at us, another way to work its way back into our Conscious attention.

This is why individuals tend to attract partners and relationships, which reflect back to them those shadow parts of themselves which they do not wish to face. And you know that you have finally learned the lesson when the next partner you attract is completely different from all the others.

Or your new job is better and different from all the dead-end jobs you have had before.

Basically, you have finally broken the pattern, you have brought a part of yourself... long hiding... back into the light and re-integrated it into your psyche, which is why you are now able to attract a different type of person into your life, or job, career, vocation....

An Astrological natal chart is, therefore, a powerful tool to help an individual understand the archetypal forces which drive their personality and identify those Planets they own and are comfortable with.

And also those Planets they are actively disowning, hiding from within, and so projecting out to the world, and then reflected back to them through other people and situations.

However, **Energy Astrology** takes this self-healing process a stage further, and also helps to speed up this process (to a certain extent), even without the need for convenient transits (although they do help focus the energy for us, bringing back to consciousness whatever we are trying to hide from).

Normally, an individual has to wait for situations and circumstances to activate a Planetary Archetype before they can discover if it is one which they own or disown (otherwise known as the right transits).

However, using the **Energy Astrology** approach, an individual can have all their primary Planetary Archetypes activated in sequence, thus allowing them to feel these distinctive energies and also observe their personality reactions to these energies.

Or they can just work on the one they feel most drawn to... or which has been identified through dowsing, muscle testing, plain old intuition, or self-observation.

If they love the energies and are relaxed around them, this is a good sign that there is no projection going on.

However, if they are squirming in their seat, and can't wait for it all to be over, this is a definite sign that something is miswired in their psyche, and misplacing or projection is occurring somewhere.

So, it's just a matter of activating the right Chakra and Meridian energy association, and that particular energy starts to flow back into your Consciousness and waiting to see how that person will react.

This means, in a short space of time, an individual can quickly define which Planetary energies they are comfortable with, and which Planetary energies they are most likely to be projecting outwards and so need to work on to own and re-claim.

Because, in life, the more integrated we are, the more successful and happy we are too. That seems to be one of the Laws of our shared Universe.

To help re-claim these projections, the **Energy Astrology** approach is structured around a four-step process to create an internal space within the psyche from which individuals can start to own their Planet + Sign / Charka + Meridian energies.

First, the individual allows themselves to **FEEL** the Planetary energies manifesting through their Charkas and Meridians.

OK, initially they may not like the energy, it may make them feel very uncomfortable... but at least they are allowing themselves to bring it into Consciousness... to **FEEL** it.

Because when you can **FEEL** it... you are not hiding from it... you are not running from it... and you are not projecting it.

Then over time, they learn to **ACCEPT** the energy.

OK... this is the stage where people start thinking... "*OK, I may not be 100% comfortable with this energy... but at least I can now see that it is me... that this is a part of me...*"

And this is an important stage in the alchemical process of self-transformation... where you are no longer pushing the energy away... and you are starting to identify with it... and allow it to rest within your Consciousness.

Which eventually leads to an **OWNERSHIP** of the energy, the ability to identify with that energy 100%.

And with **OWNERSHIP** comes the ability to see the positives in that energy... the way you can use it for good in your life... the benefits that it starts to bring you.

You start to see the energy in a much more well-rounded way.

And then finally, the energy is so well **INTEGRATED** in your psyche, that you no longer notice that you ever had a problem with it.

As the Taoist mystic, **Chung Tzu** used to say... "*When the shoe fits... you feel so at ease... that you forget all about wearing shoes...*"

The equation for the whole of **Energy Astrology** is, therefore:

- **Feeling** leads to **Acceptance**
- **Acceptance** leads to **Ownership**
- **Ownership** leads to **Integration**

Once an individual can feel and accept a Planetary energy, this can open a space for a shift in many areas of their life – relationships, abundance, health, work, spiritual growth, and creativity.

But the process has to and can only start with a feeling, with re-connecting with the energies.

One of the massive truths of our Universe, and also of being Human, is if you don't want to feel, if you are avoiding re-connecting with elements of your psyche, you cannot work with them, and self-transformation is just not possible.

Unfortunately, if someone has come to associate an energy as uncomfortable, unwelcome, even painful, for some reason, usually a belief they have inherited from their family, then they either project it out on to other people, or they push it deep down into their Unconscious Mind, and try to forget all about it.

But either of these two approaches means they have disconnected from that energy.

And how can you ever feel that which you have unplugged from your Conscious Mind.

It's a bit like taking your phone number out of the listing in the telephone directory and then sitting by the phone, waiting for it to ring.

When people disconnect from a specific feeling, they become trapped, because they cannot truly banish something like that, it always remains inside, somewhere, trying to get out, at some level of their psyche.

Psychic energy never goes away, it cannot be destroyed, even though we try very hard,

And so they continue to suffer (often no longer knowing why, because the memories and reasons have been buried so deep that they no longer remember, especially if the pain was suffered in early childhood).

And if they can no longer feel these disconnected energies, they cannot start the process of transforming them.

That's the condition and issue for so many people around our Planet.

It is perhaps true to say that Western culture, with all its anti-depressants, pain-killers, and physical, mental and emotional distractions, is not very good at dealing with and transforming inner pain, re-connecting with long, long buried feelings.

Hence, many people are totally unable to heal themselves nor able to allow others to help them heal either.

Because true inner healing can only occur when someone allows themselves to feel their inner world, even if it is initially painful to do so...

Because as the spiritual teacher and writer **David R Hawkins** has written many times... when you can observe the emotional pain... neutrally... without feeding it... then it slowly starts to dissipate... and eventually you are free of it.

However, as the Ancient Alchemists knew... if the pain is great... then it needs to be released in manageable stages... otherwise, it will explode from the Unconscious Mind like a volcanic eruption and overwhelm the Conscious Mind. That way potential madness lies. So sometimes these things need to be done slowly and carefully and in a stable way... no matter how fast our ego wants to go.

And that is exactly what **Energy Astrology** is designed to allow you to do.

* * * * * * * * *

NURTURE Vs NATURE

One of the great things about **Energy Astrology** is... that it helps provide a new and interesting angle on the whole Nature vs Nurture debate.

And the forces which create and shape an individual personality... a person's character.

Because the eternal question is...

Which is more important...

That which is programmed into us at birth, that which we bring with us?

Or that which we take on, we inherit from our parents, our family, our culture, our society?

That debate has been raging for centuries... even millennia.

But it has heated up, somewhat, in recent years, since the discovery of DNA.

So who exactly are we?

Are we more Nurture or more Nature?

Here is the **Energy Astrology** take on it.

Imagine a man... let's call him Fred... who was born at the moment of time when there were 4 Planets in **Sagittarius**.

Say... **Venus in Sagittarius, Sun in Sagittarius, Mercury in Sagittarius**, and **Mars in Sagittarius**... which is a lot of Sagittarius...

Now, from the perspective of **Energy Astrology**... as we have seen... there is a link between one of the 12 Astrological Signs, and one of the 12 Meridians... in this case.

Sagittarius = Spleen meridian

And the +ve for the Spleen meridian = Faith in Future... and the -ve = Worry & Anxiety.

Now to quote the traditional definition from TCM (Traditional Chinese Medicine)... when energy flows easily and well along a Meridian then it manifests the positive quality associated with that Meridian (in this case, Faith and Confidence)...

But if the flow is blocked for any reason, then the Meridian manifests the negative quality (in this case, Worry and Anxiety).

You see... fundamentally, it's all about the flow chi along the Meridian.

Now, if you imagine that a Meridian is like a garden hosepipe, and 4 people are standing on it, putting all of their weight on the hosepipe... what is going to happen?

Easy... the flow becomes blocked.

Which means?

Flow is not possible.

And it's kind of the same with all Meridians and Astrological Signs.

And the people standing on the hosepipe?

They're the Planets... all heavy, exerting a downward force, blocking the flow...

... Yes, you got it... and the Meridian starts to express its negative side... in this case, for **Sagittarius**/Spleen... Worry and Anxiety.

When you have 4 planets in **Sagittarius**, like Fred, (or any planet in any sign for that matter)... they are all going to press down on the Meridian they are associated with, blocking the flow of chi... and obviously, the more Planets, the greater the pressing / blocking force.

That's why we can say someone is very **Sagittarius**... or **Libran**... or **Gemini**... because they have so many Planets in that Sign... so much weight pressing down on that particular Meridian... that they are no choice but to express the positive or negative energies associated with that Sign or Meridian...

In this case, **Venus**, **Mercury**, **The Sun** and **Mars**... all in

Sagittarius... all pressing down on the Spleen Meridian... this causes its default setting to shift from the positive expression (i.e. Faith and Confidence)... towards the negative (i.e. Worry and Anxiety).

And that is basically how the Up There... gets programmed into our subtle energy field... into who we are Down Here.

But... fortunately... there is also Nurture, which can redress the balance to a point... the family we are born into, and who raise us... the culture and society which surrounds us... and so influences us from birth.

In the **John Diamond** Kinesiology system, the +ve affirmation for the Spleen Meridian (and so Sagittarius) is:

"I have faith and confidence in my future. I am secure. My future is secure."

Saying this over in your mind strengthens the Spleen Meridian, increases the flow of chi, helps to counteract the pressure from those 4 Planets... and so pushes the expression of Spleen energy back into the positive... thus increasing an individual's self-expression and inner faith.

And the thing is... if a child with 4 Planets in **Sagittarius** is fortunate to be born into a confident and optimistic family and/or culture... where beliefs, similar to that affirmation above, are planted in their Unconscious mind from an early age... it's a bit like being given an energy vaccination at birth, which helps to counteract the weight of those 4 Planets... and all through their childhood they are encouraged towards adopting a more positive outlook on their life...

"Have faith and my life will flow positively."

However, if they were unfortunate, and were born into a family of total worriers and anxietyacs (yes, you're right, no such word, just made it up)... then you would not have been surrounded by such positive affirmations and beliefs in childhood... in fact, you would have been raised opposite... and so there would have been nothing *positive* planted in their Unconscious Mind, through their early childhood, to counter the heavyweight of those 4 Planets weighing down on their Spleen Meridian... pushing them towards their own cloud of internal Worry & Anxiety.

Nature versus Nurture... and the endless debate and discussion down through the centuries...

Well, for **Energy Astrology**... *it's both!*

Basically, that's how **Energy Astrology** views it... approaches it... and even if you are born with the most complex and challenging natal chart you could ever imagine... there is always something you can do to bring things into some kind of harmony... and positive expression.

Because really... it's all about learning to shift the weight of the Planets in your natal chart.

And home isn't something we make just *out there*, with bricks and mortar... true home is what we make *within us*, through learning how to handle our own personality... our own energies best.

If you don't ever learn to be at home in your own skin... the most beautiful palace in the world can feel cold and unwelcoming. But if you find your true centre... then the smallest hovel can feel like the warmest and welcoming spot on Earth.

It's all about being able to be happy wherever you find yourself... and that is totally dependent on being at home within yourself... *only always*.

... And this is the point where/when **Energy Astrology** really does come into its own.

Because with the right information... there is so much you can practically do to turn things towards the positive in your own energy anatomy.

- Positive Thoughts
- Affirmations
- Crystal Vibrations
- Audio Essences

So you are never as helpless as you might believe yourself to be... just a matter of plugging into the right kind of information... and then working on yourself... lifting your own vibration.

Finally... going back to Fred from earlier.

From the perspective of **Energy Astrology**, and with **Venus in Sagittarius**, **Sun in Sagittarius**, **Mercury in Sagittarius**, and **Mars in Sagittarius**... our everyman Fred would find that:

- His sense of self-worth (**Venus**) is undermined/reduced by worry and anxiety, strengthened/enhanced by faith and confidence.

- His ability to step outside his comfort zone and be a fully rounded individual (**The Sun**) is undermined/reduced by worry and anxiety, strengthened and enhanced by faith and confidence.

- His ability to communicate (**Mercury**) is undermined/reduced by worry and anxiety, strengthened and enhanced by faith and confidence.

- His ability to assert himself and understand/go for his own desires (**Mars**) is undermined/reduced by worry and anxiety, strengthened and enhanced by faith and confidence.

So these are the 4 areas which make Fred an **Uber-Sagittarian**... which either undermine him... or which support him as he goes through life.

As with all of us, it's Fred's choice how he decides to play it... how he decides to play the cards he has been dealt.

Which is the same truth for us all.

That's just a little taste of the effectiveness of **Energy Astrology** Chart Interpretation... how it can get to the root of what energies, thoughts and feelings a person needs to cultivate in their own life.

The rest of this book with be building upwards from this foundation...

Chapter 1-3: The Importance Of Standing On The Earth

In any Astrological system, **The Earth** is represented by the centre of the chart, although you will never find a glyph for **The Earth** on an Astrological chart.[1]

An Astrological chart is done from the perspective of a moment in time when, if you were standing on **The Earth**, looking up and out and around, you would see and find that the other Planets in the rest of our Solar System would be in those specific locations.

It is implied that **The Earth** is in the centre of it all (but when

---

1   OK... any Astrological system based on our **Earth**, that is.

something is implied, we also tend to forget the underlying truth).

And then the Planets move on, to form new patterns, a continual Celestial motion.

So Astrology is a lot like photography.

Each Astrological Chart is a photograph... taken... captured... of a specific moment in time.

Only with Astrology, it is possible to take photographs of past moments... as well as energy photographs of moments yet to come... next week... next month... next millennium.

Now, in traditional Astrology, **The Earth** itself doesn't get mentioned much, although as we will now argue, it is perhaps the most important of all the Planets in our Solar System.

It is the 3rd Rock from **The Sun**... upon which we all live... and stand.

Upon which all lives and dramas unfold.

It is our stage and life-support system.

Hitler, Mahatma Gandhi, Genghis Khan, and **Gautama the Buddha**... high or low... rich or poor... we were and are all born in the same neighbourhood of our Solar System.

On **Planet Earth**.

It gives us all we need to prosper and survive, live out our hopes and dreams, achieve our life-purpose (or not).

Be successful, make mistakes, hopefully learn from them, love and grow.

And a platform from which to look up and contemplate the vastness of the Universe around us.

As well as a platform from which to receive the blessings of the Universe all around us.

Without **The Earth**, we wouldn't be able to appreciate the Astrological pattern and energies from the other Planets, which are woven, and continually being re-woven, all around us, or stand any chance at integrating them, as we shall soon discover.

And ours is the only Planet (...that we know of...) that is a home for life, where life has become *established*... and certainly it is the only planet where life is in *abundance*.

Whales... Elephants... Penguins... Eagles... Lamas... Kangaroos... such a vast array of different species and lifeforms... plus one particular Ape-like creature that stood upright about 3 million years, and developed a high-performance Brain.

Which meant it could start looking up at the sky above and also start to consider its true place in the Universe, plus do some sophisticated mathematics and stellar mapping.

Abundant life, and across a billion years of Evolution, leading to self-awareness, intelligence and understanding.

Only on one Planet that we know of, in a seemingly infinite Universe.

OK, there might have been life on **Mars** a billion or so years ago, and it might remain now, hidden deep in the rocks, away from the harshness of the Martian surface, with all the protective Martian atmosphere having slipped away into outer space over time.

And yes, there may be life on **The Moons of Jupiter**, or swimming in the lakes of **Titan**, a different kind of life, probably.

But despite whatever the data is sent back from our future space probes, visiting the distant worlds of our Solar System in the future.

Earth is the only Planet where life exists for definite, and where life exists in abundance, across the whole surface of our Planet (even deserts and glaciers have a faint trace of living organisms, and there may be more life at the bottom of our oceans then the rest of our Solar System combined).

And we are most definitely the only lifeform which has reached up and out, and touched the rest of the Solar System to some degree, with our telescopes, satellites and space probes, and our fierce intelligence and curiosity.

We are also, most definitely, the only creature in this Solar System to have reached up, and touched the stars with our Mind.

So **Earth** is the only Planet where a creature can look up at the night sky and go...

Wow!

Earth is the Planet on which you live, on which you are born, or can be born.

And so it is the foundation... the stage... on which we all grow and learn our life-lessons.

Without the **Earth**, you would not be able to explore and experience, you would not be able to expand your individual Consciousness, because it supports all your needs.

And as a species, without **Planet Earth**, we just wouldn't exist.

And that is an important element to recognise and remember, it is only because **The Earth** exists, that we have a platform on which to expand and grow... and a stage upon which the other Planets in our Solar System can *energetically act.*

Think of **Earth** as the stage of a theatre, and each of the other Planets is like a different coloured stage light... blue, green, red or yellow... shining down.

And all of these Planetary lights are pointing towards the stage.

Are pointing towards **You**... standing on **The Earth stage**.

Without you, without the stage on which you stand, and all the other players who you are interacting with, during your lifetime, who are also under the influence of these Planetary energies.

Without all this... **the Earth stage**... what would be the point?

The different Planetary energies would just be radiating out into empty space, without ever finding anything, or anyone, to act upon, nothing to influence and change.

All the transits in the Solar System would be meaningless.

Who would be influenced?

It would be like the rays of the Sun... radiating out into space... never connecting with living skin... with a face... that could feel their warmth... that could appreciate the experience.

Without **The Earth** as a platform on which all the dramas of Mankind, and each individual member of the Human Race, can act out.

Without a Human having a frustrating day, there is no one else in the Solar System capable of appreciating **Mercury Retrograde**, or any other transit for that matter.

I mean, the Astrological energies of **Jupiter** probably influence Saturn... and vice versa... **Pluto** and **Neptune** probably play energy tag out on the edges of our Solar System, (and I don't care if it is now considered a dwarf planet, **Pluto** still packs one hell of an energy punch, and just because an Astronomer has re-classified it as a Dwarf Planet, doesn't mean they aren't going to be put through Hell from time to time, when their wife Cindy leaves them, and takes the kids to live with her mother in Florida).

But without the existence of some kind of lifeform on **Jupiter** or **Saturn**, then it is highly unlikely that much happens when the Astrological energies, radiating out from the various Planets across our Solar System, touch the other Planets within our Solar System.

Because without life, and some kind of fluid Consciousness to act on, it is highly unlikely that Astrological energies do much when they do reach and touch another Planet.

Plus... from another Planet, **The Earth** itself is just another Planet in the sky... while that world is the centre of every Astrological chart originating from its surface.

Whether **Jupiter** or **Saturn**, or any of the other planets means the same from the perspective of another world, and what **The Earth** represents... *who can say.*

We may need to wait until the first babies born on **Mars** to find out the answer to that question...

Or on **Europa**... or **Titan**.

But what we can say.

Humans are born on **The Earth** to learn their life-lessons, and to expand their individual Consciousness, that's the best reason anyone has ever come up with... although different religions and spiritual traditions cloak it in a slightly different language.

And while we are here, the Astrological energies from the other Planets act upon us, while we exist on **The Earth**.

But there are other energies we need to factor in, the energies radiating up and out from **The Earth** itself.

Which means... **Grounding**.

But what exactly is grounding?

Well... grounding is our natural, energy connection to **The Earth** beneath us.

And it has nothing to do with gravity, and it has everything to do with electromagnetism.

And then it is the interaction between our aura, our own electromagnetic field, and the aura of **Earth**, our Planets own electromagnetic field, that is super-important... *on many levels.*

* * * * * * * * * *

Now, I can't exactly remember that much of the exact circumstances surrounding the moment when it happened, but I can remember that I was staring into space, wondering about the whole phenomenon around **grounding**.

I mean... what is grounding... and why is it so hard to describe... let alone re-create on a daily basis... and why are some people more naturally grounded than others?

And as I was glancing up into the sky, my intuition suddenly came online and said:

"You human beings are weird... you believe that grounding is a function of gravity... it's so not... it's a function of electromagnetism... which makes so much difference..."

And ever since that unexpected insight, I have come to see the profound truth in this simple fact.

Grounding has nothing to do with gravity, even though some people mistakenly think that it does.

But it does have everything to do with electromagnetism, and when you realize that, you start to understand why it works, and also why it often doesn't. Why some people are naturally grounded, while others choose not to be, or are unable to stay grounded.

Yes, grounding can make us feel as if we are solid and connected to the Planet below.

But that feeling arises from our connection to the Planet's electromagnetic field, and not its pulling us down gravity-field.

Since that out-of-the-box insight, I have shifted my own thinking in this area big time, and found... it's true (honest).

Grounding occurs and is strengthened when our own electromagnetic aura is able to connect, communicate and resonant with the E.M. field of our **Planet Earth**.

It has nothing to do with gravity... it arises when our own electromagnetic field is in direct contact, connection and resonance with the vast electromagnetic field of the Planet.

It occurs when we allow our own electromagnetic aura to connect with, and be empowered by, the natural electromagnetic field of this Planet.

But people confuse the two, they confuse grounding with being heavy, and this causes no end of problems.

Because, in our psyche, heaviness is associated with depression... being dragged down by life, and so people try to avoid that, quite naturally, and lightness is thought to be a good thing.

However, some people, mistakenly avoid grounding because they assume that it is connected with heaviness, so depression etc.

And so, through avoiding grounding and being grounded, they make their life far more difficult then it should be.

However, once you understand this simple fact, and re-connect, then unexpected doors open, as we shall see right now.

Because apart from my intuitive insight, is there any independent scientific research/experiments to back up this Grounding = Electromagnetism theory?

Well, actually... there is... as we shall discover now.

Recently, modern science has had to admit that the Human body does produce an electromagnetic aura, just as the ancients said it did, but scientists now argue that it is not integral to the continuation of life itself. They argue that this electromagnetic field is not used by life in any positive way, and is little more than a by-product of life, just as petrol fumes are a by-product of a car engine.

Personally, I do not believe this is correct, because there has been one scientific experiment, little known, which does indicate a) the existence of subtle energy and b) its importance to our continued health and well-being.

The experiment is discussed in **Valerie V. Hunt's** book *Infinite Mind: Science of the Human Vibrations of Consciousness*.

While a professor at the Physics department at University of California (Los Angeles), her team conducted an experiment, using volunteers who were placed inside a Mu field generator.

This is a human-shaped box inside which the researchers could control and manipulate the electromagnetic field within, either increasing/decreasing the electricity present, the magnetism, or both. This is the electromagnetic field which the volunteers would then be exposed to while they were inside the box. The researchers were even able to completely cancel out the electromagnetic field within the Mu space entirely, which would mean the volunteers would be inside a space with no electromagnetic field. However, the researchers were also able to increase the intensity of the field if they so desired, allowing the volunteers to experience a denser electromagnetic field.

Now, if our physical bodies do not use electromagnetic fields in any positive way, as conventional science currently suggests, then being placed inside a box where electromagnetism has been cancelled out should have no detrimental effect upon us. Neither should be increasing the levels of electromagnetism above the norm have any effect either...

However, what **Valerie Hunt** and her research team found (a team which also included a number of individuals who could 'see' the human aura), was that when individuals were placed in the Mu box and then the electric part of the E.M. field was cancelled out:

The findings were amazing. When the electrical aspect of the atmosphere in the room was withdrawn, leaving less energy, the auric fields became randomly disorganised, scattered and incoherent...

When the electromagnetism in the air was depleted, the only other electrical energy available for the subjects to interact with was the fields of other subjects in the room. As they drew upon one another's field, both fields were weakened. In the absence of an atmospheric source of electromagnetism, the interaction increased between their confused fields. At that stage, general disorganisation of both fields increased. The subjects burst into tears and sobbed, an experience, unlike these people, had ever endured.

In addition to these discoveries, **Hunt** also reports that:

• The aura reader perceived that, as the room's electromagnetic field diminished, the individual's outer aura dissipated, and it was easier to see into the inner layers, which was like a *fishnet energy* that did not correspond to the Meridian system but seemed more aligned to the connective tissue of the physical body.

• The individuals within the room lost the sense of their own body boundary and body image. As the field within the room weakened, each individual aura reached out for another electromagnetic field which it could use to fix and validate its own position. Basically, each individual field had lost its ability to locate itself in space. However, once one aura had located another aura, the stronger one soon tried to draw upon, or cannibalise, the weaker field.[2]

• When the electromagnetic field within the room was increased, then people inside the room reported that their thinking became sharper, clearer, and their consciousness expanded. The reader reported that their auras were also restored, and became more

_____

2   It is interesting to note that our energy bodies need a connection to a strong and vibrant electromagnetic field in order to verify its position in space-time... it's perhaps only a small step further to say that our energy body also uses Astrological energies in the same way... as a form of Celestial location-finding and navigation.

vibrant and colourful.

It is possible that the Human aura reader was seeing what, in Chinese energy medicine, is known as the Jing Jin, an energy system which lies below the level of the meridian system, and which is believed to be associated with our connective tissues. It is perceived as being the 'riverbed' for the qi of our meridian system. More about this can be found in **Damo Mitchell's** book *The Four Dragons: Clearing the Meridians and Awakening the Spine in Nei Gong* (Singing Dragon, 2014).[3]

Now, I would suggest that what the following experiments directly show us is that:

1. The electromagnetic field all around us does have a direct influence on our physical, emotional, and mental well-being. When we become disconnected from this field, then our ability to function is seriously impaired.

2. The origin of this electromagnetic field is our Planet Earth itself, and so we are all dependent on the electromagnetic atmosphere created by the Planet beneath us.

3. When the electromagnetic field falls below a certain level, an individual's aura will start reaching out to others, desperately trying to *cannibalise other people's energy* in order to remain stable. This could be the mechanics behind the phenomenon of someone being a psychic or energy vampire (i.e. for some reason they cannot access the E.M. field all around them, or believe that they cannot, so they start 'zapping' the other people in their location).

4. Under certain conditions, an individual can lose a sense of their own body image, their distinct boundaries and so a sense of self.

3   I have also found that this Jing Jin field... an energy field below the Meridians. but which connects all 12 Meridians... is also the level on which our House system exists and operates.

5. If the electromagnetic field within the room is increased 'above and beyond' the norm, individuals start to perform 'above and beyond' the norm, and this appears to raise their level of consciousness. This supports the idea that, according to design, position and shape it is possible to create 'sick' buildings (i.e. which make people feel unwell), and also buildings which improve and promote health and well-being.

But there are also interesting implications here in relation to how human beings live and group themselves together. As we have seen from **Valerie Hunt's** Mu Room experiment, the more the electromagnetic field diminishes, the more strain individuals are put under, the more emotional they become, the more their clarity of thought diminishes, and the more they try to 'vamp' their neighbour as the E.M. field starts to diminish.

So what does this tell us?

Well... that our connection to the electromagnetism of this Planet beneath (and around) us is just as important to our continued well-being as eating... drinking... even breathing.

But if you take the findings of these series of experiments, and use them to look deeper... then you can uncover a whole different way of looking at life on this planet, what it takes to be a successful Human being and our true potential...

* * * * * * * * * *

Valerie Hunt's experiment has some profound insights for Astrology... and **Energy Astrology** in particular.

And there's also an irony which arises from the findings of this experiment...

Which is...

The *more* grounded you are... the more you able to cope with the Astrological energies flowing down to **Planet Earth**.

And the *less* grounded you are, the less you able to cope with the Astrological transits that continually buffet our Planet, and all the 7 to 8 billion other citizens of **Planet Earth**.

I mean, Astrologers spend so much of our time looking up into the night sky... calculating the position of the other Planets from the perspective of **The Earth**.

*That they tend to forget the importance of **The Earth** itself.*

The rock we are standing on, which supports us.

On a physical *and* electromagnetic level.

The importance of being able to stand on **The Earth**, strong and supported.

Because it is our strong and stable energy connection to **The Earth** which allows us to safely work with and integrate the energies of all the other Planets in our Solar System, and from the Galaxy beyond.

Because if we are ungrounded, we have very little chance of being able to cope and succeed with the other energies in our Solar System.

So it all starts with our standing on **The Earth**... *looking up.*

Contemplating the Universe, and our place in it, from our place on this Planet.

Earth... our lifetime residence in an infinite Universe.

Because we need to understand that with Astrology, whether traditional or **Energy Astrology**, it's all about *location, relativity* and *perspective...*

Time is important, all subsequent events, and the passage of time, in relation to the moment of our birth.

But space is important too, our place of birth, the exact location, upon **The Earth**.

But the most important thing of all...

That we were born upon the Earth in the first place.

A place of life and abundance, and the only place in our Solar System that where your dreams have any chance of coming true.

And where Astrologers have all the resources they need to calculate and draw up an Astrological chart.

As Buddhist Masters used to say... and probably still do...

The Gods in the highest Heaven are envious of each Man and Woman born upon the Earth.

For when Man is born on **The Earth**, he or she has the best chance at expanding their Consciousness... expanding... evolving into something more... something higher.

So one of the primary insights with **Energy Astrology**, and what makes it different from the more traditional forms of Astrology.

The next, and maybe the most important lesson:

Don't forget the Planet on which you were born... you need to develop a relationship to the Earth too... just as much as any other planetary energy in the Solar System... in fact, more so...

Adopt a tree... plant a tree...

Walk on the grass barefoot maybe...

Look up at the blue sky above with a feeling of gratitude...

Because **The Earth** gives you a foundation... a platform from which to explore the rest of the Universe.

Not in a rocket ship maybe...

But a platform from our Universe of Consciousness.

Your connection to the Planet below you gives you the best chance at being able to successfully surf the celestial energies you will meet on your journey of a lifetime.

And you definitely **don't** need a spaceship to explore your inner world within.

The Earth beneath gives us all the best platform we have and ever need to stand and look up at the stars overhead... wondering at the night sky, the same as our far distant ancestors once did... across three million years of time.

* * * * * * * * * *

Finally... the Astrological glyph for **The Earth** is a circle, with a square running through its centre... or a circle with an inner cross.

Which is kind of saying... you stand in the centre... X makes the spot.

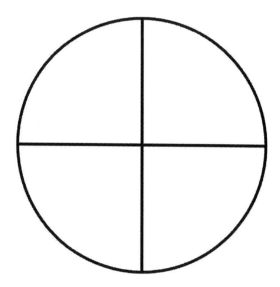

Obviously... if there are Astrologers on other worlds... far from here... they will see things completely different to us...

"The Planet Varg is about to enter the Sign of Clatch in the 17th House of your chart... so in the next 39 hours, before tomorrow, you will meet a flat, dark hadsome stranger, with many sensitive tentacles... plus... your luck will change and you'll win the Planetary Lottery!"

Well... maybe not so different after all...

Chapter 1-4: The 2 Hemispheres of Energy Astrology

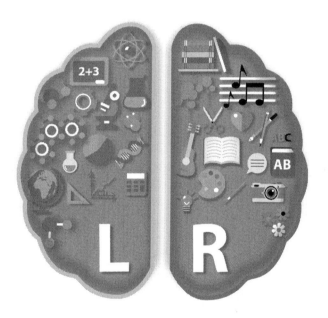

Now, it may not be initially apparent, but there are two sides to **Energy Astrology**.

Just as there are two sides to our Human Brain.

Two Hemispheres.

And this metaphor is really quite apt.

The left hemisphere of the Human Brain is linked to rational thought and our intellect.

While the right hemisphere of our Brain links to feelings, our ability to discern patterns, to our intuition, and our ability to think outside the box.

And this is equally as true for the two sides of **Energy Astrology**.

We could say that the left side of **Energy Astrology** is an approach which allows us to see and interpret an Astrological chart in a new way, through the relationship between the Planets and Chakras, the Signs and Meridians, and the energy patterns they create.

While on the right side of **Energy Astrology** there is an approach which is more energy and feeling related, an approach which allows an individual to step into different Astrological energies, an approach which allows an individual to directly *feel* their own Natal chart, plus energies which lie outside their own Natal chart (which can be quite a liberating experience).

An approach which allows people to directly experience what a Planet in a particular Sign and House feels like.

Or feel the tension and harmony between two Planets, a tension or harmony which is hot-wired into their own energy anatomy perhaps, and so forms the bedrock for their own personality and approach to life.

Sometimes, it is not until we can directly *feel* an energy that we can figure out how to work with it effectively, move forward, and transform.

Because any theory is just an idea floating in our head, but feelings make things real and tangible.

And feelings and emotions... for good or ill... provide the energy necessary to manifest ideas out into the world.

In fact, **Energy Astrology** is one of the few developmental systems, that I know of, which has this dual nature at its heart.

And if the left-hand side of **Energy Astrology** is transformational, then the right-hand side of **Energy Astrology** is transformational squared.

Now, in life, it is said that some people are more thinkers, more reason-orientated, while others are more feelers, feeling orientated. Some people are more intellectual, while others are more intuitive. Some are more extrovert, and others more introvert.

And this is all true.

But it has also been said that there are two types of Astrologers.

There are Saturn types of Astrologers, who like all the maths and geometric patterns which Astrology can provide and create. These are the type of people who definitely make their bed in the morning, and the lines are all perfectly straight.

And then there are also the Uranian types of Astrologers, who like the different intellectual realms which Astrology can take you to, but are not overly attracted to the maths and geometry, and who probably breathed a big sigh of relief when someone created the first Astrological computer programme, so they no longer had to waste time drawing up all those charts by hand (i.e. they could start focusing in on the important stuff).

But personally, I think this whole 2 Types of Astrologers argument is actually wrong.

Or rather... *incomplete.*

Because it ignores all the *feeling types.*

Those Astrology types who are more aligned to Neptune and Venus.

For centuries, maybe millennia, these feeling types were unable to find a doorway into a subject which was dominated by intellectual pursuits and reasoning, because their consciousness and approach was alien to the Astrology of the time.

And that is exactly what I found when I first put **Energy Astrology** out into the world.

It really connected with all the feeling types, who suddenly found a type of Astrology they could connect with, and which wasn't based around reading lots and lots of books.

So many people were saying:

*"I have always felt attracted to Astrology, but was turned off whenever I picked up a book because it was all so dry and rational, there was no Heart involved for me, and I just couldn't find a way into the subject. But now, with **Energy Astrology**, it is all starting to resonate with me. And the intellectual stuff is also starting to make sense too because my head can now link it to the feelings, I have found a way into Astrology that works for me."*

Putting **Energy Astrology** out into the world, I found that the right-hand side of **Energy Astrology** really appealed, connected with, and was attractive to all those individuals who are more into feelings.

But then, on top of that, being able to work with feelings, regardless of your type, opens up a new and unexpected door.

OK, back when I was first exploring/developing the approach of **Energy Astrology**, my inner guidance gave me the following formula...

- Feeling leads to Acceptance
- Acceptance leads to Ownership
- Ownership leads to Integration

And I have found this formula to be totally true.

You see, many people push an uncomfortable feeling out of their Conscious mind, push it down into their Unconscious, and this is true for love as much as anger say, for both what we call the positive as well as the negative.

We humans can suppress love just as much as we can suppress anger or hate. Basically, ANY feeling can be suppressed for so many different reasons.

But all feelings are basically energy, and when we suppress them, whatever they are, we are only suppressing our core energy, and that is never good because it's like we're only operating, owning, a small percentage of who we are.

It costs a lot of taxpayers money to lock someone up in prison.

And similarly, whenever we suppress something, we are using our core energy, to trap and lock down our own core energy.

And that's energy that can't be used for anything else... anything more positive...

So we want to reclaim those parts, plug them back in, if only because we are more healthy, vital, and happy when we are functioning on the majority of our core energy.

But to do that... we need to re-claim feelings which, for some reason, we have defined as *unacceptable*.

And to do that... 1st stage... we need to **Feel** them.

Now, that doesn't mean you need to wallow in the pain or get all masochistic.

But once you start doing that, allowing simple feeling... a strange thing occurs... 2nd stage... **Acceptance**... you start to accept that this feeling is you, and so stop pushing it away.

You start to accept that this feeling is your core energy too.

Which then leads to the 3rd stage... **Ownership**... where you start to see that maybe this feeling has things to offer you.. it is a part of you, and so you start to own it.

And finally, 4th stage... **Integration**... a point where you stop thinking about the feeling which once caused you issues, it is so integrated into your energy field, that it is no longer a problem, because when the shoe fits, whoever thinks about their shoes (as the Ancient Taoists used to say).

But the thing is, while you are running away from the unpleasant feeling, then this process of alchemical transformation can *never* start.

Because all unpleasant feelings are telling us something, they contain information and energy... OUR energy.

And to be happy and successful in life, to achieve our goals and dreams, we need as much of our core energy as we can lay our psychic hands upon.

Which is why... in the long-run... suppressing our own core energy, using other core energy to suppress it, is never a good strategy for life, we just end up being tied up in psychic knots, and unable to move, and with far less energy then you should have.

Now, there is a law of the Human psyche known as Projection that states that when an individual does not acknowledge and own an energy within themselves, that energy is projected outwards and manifests in some area of their life, usually in the form of challenging situations or recurring conflict, until that person is able to acknowledge and integrate those energies within their own psyche consciously.

This is why individuals tend to attract partners and relationships which reflect back to them those shadow parts of themselves which they do not wish to face. And you know that you have finally learned the lesson when the next partner you attract is completely different from all the others... i.e. you have finally broken the pattern.

An Astrological natal chart is, therefore, a powerful tool to help an individual understand the archetypal forces which drive their personality and identify those planets they own and are comfortable with.

And those Planets they are actively disowning and projecting out on to other people and situations.

However, on the right-hand side, **Energy Astrology** takes this self-healing process a stage further and also helps to speed up this process, which is very win-win.

Normally, an individual has to wait for situations and circumstances to activate a Planetary archetype before they can discover if it is one which they own or disown (otherwise known as the right transits).

However, using the **Energy Astrology** approach, an individual can have all their primary Planetary archetypes activated in sequence, thus allowing them to feel these distinctive energies and also observe their personality reactions to these energies (this all occurs on an Energy Astrology Stage 1 weekend).

It's just a matter of activating the right Chakra/Meridian energy associations.

This means, in a short space of time, an individual can quickly define which Planetary energies they are comfortable with, and which planetary energies they are most likely to be projecting outwards and so need to work on.

To help re-claim these projections, the **Energy Astrology** approach is structured around a four-step process to create an internal space within the psyche from which individuals can start to own their planetary + sign/charka + meridian energies.

First, the individual allows themselves to **FEEL** the Planetary energies manifesting through their Charkas and Meridians.

OK, initially they may not like the energy, it may make them feel very uncomfortable, but at least they are allowing them to bring it into consciousness, to **FEEL** it. Then over time, they learn to **ACCEPT** the energy.

Which eventually leads to an **OWNERSHIP** of the energy, the ability to identify with that energy.

And then finally, the energy is so well **INTEGRATED** into their psyche, the individual no longer notices that they ever had a problem with it.

The equation for the whole of **Energy Astrology** process is, therefore:

- Feeling leads to Acceptance
- Acceptance leads to Ownership
- Ownership leads to Integration

Once an individual can feel and accept Planetary energy, this can open a space for a shift in many areas of their life – relationships, abundance, health, work, spiritual growth, and creativity.

Unfortunately, if someone has come to associate any specific energy as uncomfortable, unwelcome, even painful... for some reason... usually a belief they have inherited from their family, then they either project it out on to other people, or they push it deep down into their Unconscious Mind.

But either of these two approaches means they have disconnected from the energy.

And how can you **FEEL** that which you have unplugged from your Conscious Mind?

Hence people become trapped. They cannot truly banish something, and so continue to suffer (often no longer knowing why, because the memories and reasons have been buried so deep, they are lost).

And if they can no longer **FEEL** those disconnected energies, they cannot start the process of transforming them.

That's the condition and issue for so many people around our planet.

It is perhaps true to say that Western culture, with all its anti-depressants, pain-killers, and physical, mental and emotional distractions, is not very good at dealing with and transforming inner pain.

Hence, many people are totally unable to heal themselves nor able to allow others to help them heal.

Because true inner healing can only occur when someone allows themselves to **FEEL** their inner world, even if it is initially painful to do so.

A journey of a thousand miles has to start with the first step, as many Spiritual traditions say.

And as the spiritual teacher and writer **David R Hawkins** has written many times when you can observe the emotional pain... neutrally... without feeding it... then it slowly starts to dissipate, and eventually, you become free of it.

However, as the Ancient Alchemists knew, if the pain is great, then it needs to be released in manageable stages. Otherwise, it will explode from the Unconscious Mind like a volcanic eruption and overwhelm the Conscious Mind. That way potential madness lies. So sometimes these things need to be done slowly and carefully and in a stable way, no matter how fast our ego wants to go.

And that is exactly what the right-hand side of **Energy Astrology** is designed to allow you to do.

Chapter 1-5: What Is An Audio Essence?

The writer and mythologist **Joseph Campbell** believed that Mankind isn't looking for a meaning to life, *but a feeling that will make our lives meaningful.*

If he is correct, all our religious and spiritual pursuits, down through the ages, is, therefore, simply a pursuit of *a meaningful feeling.*

A feeling that will erase all our fears and pain.

A feeling so deep and wide, so beautiful and ecstatic that it lifts us up and enfolds us in its meaning and purpose.

And the Ancient Greek definition of Ecstasy was *a feeling which allowed you to step outside of yourself, and into something bigger.*

But do such feelings truly exist?

And if they do, where can we find such feelings in our modern, hyper, tense and fractured world?

For many people, the closest they ever come to such a state is through sound and music.

But what if sound could do so much more?

What if sound could be the key to a whole range of uplifting and positive feelings?

As a crystal therapist, kinesiologist and light body teacher, my personal journey, life quest perhaps, has been to explore different vibrational healing systems, to identify those which are the most beneficial.

As our Planet increasingly moves into the digital age, I now believe new forms of vibrational healing and personal growth *must* emerge which don't require us to plunder the limited resources of the planet, and which make vibrational healing available to everyone, from Somerset, Saskatchewan and to Senegal.

This is the main purpose behind **Audio Essences**.

Audio Essences was born on a day in February 2012, when I was walking across a carpark, in Exeter, in the United Kingdom, on a rainy day, and the thought suddenly floated into my head...

" *Why don't you try doing this? It's a way to translate subtle vibrations into an MP3 sound file. So that whenever you listen to the*

MP3 track, you will be able to access the subtle vibration contained within."

OK, quite a claim from my intuition perhaps, but when I got home that night, I did exactly what I was shown in my Mind.

And so the first **Audio Essence** was created.

I listened to it, and received the energy benefit my intuition had promised, I played it to other people, and they received a very similar experience to my own.

Whenever you listen to the MP3 track, you will be able to access the subtle vibration contained within... the original vibration which was recorded.

In the intervening years, I have worked with a great number of different people and Groups, in person and online, and proved that **Audio Essences** *do work* and are effective, time and time again. I have also been able to refine them, discover how they influence and interact with an individual's subtle energy anatomy, and based on that, how they can be made even more effective, and so are currently effective for around 90% of people.

Just as, for centuries, people have been using sunlight to capture vibrations in pure spring water to create water essences, now the technology exists to capture and transmit a whole range of unique vibrations through digital sound, known as an **Audio Essences**. And if you can change your vibration you can, therefore, easily change your feeling state, and you can now change your vibration just through the act of listening because **Audio Essences** *use sounds as the carrier wave for subtle vibrations.*

Many ancient traditions around the world talk about subtle vibrations, which cannot be heard with the human ears, or created through the human voice, or even through musical instruments, but which influence how the universe works and coalesces.

These subtle vibrations often exist above and beyond the range of normal human hearing (20 to 20,000 Hz).

Using the **Audio Essence** process, these subtle vibrations can be captured from many different sources: single crystals, crystal patterns, flowers, trees, essential oils, homoeopathic remedies, even the past words of enlightened masters (the **Audio Satsang** range).

An **Audio Essence** track can then be embedded into any piece of music or spoken track because the **Audio Essence** effect does not arise from the music itself but from the subtle vibrations contained beneath the music/words.

It is these subtle vibrations which create the **Audio Essence** effect and open the listener up to a whole new world of possibilities.

There are many positive benefits with this approach:

- An **Audio Essence** can be instantly downloaded from the internet whenever needed, to anywhere on the planet with a signal, and loaded on to many different kinds of electronic devices – mobile phones, laptops, tablets, MP3 players (or whatever device comes next)
- **Audio Essences** can be used to capture the vibrations of rare and expensive crystals, flowers, or essential oils, so making them available to many more people who could benefit from them
- **Audio Essences** can be added to guided journeys so that the subtle vibration resonates with the intention and purpose of the journey, so making the journey more effective
- **Audio Essences** can be used in many different ways – relaxation, meditation, balancing and healing, personal protection, manifestation or inner exploration. They can be actively worked with, or passively played in the background, although we always stress it is polite and good manners to make

listeners aware of what is happening to them, even ask their permission first.

• With **Audio Essences** you can merge and combine different subtle vibrations, thus creating some very interesting energy spaces to explore and work with.

And that last point, that you can merge and combine different tracks, is what makes the energy side of **Energy Astrology** real and possible.

As we have said earlier, there is a *left* and *right* side to **Energy Astrology**, two different approaches, which compliment each other.

The *left side* is all about a different way of doing Chart Interpretation.

The *right side* is all about feeling and allowing people to step into the exact energies of a particular Planet in Sign and House.

But then the question becomes?

How exactly do you *do* that, how can you transmit the energies relating to a Planet + Sign + House so that people can really *feel* what that vibration is like?

OK, hopefully you now understand that the main foundation of **Energy Astrology** is Planets = Chakras and Signs = Meridians.

So the final question is:

How do you combine and transmit them?

Well, the simple answer is that it's all done through **Audio Essences**.

Different **Audio Essence**s... layered... combined... merged... to create the required energies for an Astrological combination.

Example 1: The **Audio Essence** for Sun in Taurus in the 7th House is the merging of:

- The **Audio Essence** for the Sun/Heart Chakra
- The **Audio Essence** for Taurus/Triple Warmer Meridian
- The **Audio Essence** for the 7th House (Heart Protector Meridian)

Example 2: The Audio Essence for Jupiter in Aries in the 11th House is the merging of:

- The **Audio Essence** for Jupiter/Base Chakra
- The **Audio Essence** for Aries/Kidney Meridian
- The **Audio Essence** for the 11th House (Lung Meridian)

Example 3: The Audio Essence for South Node in Cancer in the 5th House is the merging of:

- The **Audio Essence** for the South Node/Linking of Pingala and Ida Nadis at Base Chakra
- The **Audio Essence** for Cancer/Stomach Meridian
- The **Audio Essence** for the 5th House (Heart Meridian)

And this is the point at which no amount of words may truly convince you... you need some concrete experience.

So...

The full range of **Audio Essences** are available from our 2 websites **www.audio-medication.com**... and **www.energy-astrology.com**... to purchase and download.

Our YouTube Channel **The How To Club** contains a number of free to access **Audio Essences**... plus ones which relate to **Energy Astrology** Planets... for people to try out for themselves.

And a number of eCourses... which utilise **Audio Essence** technology... will soon be available too.

All of which will allow people to work with the feeling side of **Energy Astrology** *in very practical and beneficial ways!*

PART TWO:
THE ASTROLOGICAL SIGNS

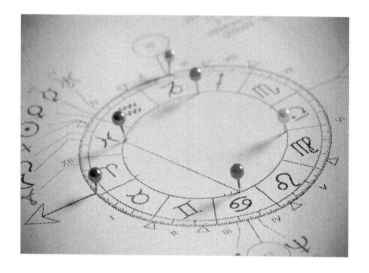

Chapter 2-1: Astrological Signs & Meridians

The 1st major pillar of **Energy Astrology** is:

Signs = Meridians

That each of the 12 Astrological Signs can be associated with one of the 12 Meridians from Chinese energy practices.

In **Energy Astrology**, the 12 Astrological Signs directly equate to the 12 Meridians in a one-on-one way.

The above image shows the standard Glyphs for each of the 12 Astrological Signs: 1st Row (left to right) **Aries**, **Leo**, **Sagittarius**, *the 3 Fire Signs... 2nd Row (left to right),* **Taurus**, **Virgo**, **Capricorn**, *the 3 Earth Signs... 3rd Row (left to right),* **Gemini**, **Libra**, **Aquarius**, *the 3 Air Signs... 4th Row (left to right),* **Cancer**, **Scorpio**, **Pisces**, *the 3 Water Signs.*

This is based on the work of the German Astrologer, **Reinhold Ebertin** (1901 to 1988), the founder of **Cosmobiology**, who mapped out the association between the Meridians and Astrological Signs in his influential book *The Combination of Stellar Influences*.

Basically, I have taken his discoveries to the next logical level.

In Part Two of this book, we will now dive deeper into this Astrological Sign and Meridian relationship, explaining the pros and cons of each Sign, the advantages and disadvantages, from an energy perspective, and how we can work with each Sign and Meridian for our own maximum benefit.

Plus, we will also be exploring the energy relationship and resonance between each of the 12 Astrological Signs, and how they work together in:

- **Elemental Relationship**
- **Polarity Relationship**
- **Modality**

And finally, how it is also possible to conceive of new and different relationships between the 12 Astrological Signs, relationships which don't appear in the traditional Western Astrological mappings, but are indeed possible if you look at what is possible from an Eastern perspective (Chapters 2-17 and 2-18).

So to get us started, once again, the connection between the 12 Astrological Signs and the 12 Meridians are as follows, based on the work of **Reinhold Ebertin**:

- **Aries** = Kidney Meridian
- **Taurus** = Triple Warmer Meridian (aka Triple Burner or Triple Heater)
- **Gemini** = Liver Meridian

- **Cancer** = Stomach Meridian
- **Leo** = Heart Meridian
- **Virgo** = Large Intestine Meridian
- **Libra** = Heart Protector Meridian (aka Heart Constrictor or Circulation-Sex)
- **Scorpio** = Bladder Meridian
- **Sagittarius** = Spleen Meridian
- **Capricorn** = Gallbladder Meridian
- **Aquarius** = Lung Meridian
- **Pisces** = Small Intestine Meridian

Now, each of the above 12 Glyphs is an ancient image, associated with a particular Astrological Sign, going all the way back to Ancient Babylonian times, where the ancient Astrologers of times past identified each of the Astrological Signs with their respective image *for a reason.*

So understanding why they chose that particular Glyph for that particular Astrological Sign, why that particular metaphor and image is the best fit, goes a long way to understanding the archetypal energy at work at the core of that particular Sign.

But we also need to remember that, from the perspective of Chinese medicine and energy practices, a Meridian is basically *a pipeline along which energy... or Chi... flows...* as we explored back in Chapter 1-2.

According to the ancient Chinese Sages, when energy is flowing along a Meridian smoothly and without hindrance, then it manifests positive qualities, the positive thoughts and emotions associated with that particular Meridian.

However, when energy cannot easily flow along that Meridian... or becomes totally blocked, then it starts to manifest negative qualities, the negative thoughts and emotions associated with that particular Meridian.

Now, that is basic Meridian theory... as passed down to us from those Ancient Chinese Sages, and we will be exploring the positive and negative qualities for each of these Sign-Meridian combinations next.

And I don't have a problem with that approach and metaphor.

Accept it is a very binary approach.

Yes or No... On or Off... 1 or 0.

Either the Chi is flowing... or it is not.

And from my own work with the Meridians, over the past two decades, I have found that they are more complex then that, and so the metaphor which I use to describe them isn't *water flowing along a bamboo pipe*, say.

For me, now... living in the 21st Century... I see them more like *fibre optic cables... along which travel millions of pieces of data... all traveling on a myriad of laser beams.*

Where Chi is the lazer beam, carrying a whole host of different data streams.

Five or six thousand years ago, the Ancient Chinese Seers had to use metaphors, from the world around them, to describe and explain how the Meridians worked.

Like... *water flowing along a bamboo tube.*

But that doesn't mean that this metaphor is an *exact fit* for what is really happening.

Just that, around five or six thousand years ago, it was the *best metaphor* they had available.

Just like the wheel was the best form of transport, along with horses and oxen.

And there is no reason why we must stick to this ancient bamboo metaphor, now we have reached more Modern times, when we have more apt descriptions available to us to describe the workings of the Meridians.

Like... *data flowing down a fibre optic cable on a myriad of lazer beams.*

And maybe, in a thousand years from now, Humans will be able to upgrade that fibre optic metaphor as well.

Things are always changing, and that is also true for the metaphors we use to describe our inner world, as well as our inner world itself, that evolves too, slowly, over millennia, but it also changes.

You see, when you stand back and consider all the things which the 12 Meridians are meant to do, all their different functions.

And on different levels... physical... emotional... mental... and spiritual.

A simple binary system... On or Off... 1 or 0... to my mind... just wouldn't be able to cope.

It wouldn't be sophisticated enough to run and control everything needed in our energy anatomy.

That is why I prefer the fibre optic cable metaphor for the 12 Meridians.

One... the fibre optic cable analogy allows for each Meridian to have multiple functions, all occurring at the same time, on multiple levels, which is something I have found to be true with the Meridians.

They are not just about performing a single task, each Meridian is multi-tasking each micro-second of the day.

But also, with a fibre optic cable metaphor, if you press down on the cable, yes, some of the signals may get blocked, some signals may be distorted, but other signals will still get through.

So it isn't an On or Off... Yes or No... set-up.

There just isn't enough complexity, and flexibility, and adaptability, built into that kind of Yes/No system to ensure that each individual can keep going.

Keeping going in difficult circumstances.

And despite whatever harm they are doing to themselves...

Because... and let's be honest here... Humans are one of the few creatures where the physical body has to deal with the harm it is receiving from the world around it.

And also, the harm which that particular owner may also be doing to their own physical body, through some kind of self-abuse... lack of exercise... over-eating... under-eating... smoking... drinking too little... drinking too much... eating the wrong sort of foods.

And that's just on the physical level.

There are other kinds of abuse which can occur on the emotional... mental levels... or even higher.

All of which our energy anatomy has to absorb and find a way to deal with.

So our energy anatomy also needs to be robust enough to cope with how the individual owner uses their body, just as much as the stress and strain it has to handle from the external world around us.

And that's why I prefer *the fibre optic cable metaphor* over *the water down a pipe metaphor.*

Because I seriously doubt that a simple On-Off system could survive long having to deal with all the abuse with your average individual deals out to their energy anatomy on a daily basis.

To survive and continue to exist, our system needs to be more flexible and adaptable then that.

Which is why, as we start now to explore the relationship between each of the 12 Meridians and the 12 Astrological Signs, we will discover a system which is full of beautiful depth and complexity.

And where things are also designed to be rugged and robust.

Where our energy system is designed to keep us alive for as long as possible, despite what we may be doing, thinking or feeling.

Because... you never know... 10 years down the line... we might decide to change our ways.

And start to live a completely different life entirely.

And fix and heal ourselves... and eat more healthily, and be more loving and caring to ourselves and other people etc...

Because our Meridian system, just like our Chakra system, is designed to be robust enough to keep us alive long enough, in the hope that one day we will go:

"I think I am going to let go of my past destructive behavior... I want to change... I want to grow..."

And start to explore the inner potential hidden within our Astrological Natal Chart.

So now, let's dive into an exploration of each of the 12 Astrological Sign and Meridian combinations.

Chapter 2-2: Aries & Kidney Meridian

OK, hands up, who out there in reader land consider the idea of climbing a mountain... *scary?*

And even worse, who finds the idea of climbing it with the merest of safety equipment, indeed, climbing it with just your bare hands... *utterly terrifying?*

If that is the case... I would put money on the fact you don't have a lot of planets in **Aries** in your Astrological natal chart.

Because if I were to ask that question of a true-blooded, full-on **Aries**, their reply would probably be:

ARIES

*The Astrological Glyph which the Ancient Astrologers associated with the Sign of **Aries** was the Ram. For people in pre-history, Rams were a symbol of fertility and power, assertiveness and aggression. I found this advice from a website on rearing farm animals: "The best way to raise nonaggressive rams is to LEAVE THEM ALONE! Do not try to make friends with them, do not scratch or rub or push on their heads, do not tease them, do not treat them roughly, and do not play with them. LEAVE THEM ALONE!" Which gives a massive pointer to the true nature of **Aries**. They are loners, individuals, and don't rub them up the wrong way. Farmers and goat-herders, back in pre-history, would have known this well and passed the knowledge on to the Ancient Astrologers.*

* * * * * * * * * *

"Hang on… don't rush me… I'm thinking about it… I am free tomorrow afternoon… which mountain range are we heading out too?"

In fact, an **Uber-Aries** wouldn't even need time to think about it… they'd be off… act now, think later.

Aries has the reputation of being the daredevil, stunt man, and fearless explorer of the Zodiac.

And the reason for this is because **Aries** has a unique and unusual relationship to that thing which would paralyze other Zodiac signs.

And that thing is… Fear.

It's also the reason why you don't mess with an **Aries**, because they're not afraid of you, no matter how big you may think you are.

Let me explain.

The German astrologer **Reinhold Ebertin** originally made the connection between **Aries** and the Kidney meridian, and this link allows us to make a further link, drawing upon the work of the kinesiologist, **John Diamond**, because in his energy system/ approach the Kidney meridian is linked to the positive quality of Sexual Assuredness, and the negative quality of Sexual Unassuredness.

But this is one of the two times in this book when I am not going to follow-up on **John Diamond's** findings to the letter.

Why?

Because a) I feel the Traditional Chinese Medicine classification for the negative Kidney quality of Fear is much more useful to an understanding of **Aries**, and b) I also believe that it's not just Sexual Assuredness which is the key, but Assuredness in general.

The Dictionary definition of Assuredness is usually something like:

Made certain, exhibiting confidence and authority.

Which does point to the fact that they have a direct and unique relationship to Self-confidence and Fear.

And having said that… if I may… throwing in the Elemental Archetype for **Aries** from **Energy Astrology**… *Spirit into Spirit.*

With **Aries**, we are dealing with an energy/individual that is very much *newborn.*

The newborn baby… the rebellious individual with original thinking… **Aphrodite** arising newborn from the waves off the coast of Cyprus in the Mediterranean… all are images which resonate with **Aries**.

Because in many ways, **Aries** approaches the world around them as if they were a newborn baby, in both a positive and a negative sense.

Newborn babies are only born with two fears which are pre-programmed into them by Evolution: a) the fear of falling, and b) the fear of loud noises, for various reasons, These two fears are programmed into all babies… no exceptions.

Even **Arnold Schwarzenegger** was afraid of being dropped when a baby.

All other fears a baby picks up from its family and environment and society.

It's not born with those fears.

So, as a baby-mind, **Aries** is more resistant to fears than other people.

And when I say it's a baby-mind, I don't mean that in a derogatory way, but it's a Mind which is fresh and clean, and isn't carrying prior conditioning, and is only really afraid of falling and loud noises.

And what does a newborn baby do, apart from eating, sleeping, occasionally crying, and pooping?

Well, it starts to explore the world around it, and it starts to test the world it starts to test itself against the limitations of the world around it.

Behavioral scientists have discovered that all babies run mini-experiments, designed to work out what kind of world + soceity + culture + family they have been born into, but to do that it needs **Aries** energy.

Every small child is a mini **Aries** adventurer, pitting itself against the world into which it has been born, challenging itself to crawl further, stand taller, smile brighter, finding out what it can and cannot do.

And through this active growth process, of trial and error, of testing itself against the external world, the baby/small child comes to define itself, define its unique personality, and this is true for all the Zodiac signs, for every human individual who has ever lived.

But with an **Aries**, that process doesn't end at childhood, that process continues on into adult life. They are continually on the look-out for new challenges through which to test and define themselves.

In fact, in a strange way, they need constant challenges, the adrenaline rush, the constant doing, as a way to convince themselves that they are still alive, that they still exist. Whereas the other personality Zodiac signs, define their basic personality during childhood and then leave it at that for the rest of their life (on average), an **Aries** continues to test themselves throughout their entire life. *If I put myself in this challenging situation, in this difficult environment, what will happen, how will I perform, what will I do?*

Aries is not an individual who wants to live their life, sitting at home, on the sofa, watching TV. No, this Sign would be too bored, they would literally be bored to death, they want action and motion, they want to be in the Documentary Channel series, with themselves as the star performer, and the odd thing is, they wouldn't care if no one else ever watched the programme after it was complete, because for them the fun was in the making, in going on the adventure. They really don't care what others think, and for this reason, they can come across as quite self-centered, even selfish, because it is all about them and their own personal adventure.

For them, life is about action and active participation, and this very much defines their relationship to the world around them, which is seen as an adventure playground. Even other people can be seen as a resource to help them to be successful on their adventure, their solo quest (which really winds up many of the other Zodiac signs, who hate being seen as little more than a resource for someone else's selfish adventure. However, for **Aries**, it's nothing personal, just the way things are).

For the majority of the Zodiac signs, if they see a far off mountain, that has never before been climbed in the whole history of the world, they will think to themselves... *What a beautiful mountain!*

A **Capricorn** might think... *If I climb that mountain, then I will be famous, and it will help to further my career!*

But an **Aries** will think... *If I climb and conquer that mountain, then I will prove to myself... once again... that I am Number 1, and still successful... that I have still got what it takes!*

In a sense, **Aries** isn't concerned with what others think or want, it's not about them seeking adulation or emotional payback... what they do is always for themselves... whenever they conquer a mountain, whenever they go out on a limb, they are doing it for themselves, and social prestige means very little to them (in fact, having to worry about other people, that would be seen as a hindrance, something holding them back from achieving all they might be).

OK, they may make a survival documentary or three, but they are always itching to get back into the jungle, to test and prove themselves in a new environment over again. They're not ones to stick around for the press launch of their new Documentary series... and they're not very active on social-media either.

They are always pushing their individual boundaries and limits in whatever field they are personally engaged in... whether sport or painting... science or making money.

Once again, the positive emotion which **Aries** is searching for is Assuredness (i.e. a state of mind in which one is free from doubt), and the negative emotions which they are trying to banish and kill-off is Doubt and Fear.

Which sounds kind of odd, until you remember the mantra of an **Aries** from **Susan Jeffers'** famous book title *Feel the fear... and do it anyway!*

Whenever they climb and conquer that far-off mountain, they re-instate and re-confirm their Assuredness, and they kill-off Fear once again... because they did it anyway.

Something a very wise **Aries** told me (4 Planets **Aries**)... is that the energy difference between Fear and Excitement is very close on the spectrum, and so it is possible to switch one type of energy into another.

And if you read **Geoff Thompsons'** book *Fear – The Friend of Exceptional People*, you will see a whole host of characters... boxers, martial arts masters, special forces... who have found the way to literally turn Fear on its head and use it to their advantage, to help focus and motivate them.

You will also see this reflected in **Ant Middleton's** book, *The Fear Bubble: Harness Fear and Live Without Limits*, where he explains how his time in the SAS helped him to understand and better surf his own fears in active service and combat.

However, I have a feeling that this type of switching only comes easily to fully functional **Aries** types, or people with a good and solid connection with their own inner **Aries**, and that the rest of the Zodiac signs don't even know that switch exists, let alone where to find it.

OK... OK... I can hear someone complaining from the back row... "*If **Aries** are so good at dealing with Fear, why is it a handicap and an issue... ?*"

Good question... definitely needs answering...

The thing is, an **Aries** still feels the Fear and even though they are the best Zodiac sign at overcoming it so that it doesn't hold them back. It is still present in their psyche, and it still distorts their energy system, and that's the problem for an **Aries**... the lurking Fear is always present at the back of their mind... and pushes them into ever new adventures/actions to prove to themselves who is the master.

In a sense, an average **Aries** is a slave to their Fear because they are always having to overcome it... that is their greatest weakness... they can never take a holiday from their inner, lurking Fear... (and it is often impossible to get an average **Aries** to admit they have any Fears at all... "*Me, afraid of what exactly? If I was afraid, how could I do all the scary things I do? Don't talk so ridiculous!*" ... especially as they pack the climbing ropes into the Land Rover, about to embark on their next climbing trip to a remote region of the Andes).

Which is easy to achieve when you are young, fit and healthy... but as you age... the body weakens... Fear will start to get the upper hand... unless the **Aries** can learn how to transmute it... which is difficult for your average **Aries** to do... because it requires that you stop rushing around out there... and go within.

If an **Aries** wants to grow spiritually, at some stage, they must close their eyes, and venture back into the Universal sea of consciousness from which they emerged... and so face and conquer a different type of Fear entirely.

Chapter 2-3: Taurus & Triple Warmer Meridian

As I write this... my Mother is outside in her garden, rushing around, doing all those last minute things which need to be completed before Winter.

Digging stuff up... planting... re-planting...

Doing whatever a good gardener needs to do at this time of year.

You see, its October, and Winter is fast approaching, and she wants *"to be prepared"* (her words).

TAURUS

*The Astrological Glyph which the Ancient Astrologers associated with the Sign of **Taurus** was the Bull. For people in pre-history, Bulls were a symbol of strength, power and fertility... which are all qualities associated with **Taurus**... and they were also super-important for maintaining the size of your herd... Without a healthy and fertile Bull, your family herd would soon suffer and diminish in size, and so your family's wealth and prosperity would also quickly decrease too. So Bulls were probably also seen as the key to continued physical abundance and prosperity. And if you don't approach them with care... they will charge... they're dangerous if you don't know how to handle them best... they have sharp horns. In the modern world, a sign of material prosperity and success is an expensive car. In ancient times, it was probably a strong, healthy and fertile Bull, that could double or triple the size of your herd, and who all your farmer neighbours wanted to breed with. That's probably why **Taurus** is linked with material prosperity.*

* * * * * * * * * *

However, she's in her late-80s, doesn't trust anyone else to do it *properly...* (although I am allowed to cut the grass... as long as I do it *properly*).

My Mother should be at a time of in her life when she is *taking it easy...* but she goes about her garden like a *demon.*

And the funny thing is...

I don't mind at all... (although I do have to keep an eye on her to ensure that she doesn't over do it...)

Because I understand what is really going on, what her garden really means to her.

As an extreme **Taurean**, my Mother perceives her garden as one of the few things she has left that gets her out of bed in the morning, which truly motivates her... keeps her going... that she has left to look forward to... that fills her with Hope.

Because her garden is her last real connection left to Physical Beauty.

But why should that be? Why do **Taureans** need Physical Beauty and some kind of future Hope to motivate them?

OK, the German astrologer **Reinhold Ebertin** originally made the connection between **Taurus** and the Triple Warmer Meridian (aka Triple Burner, also Triple Heater), and this link allows us to make a further connection, drawing upon the work of the Kinesiologist, **John Diamond**, because in his energy system/approach, the Triple Warmer Meridian is linked to the positive quality of Hope, and the negative quality of Hopelessness and Despair.

And if I may, throwing in the **Elemental Archetype** for **Taurus** from **Energy Astrology** at this point... Physical Beauty (and the desperate need to avoid Physical Ugliness).

OK... hands up anyone who can remember their Ancient Greek Mythology... especially the story of **Pandora's box?**

Pandora opens the box... and all number of illnesses and misfortunes are let loose on Mankind, but fortunately, the box is closed and locked in time to prevent Hope from escaping as well.

The moral being... as long as Man has Hope then he can face and endure most misfortunes in life.

We can also see this truth also reflected in the parable of Job from the Bible...

And something which **Oprah Winfrey** said in her 2017 Golden Globe Acceptance speech.

That she had interviewed people in her career, who had suffered many of the worst things that life could throw at you.

But the one quality she had found that they all seemed to share... the ability to hold on to Hope for a better day, even during their darkest hours.

And this truth is literally writ large in our own Meridians, Hope is the essential fuel which helps us to keep going, especially when the world around us has turned bleak and bare and dark.

You see, it's all to do with the Triple Warmer Meridian, which in many ways is the solid spine of our energy frame.

If the Triple Warmer collapses, if we lose Hope, then 99.9% of the time, it'll take the rest of our energy system down with it.

And so without Hope, the majority of people will just *give up...*

Stop trying... because what's the point of continuing on...

When someone finally loses all Hope for the future... it can be tragic... it can be a definite ending for them.

The Triple Warmer Meridian is *that* important.

For example, **U.S. Admiral John Stockdale**, writing about his experiences in a Vietnamese prisoner of war camp during the 1960s, made a very interesting observation... (**Admiral John Stockdale** quoted in **Ben Sherwood's** *The Survivors Club: The Secrets & Science That Could Save Your Life*).

When asked to explain which American prisoners perished in captivity in Vietnam, the Admiral replied, "*Oh, that's easy. The optimists.*" ... the optimists "*Were the ones who said 'we're going to be out by Christmas.' And Christmas would come, and Christmas would go. And then Thanksgiving, and then it would be Christmas again. And they died of a broken heart.*" Stockdale went on: "*This is a very important lesson. You must never confuse faith that you will prevail in the end – which you can never afford to lose – with the discipline to confront the most brutal facts of your current reality, whatever they may be.*"

So what is **John Stockdale** saying?

Well, in life, you need Hope to keep going, have faith that you will prevail in the end.

But that Hope needs to be realistic, and not just a way to escape a harsh reality. Not just an escape into fantasy land.

Because when you lose Hope, you also lose the spark of life itself, the momentum that allows you to continue in spite of the hardships you are facing.

So when our Hope is strong, the energy flowing through the Triple Warmer Meridian is strong.

But when we are plunged into total Hopelessness and Despair, then the Triple Warmer Meridian crashes, and it pulls the rest of our energy system down with it.

And one of the things which I have personally found is that the Triple Warmer Meridian is also linked to our *Fight, Flight, or Freeze response*... and so it is central to the basic functioning of our physical organism, because this response circuit was laid down in the brains of all living creatures at the start of Evolution on this planet... over 1 billion years ago.

It is what makes us fight to keep on living, it is our drive to fight for survival.

It is the survival spark within any creature who has ever lived... or will ever live...

Even in the brain of Human Beings... the most evolved creature on the planet at this time... that most primitive of response circuits... that survival spark... is also there and will activate when the right conditions present themselves.

In fact, the *Fight, Flight or Freeze circuit* is designed to override all other brain circuits, all other activities, if danger is detected... and we need to fight for our continued existence.

But the thing is... when and where there is Hope, our energy system keeps going... we will keep on fighting and struggling... in spite of the harsh circumstances we find ourselves in.

But when we lose Hope, then it is as if our energy system goes into a nosedive and crashes... Big time.

Because what keeps the gazelle running from the cheetah?

I would put money on it being the Hope of escape, the Hope that it can outrun the predator, because, without Hope, you give up, you lie down, you stop trying, because what is the point.

And this is what psychologists like **Leonard Seligman** call *learned helplessness*... where a person gives up... believes there is no Hope... so why bother to keep trying.[1]

I have seen it time and time again when someone with a lot of **Taurus** in their chart loses Hope... for something, whatever their Hope may be, and it will vary from person to person... but once they lose their Hope, they crash headlong into Despair and Depression... and to motivate them once again, you need to find something for them to Hope for.[2]

The other thing about **Taurus**... to help us understand it more completely... the **Elemental Archetype** is... *Physical Beauty*... **Taureans** get themselves fueled up inside by Physical Beauty from the outside world.

Their deep appreciation for Physical Beauty... in all its various forms... supports and sustains them, it is the fuel which fills their energy tank, allows them to keep going.

However, this provides **Taureans** with both a major advantage and a big disadvantage.

---

1   **Leonard Seligman** is widely recognised as the founder of *Positive Psychology*.

2   And this leads me to conclude that there are 2 types of Depression... one kind linked to **Taurus** / the Triple Warmer Meridian, which is caused by the loss of Hope... and the other kind linked to **Gemini** / the Liver Meridian, which is caused by the loss of movement in life (... more about this later).

If you ever need to kick start the inner motor of a **Taurean**… easy… feed their desire / need for Physical Beauty:

- Good food and drink
- A wonderful massage complete… with aromatherapy oils maybe
- A walk in nature, or through a beautiful, colourful garden on a lovely Spring day… or a garden you have lovingly created
- Great sex (… which can also be a great physical experience)
- A beautiful house + furnishings
- A great and loving hug from a friend
- A longed-for holiday to beautiful, exotic climes
- Plus… other examples of Physical Beauty

OK… true… the sex part can be tricky… especially if you live in certain parts of the world… but there are very few places were gardening is unlawful.

The advantage is that all/most of these things listed above are fairly easy to obtain… some are free… although some require money (which is why I believe **Taureans** love money… not for its own sake, but for what it can obtain for them)…

The disadvantage… as they get older… the avenues through which they can access this Physical Beauty starts to lessen. It becomes harder to access the things which feed their need for Physical Beauty, old age and dwindling health/money/resources denies them of the ways which they used to enjoy and use.

And an elderly **Taurean**, trapped in an old age peoples home, in a failing body… it must be a living nightmare.

Because many of those places are gloomy and depressing, with poor and grey interior decor.

And so as the body fails… Hope starts to diminish.

Unless… they still have something left to enjoy… or… they are being cared for by someone caring and understanding…

Which is why elderly **Taureans**, who still can, take so much pleasure in their gardens… because once life starts stripping you down, and closing down other avenues for Physical Beauty… being able to work in and enjoy your garden, the Physical Beauty of nature on your doorstep takes on an enormous value to you.

A value beyond that which any of the other Signs can really understand.

Chapter 2-4: Gemini & Liver Meridian

Going to start this chapter with 4 Big statements:

- **Geminis** are a mental sign, and so they are focused 99% on mental activity
- **Geminis** are jack of all trades, and they just don't have time to master anything like a **Sagittarius** would... and wouldn't want to anyway... it's just not their way
- Right now, during the Age of the Internet, **Geminis** are having the time of their lives... right now, is the best time there has ever been to be a **Gemini** (even better than the 15th Century when **Johannes Gutenberg** invented the printing press... way better then that)
- **Geminis** are the sign of the Zodiac who are meant to never stand still.. in fact, they're hard-wired to keep moving

GEMINI

*The Astrological Glyph which the Ancient Astrologers associated with the Sign of **Gemini** was Twins. Once again, we need to cast our minds back to Ancient Mesopotamia and Egypt to understand what this Glyph may mean in terms of the Sign of **Gemini**. And back then, the successful birth of Twins would have been a rare event... especially when you factor in the danger involved with ancient childbirth from even a single baby. So Twins were special.. and rare. Now... this is one which I cannot ever prove... but I have a suspicion that the Ancient Seers had some kind of understanding about our 2 Brains... the left and right hemispheres... and the specialisation between the two sides of our nature. And, they most probably did know all about the two sides of the Mind... the Rational + Intellectual... and the Feeling + Intuitive... and so came up with the image of Twins to capture and demonstrate this duality in our psyche... identical and yet different.*

* * * * * * * * * *

Right now, **Geminis** are just too busy surfing the web, taking in everything there is to learn to have time to complete that PhD... they don't have time to specialize... and why should they when they're having so much fun?

Right now, where the other 11 Zodiac signs are suffering from information overload, **Gemini** is loving it all.

Bring it on!... Hey, you guys keep up... What's information overload? ... This is so amazing!

Like I said, right now, **Geminis** are having the time of their lives... so much to learn, so much that is new, so much constant change and mental stimulation.

Look... someone has posted a new theory on Black Holes... and that famous actress-singer has dumped her latest boyfriend... and look another cute cat video!

Gemini's love being so plugged in.

But there is a catch... unfortunately.

Because is the point of our life a quest to achieve a definite goal... or is it to just keep on questing... and we don't care about what?

At the end of the day... at the end of your life... what have you got to show for it all?

Or put another way... is it just about accessing bucket loads of information... or is the quality and content of the information important?

In those 2 questions... lies the whole dilemma for a **Gemini**.

Let me explain.

OK, the German astrologer **Reinhold Ebertin** originally made the connection between **Gemini** and the Liver Meridian, and this link allows us to make a further link, drawing upon the work of the kinesiologist, **John Diamond**, because in his energy system/ approach the Liver Meridian is linked to the positive quality of Happiness, and the negative quality of Unhappiness.

And if I may... throwing in the **Elemental Archetype** for **Gemini** from **Energy Astrology**...*Energizing the Mind*... (in fact, with a **Gemini**, their mental body is so energetically stimulated that they can't switch it off, and they need to find something to occupy and entertain it... they require constant mental stimulation).

To understand **Gemini**... and it took me a while to figure this out... we need to understand that they are a Sign that needs constant motion... mental stimulation... they are on a continual quest... and even if they where to achieve the desired goal of the quest, the very next second they would be packing up for their next quest.

And all their many quests are really all about finding Happiness.

Now, **Aries** is also on a quest... as we have already seen... but their quests are to do with the physical world in some way, and they are looking for some kind of physical challenge to help them conquer their fear.

In contrast, **Gemini** quests are always to do with the Mind, they want to learn something new, a piece of information which will stimulate them... and help them to hold back the boredom.

But the next **Gemini** question now becomes... *What exactly is Happiness?*

Well... although is may sound like a closed-loop answer... for a **Gemini**, Happiness = Motion, and Motion = Happiness... and because **Gemini** is a mental Sign, that motion needs to have a mental / interesting and stimulating ideas component.

The very fact they are on a quest is what makes them happy…
not on achieving the end goal… which is useful, helps to give a
direction and mental focus… but the goal is definitely not what
makes them Happy.

It's the quest, the journey itself, which is the source of their
Happiness.

As the famous poem *Ithaca* by **C.P. Cavafy** states:

… Always keep Ithaca in your mind;
to reach her is your destiny.
But do not rush your journey in the least.
Better that it last for many years;
that you drop anchor at the island an old man,
rich with all you've gotten on the way,
not expecting Ithaca to make you rich.

Ithaca gave to you the beautiful journey;
without her you'd not have set upon the road.
But she has nothing left to give you any more.

That is a travel poem almost written for all **Geminis**.

They are not like **Sagittarius**, who wants to stand still and study a
topic in depth for their whole life. No, for **Gemini**, that would be too
boring, too static, too limiting…

For a **Gemini**… it would be their version of Hell!!!

So to say "*Jack of all trades, master of none*"… which is often said
about **Gemini**… isn't really fair, because they were never put on
this earth to master any trade… that's not their function, not their
unique gift or talent… and all the Astrological signs have a unique
gift (what would be the point of any of the 12 Astrological Signs
doing or being exactly the same?)

And that's what confused me about **Gemini** for a long time… you see, seen from the eyes of a **Sagittarius** say, it's as if **Geminis** are fickle, easily bored… can't settle down… probably because they haven't found the right topic/subject yet… but when they do, they'll be able to mentally settle and put down roots…

In other words, it is assumed by a **Sagittarius** or **Virgo** that when a **Gemini** finds the right subject to occupy their mental energies they will evolve.

Wrong, wrong… wrong… and wrong.

Geminis will never settle down and become a **Sagittarius** say… focusing on one topic forever after…

By their very nature, they can't… and why should they?

Because a **Gemini** is not designed or intended to carry out that function within our psyche… or within society at large.

And if you think about it from an Evolutionary point of view, Humanity would never have evolved, have never got to where we are if there wasn't something within us which wasn't *infinitely restless*… if there wasn't something inside ourselves which would continually settle for the old & reliable… and instead, didn't keep pushing to see what was beyond the next mountain…

And that part of us is **Gemini**… and an **Uber-Gemini** feels that inner force, that continual need for momentum, most keenly.

I wouldn't be surprised if it wasn't a **Gemini** who kick-started human Evolution a million odd years ago… "*Look, I was suddenly struck by the idea to see what would happen if I put the raw meat over the fire… just taste it… there… it tastes a whole lot better…*"

Gemini can never keep still... is always moving... especially on the mental plane... because that is its role... to keep us moving forward in life... as individuals, as a society and as a species.

And when you have 4 books on the go at any one time... when you have been interested in and studied 7 different subjects in the last 12 months... then it is also becomes possible to *link ideas between different areas... find connections... make new discoveries... perceive wider and deeper patterns...*

In his book, *Dragon Rises, Red Bird Flies: Psychology & Chinese Medicine*, the psychiatrist and acupuncturist **Leon Hammer**... (yes, such a hybrid does actually exist)... also states that the Liver Meridian is all about *motion*.

Which is kind of what the 21st Century is all about... it's no longer just about making a new discovery... but progress is more often about liking Idea A with Idea B to come up with a different way of doing things... even if those 2 Ideas come from different sciences and / or disciplines...

Which is kind of what **Energy Astrology** is all about, how they developed (plus Audio Essences)...

The Ancient Greek Mystic **Heraclitus** once said... "*You can never step in the same river twice...*" ... because the river is always flowing, the water is always changing... nothing remains the same.

But for a **Gemini**, it is more about stepping into as many rivers as possible... and the more change the better.

The majority of the time the motion is forward, but occasionally the motion has to be backwards because in life there are times when it is necessary to retreat to avoid an obstacle... and if all motion is lost, then the individual is plunged into depression... which for a **Gemini** is a total loss of motion, a feeling of being not only bored but stuck and totally trapped.

It is interesting that this kind of depression (and I believe there are 2 types basically) is usually depicted as being locked in a prison, with no chance of escape... no chance of movement... no brightness, all is grey and totally devoid of colour and mental stimulation... i.e. a **Gemini** description of Hell... total lock-down boring.

And so our next question has to be... well, if **Gemini** is a mind-orientated sign... where exactly is it going to look for Happiness?

In the realm of emotions, like **Cancer**... or in the realm of the physical, like **Taurus**...?

No... **Gemini** is a mind-orientated sign... so Happiness can only be found in the realm of the mind...

Gemini will always associate Happiness with some kind of mental stimulation.

And this also implies that Unhappiness occurs when a **Gemini** is locked into any boring environment... trapped...

Have you ever tried to manage a bored **Gemini**? When your back is turned... immediately they're on to the Internet, surfing... trying to find fresh mental stimulation...

Which they can't find in any boring, monotonous task you give them... no matter how hard they try. (That's why the perfect job for a **Gemini** is probably journalist... where the newsfeed is changing daily, even hourly.)

To be honest, they're not being disrespectful... or out to undermine your authority... it's just that the work you're providing them with is boring, and they have a desperate need for mental stimulation... it's like a mental drug to them.

Their Mind literally seizes up when they are bored... and they find it painful.

If you are to stand any chance of success... **Geminis** need roles that lend themselve to multi-tasking... they perform better when they are juggling several different tasks at the same time...

Helps them to keep the boredom at bay.

(Although there is a case to be made for saying "*Maybe you are in the wrong job entirely... maybe you need to find a way of earning money that is more mentally stimulating for you...*")

It used to be that a way to feed their constant need for mental stimulation, a **Gemini** would have 3 or 4 books on the go at any one time (and they probably still do)... but in the 21st Century... why start/finish a book when you can plunge into the Internet for any fresh data-fix you need... and social media... a **Geminis** total dream.

Look... someone has posted a new theory on Black Holes... and that famous actress-singer has dumped her latest boyfriend... and look another cute cat video!

In fact, in the 21st Century, your average **Gemini** is probably the happiest they have ever been in the whole long history of Humanity... ever since they got Human civilization started long ago.

I mean... the discovery of fire... and the invention of the wheel seemed very interesting at the time... and the discovery of the printing press was a blast for a while...

But for a **Gemini** now, that's nothing compared to an afternoon spent surfing the Net.

Chapter 2-5: Cancer & Stomach Meridian

Westerners often have a hard time getting their heads around the Meridian system... because in our medical tradition, over the last 300 years, organs definitely *did not* and *do not* have an emotional, mental, and even spiritual component...

They were (and still are in some people's minds) just mechanical body parts... nothing more, and nothing less.

But for many of our Ancient Ancestors... well, they had a completely different attitude to the physical body...

To the Ancients, they had a completely different set of priorities then we do in the Modern World... For example...

CANCER

*The Astrological Glyph which the Ancient Astrologers associated with the Sign of **Cancer** was the Crab. Now... I did once wonder how the Ancient Mesopotamians and Egyptians had access to Crabs... but apparently there are fresh water Crabs in the Nile... and so I assume the same is also true for the Tigris and Euphrates. So if the Ancient Seers were able to observe Crabs... which need water to survive, are heavily protected, walk sideways... and need to shed their skin and armour to grow... which leaves them vulnerable for a time... perfect image for **Cancer**.*

* * * * * * * * * *

The Ancient Tibetans did develop a rudimentary form of surgery... but discarded it from their medical tradition... because they felt that through harming the physical body with a knife... you were also harming the Soul...

So they dropped surgery from their medical tradition... because the continued health of the Soul was more important to them then the healh the physical body. After all, a Soul can always re-incarnate into a brand new body after death...

And also... from a different culture and tradition...

The Ancient Egyptians believed the Heart was the most important organ within the body, which is why they went to such pains to preserve it during the mummification process. The Brain they just threw away.

It is interesting how many ancient civilizations regarded the Heart to be more important than the Brain. Today, now that we are aware of what the Brain does, modern science just assumes that these ancient civilizations were blind and ignorant of the facts... but what if it is we who are missing something quite important, something that to our ancestors was blindingly obvious?

To understand the difference between the Heart and the Brain, it is perhaps useful to use the phenomenon of electromagnetism as an analogy. The Brain generates thought, which is like electricity, and the Heart generates a magnetic field, which is equivalent to our emotional states. Modern science teaches us that electricity and magnetism are two sides of the same phenomenon, which is known as an electromagnetic field, and that electricity can create magnetic fields, and magnetic fields can create electricity. It's a two-way process, and it is the basis for much of our modern technology.

Now, science has also shown that our Brain/thoughts can influence our Heart/emotions and our energy field. Is it therefore too big a step to consider that the Heart's magnetic field might not also be able to influence and control the type of thoughts that the Brain generates?

And if a culture was more orientated towards the spiritual, such as the Ancient Egyptians and Chinese... or Tibetans, then it would not be a total surprise to discover that they would place less emphasis upon the Brain's ability to think, and more upon the Heart's ability to love and magnetically influence the Brain?

Recent scientific discoveries have also shown that the Small Intestine is also a far more interesting organ then first thought... and produces neurochemicals, similar to the Brain... and so gives some credence to the Ancient's idea of an Abdominal Brain.

This starts to take us into a world where organs are more than just mechanical... and the emotional and mental is definitely woven into the fabric of the physical... we're so not in Kansas anymore... and much closer to how the original Ancient Chinese discoverers thought about the Meridian system.

But there is one organ where its physical function is very close to its emotional, mental, and spiritual functions.

Yep, you guessed... it's the Stomach meridian.

OK, the German astrologer **Reinhold Ebertin** originally made the connection between **Cancer** and the Stomach meridian, and this link allows us to make a further association, drawing upon the work of the kinesiologist, **John Diamond**, because in his energy system/ approach the Stomach meridian is linked to the positive quality of Contentment, and the negative quality of Emptiness and Hunger...

However... This is the second Meridian where I find using the concept of Nurturing is more useful to an understanding of the Meridian then **Diamond's** association of Contentment... although Contentment also has truth from a different perspective.

And if I may... throwing in the Elemental Archetype for **Cancer** from Energy Astrology... *Grounding Emotions* (as we shall see, Cancer feels emotions more deeply than any other Zodiac sign... in fact, you could say that for a **Cancerian**, emotions have a tangible, physical reality... and bad emotion is felt and hurts in the same way a sharp pin thrust into skin hurts).

Now... have you ever been hungry... no, not just a little bit hungry... but really, *really*, **really hungry**?

It feels terrible... and is literally all-consuming.

If it continues, the body has no option but to start drawing upon its fat reserves... if they exist... and if food is not found after that, then non-vital systems start to close down, as it starts to draw in its other emergency stored resources.

When you are hungry, you cannot think about anything else... your body won't let you... and that is part of its survival mechanism.

All you can think about, and feel, is the emptiness *within*... and all your psychic energy is focused on ending that hunger and emptiness.

If you have watched Survival programmes on the Documentary TV channel... the programmes where one or two survivalists are dropped off in a very remote location and have to fend for themselves, catching and eating whatever they can find.

Well, more often then not, the naturally sourced food isn't readily available... and so they go hungry... *really hungry*... and they become obsesssed with finding food.

The importance of finding food is literally hard-wired into every cell of our body... across a billion years of evolution... it is of primary importance... and it starts to scream in our brain.

When someone experiences being hungry, they soon discover it is all consuming... literally. If you cannot consume without... then you start to consume within.

In fact, most individuals living in our relatively the affluent Western world have no idea of the crucifying effects of real/true hunger.

You can't think straight, you don't have the energy... and what little mental energy that you can gather is focused on one thing... *finding food*... it consumes every waking moment, and sleep becomes an impossibility, you are too hungry... but the weaker you become physically, the harder it is to achieve... you desperately need food, but just can't gather enough strength/focus to get it...

A deadly downward spiral.

And if you are surrounded by your family, small children, babies... all of whom are suffering the same fate... it gets even worse... and as energy levels fall, tribal and family loyalty is also put to the test.

Real sustained hunger can even break tribal and family bonds.

In the Modern World, we tend to forget that one of the four Horsemen of the Apocalypse was famine... one of the constants of Human history until very recently in the West... but still stalking people in many other parts of the world.

Back in Ancient Egypt, there is evidence of a terrible famine which lasted 10 years... and it brought the successful and affluent Old Kingdom to an end... and there is strong evidence that people resorted to eating rats, even cannibalism... and that society came to a complete halt during this period.

A similar fate befell the Ancient Maya, in their stone cities dotted across the Yucatan Peninsula... with all the warfare and the Human sacrifice... they weren't able to see the simple truth... their farmers weren't able to grow food enough to feed their continually expanding population...

Hunger can literally level whole civilizations ... brings us to our knees... and what is true for human society is also true for any individual.

Hunger can stop us in our tracks... turn all our hopes and dreams meaningless for the duration.

So let's spin that up a level or two... to the emotional and mental levels... to understand how **Cancer** feels and thinks.

For a **Cancer**, there are certain feelings.... and certain ideas... which it needs to survive and continue... which sustain and nurture it.

And when we say *survive*... that's exactly what we mean... a matter of life and death.

Or perhaps a better way is to say that a **Cancer** believes that certain feelings and ideas are nurturing... and so it associates those feelings/ ideas with being nurtured... and so they are the only things which can end their inner hunger (for a while)... fill the inner emptiness.

... But if those feelings/ideas are not forthcoming from the environment, then **Cancer** feels their absence intensely, as a hunger... a deep craving... an emotional emptiness which needs to be filled...

And which continues to hurt them... cause them pain... while it remains unfilled...

And this emotional/mental hunger can become just as all-consuming as any physical hunger.

It totally focuses the mind of a **Cancer**... how can I fill this emotional and mental emptiness?

And if the Universe will not deliver what a **Cancer** needs... then fine... it has a whole box of subtle games and manipulations to make the other people give it what it needs... (something coerced is never as sweet and fulfilling as something given freely... although if you are a desperate and needy **Cancer**, you'll take any emotional food you can get... a desperate **Cancer** will even take anger instead of love, because at least it is some kind of emotional response from the beloved).

Even if **Cancer** is lucky enough to find a partner who is able to fill their emotional emptiness... there is always the fear they might leave... which is why some **Cancerians** become clingy... trying to weave a web of emotional bonds from which another person can never escape.

A **Cancerian** can be like a sipder in the centre of an emotional web... which is spins to capture and ensnare others... because **Cancer**, so at home in the world of emotions, knows how to be emotionally manipulative to get its own way... probably better then any other Sign... with the possible exception of **Scorpio**.

The thing which you need to really understand about **Cancer**... their desperate need for emotional and mental nurturing... and if deprived... the desperate lengths it will go to feed the emptiness within (even if it means they're not thinking straight... which technically, they're not)... and how sometimes their nurturing of others is a way to connect with the same feeling they also desperately desire within.

Now, as with many of the other signs, the trick is to learn to give yourself what you need... but when you are a desperate **Cancer**, and you're not thinking right... what are the chances of that happening?

Interesting side thought... perhaps one of the reasons why humanity stayed with the hunter-gatherer culture for millennia was because the desperate need to continually find food, to keep the hunger at bay, locked people into **Cancerian** / tribal consciousness throughout this period. It wasn't until the Agrarian revolution occurred, and food production went into surplus and over-abundance mode, that for better or worse, humanity left the tribal culture behind... its **Cancerian** roots... and our expansive culture and cities could begin and spread.

Just a thought...

Chapter 2-6: Leo & Heart Meridian

I have a colleague whose ex-partner is in a Beatles tribute band.

... and she once explained, that even though she knew he was an average kind of guy... as soon as he stepped out on stage as John, Paul, George or Ringo... (he was very versatile, and in his career had played each member of the Fab 4)... some strange transformation happened...

It was as if all the energy and adoration which was being projected from the audience towards the stage transformed him and his bandmates into something *larger*... more *expanded*... more *elevated*... And, of course, he totally loved it... all that energy... all that attention... flowing his way...

LEO

The Astrological Glyph which the Ancient Astrologers associated with the Sign of Leo was a Lion. Once again, we need to cast our minds back to Ancient Mesopotamia and Egypt to understand what this Glyph may mean in terms of the Sign of Leo. And back then, Lions were much more common then they are now... especially across the Middle East... and so where dangerous. And they were associated with Kingship... not only through being top of the pecking order... but because it was considered kingly for a King to hunt and kill a Lion... which is something you see depicted several times in Egyptian hieroglyphics. So the Astrological Sign of Leo is really all about being top... being the centre... being the best.

* * * * * * * * * *

She said that even after coming off stage, signing autographs, people still saw him as a genuine Beatle...

It was an in the eye of the beholder kind of thing.

And in that transformation... I believe you get a glimpse into the heart of every true **Leo** alive.

You see... people often read that **Leo** is a sign that is linked to acting... and they naturally assume it is because **Leos** like playing different roles... but actually, that's not really it at all...

Yes, they like standing on the stage, in front of an audience...
but not necessarily because they are playing a part (and they are certainly not playing any role to escape from an inadequate sense of self... well, certainly not all of them...)

No, it's because when you are on stage... in front of an audience... *all eyes are on you...* you are the centre of attention... all the psychic energy is focused on you... and as a result, you feel more alive.

That's what a true **Leo** is looking for... that sense of love and aliveness.

It's all about the love of attention... both on a personality level... and also on an energy or psychic level.

... And it took me a while to figure it out... but I think it's because the energy boost they get from others... focusing on them... helps them to connect with their inner/true core... the energy boost and lift they get whenever someone loves and adores them...

That's why I find that **Leos** are actually... weirdly... one of the most energetically complex of all the 12 Astrological Signs... (... and who would have thought... they kept that well hidden, didn't they).

They want to be... they desire to be... the centre of attention... for a definite reason.

... Let me explain.

OK, the German astrologer **Reinhold Ebertin** originally made the connection between **Leo** and the Heart Meridian, and this link allows us to make a further association, drawing upon the work of the kinesiologist, **John Diamond**, because in his energy system/ approach the Heart Meridian is linked to the positive quality of Love, and the negative quality of Anger...

And if I may... throwing in the Elemental Archetype for **Leo** from **Energy Astrology**...*Spiritual Beauty* (and the desperate need to avoid spiritual ugliness).

For a long time, that was the problem... when I worked out the formula for the Elemental Archetype for **Leo**... out came the answer... Spiritual Beauty...

But then this raised the question...

What exactly is Spiritual Beauty?

That had me stalled for a long time.

And I got the answer... and a clear understanding of the core of **Leo**... from an unlikely source... the ancient story of the fallen archangel **Lucifer**.

Now... I am not saying that **Leos** are demons... hear me out here... (although I am sure some people will have encountered **Leo** boyfriends/girlfriends/partners who were definitely anything but angels).

You see, **Lucifer** was originally the highest of God's angels... the most glorious and beautiful... and his name means *light-bringer*.

However, one day God produced a baby-brother for the angels... Mankind... and ordered the angels and arch-angels to bow down and worship man...

To which **Lucifer** replied... "*What! No way am I bowing down and worshiping that frail and puny creature...*"

This may have been the first ever appearance of **Leo's** inherent pride and hard-wired ego... but let's skip over that for the moment...

For refusing to bow down to Mankind (i.e. us), **Lucifer** was cast out of Heaven and into the depths of Hell.

Because in Heaven, the whole obeying thing is taken quite seriously...

He was cast beyond the Divine Light... into the darkest pit possible.

And after **Lucifer** literally hit rock bottom... he was so angry... in fact, all his acts of badness ever since, his desire to wreak revenge through those small ape creatures he refused to worship, have been fueled by his raging resentment... and the fact that he is really pissed off at God (as anyone who has watched all the series of the TV show *Supernatural* will know full well... theirs is the ultimate father-son battle).

Lucifer has fallen from the Loving Bliss of Heaven into the Angry Fires of Hell... which is the same potential spectrum which all **Leos** experience in their life.

Now in that above story... there are so many clues as to the true energy nature of **Leo**... if you know where to look.

Firstly... **Lucifer** was cast down into Hell... but question... why had God created Hell to begin with... previous to **Lucifer** being banished into it?

Unless Hell is a metaphor for something... the falling into, and being trapped, by lower vibrational emotions, such as Anger perhaps?

And if Hell = Anger... then Heaven = Love?

So I have come to believe that **Leo** represents that part of us which remembers, vaguely perhaps, the higher dimensions of Love... our inner Heaven... and longs to return there... desperately longs to re-connect with transcending/transforming Love... and experiences Anger when we are deprived... when we are locked out of vibrational Heaven.

Because **Leo** is the part of us which remembers what Heaven was like...

... And **Leos** are eternally searching for a way back... and believe that if they can gather enough love and attention from other people... that energy blast will help to raise them up... help them to open the inner door to Heaven within themselves.

There is a Zen story on this very subject... how Heaven lies within.

A Samurai Warrior goes to a Zen Master and says *"Show me Heaven & Hell."*

The Zen Master says... *"You are an ignorant fool."*

The Samurai Warrior draws his swords shouting... *"How dare you insult me!"*

The Zen Master looks at him calmly saying... *"Your anger is Hell."*

Suddenly the Warrior understands, and sheaths his sword.

To which the Zen Master responds... *"And that is Heaven."*

For example... just suppose...

Picture a celestial travel agency up above... where Souls go to read all the latest brochures about this amazing destination called... Planet Earth... a fantastic place where you can learn all kinds of life lessons... and process karma... and... stuff like that...

Wow... incredible... there is nothing like that in the rest of manifest Creation... where do we sign?

And so Souls sign up for a few incarnations on Planet Earth... and when they arrive... they discover it's nothing like what the brochure said... it's 100% horrible... there are all these lower emotions, and people are mean and nasty to one another... and bad karma clings to you, lifetime after lifetime... trapping you into physical incarnation.

Yep, lifetime after lifetime... after lifetime.

Talk about a Holiday from Hell.

But then... sometimes Earth is Hell... especially if you are born into an area of the planet locked into anger, revenge and rage...

And so it would not be surprising if a part of our Soul gets angry at the fact that they left dimensions of Unconditional Love and Bliss for... *an experience down here?*

But of course... that's just a metaphor... no truth in it, is there?

Well... maybe... a lot depends on your belief system I suppose...

But I have come to believe that **Leo** is the part of us that longs for a return to Love and Unconditional Love... the higher dimensions and energy spaces... and feels Anger at being trapped in these lower vibrational planes... *down here*... stuck in the energy mud of fear, and worry, and lack, apathy, guilt, and shame... and < *fill in any other favourite limiting emotions here*>.

So how do you get back up there... back up to energy heaven?

By changing your vibration, re-tuning your Heart to Love... and as with the other 11 Astrological Signs... a **Leo** can either create it within for themselves... or search for it without... i.e. find a way to get other people to give it to them... to Love them... to shower them with Love and energy and attention... to turn the spotlight towards them.

But through finding Love within... you are always *self-sufficient*, and so can cope with whatever life throws at you (this is the highly evolved kind of **Leos**).

However, there is the other way... **Leos** who get their Love fix through getting other people to shine their love light on them.

These are the **Leos** who need to stand out... who need to stand centre stage... who need to be the centre of attention...

Because for this energy strategy to work... these **Leos** need to be seen... (other people can't love a **Leo** who is in hiding, can they?)

And this strategy can work very effectively... until the inevitable happens, and the spotlight is suddenly taken away, for whatever reason... and then it is...

Total meltdown... with the **Leo** plunging back down into Anger Hell.

"How dare they ignore me... how dare they leave me alone... how dare they... I am so angry at them for treating me this way!!! ... Don't they know who I am???"

Just like **Lucifer** being cast out of Heaven... *so unfair!*

Like I said... **Leos** are one of the most complex Astrological Signs...

much more complex then you would think at first glance.

A **Leo** ignored... it feels to them like someone has turned off the spotlight, leaving them in the dark.

Note: After hitting rock bottom in Hell, why **Lucifer** didn't shout... *"Sorry!... Can I have a second chance please... those man-puppies... I am sure they have many redeeming features that are not initially apparent... Can I come back upstairs now please? Any chance of some forgiveness for me down here?"* ... we shall never know.

Leo pride, I guess.

It is also interesting to note that the Heart Meridian, in the Chinese energy systems, is considered to be the centre... the Emperor... of all the Meridians...

In a similar way that the Astrological Sign of **Leo** is associated with a Lion... who is the King of the beasts...

So perhaps the Astrological Sign of **Leo** is also about stepping into your true, inner power...

About re-discovering your angel wings...

About re-discovering your inner Love...

Which are the vibrational wings which can allow you to fly back to Heaven...

Where you soon discover that God was never angry at you to begin with...

It was all a mistake of your mis-perception...

Chapter 2-7: Virgo & Large Intestine Meridian

In the above photo, a puppy has just destroyed a cushion, ripping it apart, feathers all over the place... and you can just imagine its owner, standing over it, saying... *"Bad dog!... Naughty dog!"*

Trying to make the puppy feel guilty... which is pretty much the same tactic which people try to use on other people when they want to control their behaviour.

Because when you make someone else feel guilty, it becomes easier to undermine them and control them, because people will do almost anything to avoid the low and horrible feeling of guilt.

Why?

VIRGO

*The Astrological Glyph which the Ancient Astrologers associated with the Sign of **Virgo** was the Virgin. Now... Astrology was born in lands, such as Egypt and Mesopotamia... and back then, women were expected to spend a period of time as a Sacred Prostitute, aligned to a Temple... providing a service to the God or Goddess. So we shouldn't let our Modern concept of virginity colour how it was perceived millennia ago... where it represented a woman who slept with many men... but who never gave away their sacred, inner nature and energies to any man... they never gave away, within them, what belonged to the Divine.*

* * * * * * * * * *

Well, let's begin disentangling that by tracking the link between the Astrological Sign of **Virgo** to the issue of Guilt.

OK, the German astrologer **Reinhold Ebertin** originally made the connection between **Virgo** and the Large Intestine Meridian, and this link allows us to make a further association, drawing upon the work of the kinesiologist, **John Diamond**, because in his energy system/approach the Large Intestine is linked to the positive quality of Self-Worth, and the negative quality of Guilt.

In a psychosomatic approach, the Large Intestine is where we process our waste before it is expelled, so it is the place where we energetically place all the psychic material we do not want to face, the psychic material we feel guilty about.

Or to simplify that equation a little... -ve **Virgo** = Guilt, +ve **Virgo** = Self-Worth.

But now we have the equation, the next question... *what exactly is guilt?*

Well, a useful definition is that an individual feels guilt when they know they have done something bad/wrong, as opposed to shame, which occurs when an individual believes themselves to be bad/wrong, and so everything they do is also bound to be bad/wrong.

So shame is even more toxic then guilt, because at least with guilt you can say "*I have done a bad thing... but I am still a good person*", with shame that defence is taken away totally from you, because you define yourself as being bad through and through.

Parents try to educate their kids... and puppies... by defining certain actions as bad, and creating a sense of guilt, so that the kids/puppies won't repeat those actions because of the bad feeling attached to the action.

Both shame and guilt are very low vibration, which results in two things:

Guilt feels so awful that people will do anything to avoid feeling guilty, something which priests down the millennia have used to control their tribes, as has mothers/fathers for untold generations. Unfortunately, a small child doesn't always understand the difference between an action they have carried out, and their own independent sense of self, so often at an early age guilt is accompanied by a fair degree of shame, which is actually the most toxic of all emotions, because it cuts into the root of who we believe ourselves to be.

Now, one of the things which **Virgo** is known for is... *perfectionism* on a good day... and *procrastination* on a bad day.

But both of these can be traced back to guilt.

Perfectionism is a way of avoiding guilt, or at least, people hope it is, because you constantly strive so that your actions/creations will be perfect, because then no one can ever then find fault with them, and if no one can find fault with them, no one can ever criticize you, and if no one can ever criticize you, then you are never going to ever feel guilty.

See how it works?

That's why **Virgo's** strive for perfection, because it is a way, they believe or hope, of avoiding the guilt they dread.

Procrastination works in a similar way... if you never finish anything, no one can ever criticize it, because it is always a work in progress, which means no one can ever criticize you, then you are never going to ever feel guilt.

See how that approach works?

Virgo's have a tendency to avoid finishing anything, not because they can't (actually they are very capable fellows), but because if / when they do finish something, they are open to people judging their creation... which... etc... etc... could end up in their feeling guilty.

Virgo's have a reputation of being able to find fault with anything... but they live in fear of the same precise eye being turned on them...

because if they are found to be at fault... yep, you guessed it... a tsunami of guilt.

Strangely, if you are very **Virgoan** (i.e. several planets in **Virgo** say), from early childhood you have usually discovered that you would rather **not try**... and so settle on feeling the frustration of never completing anything, rather than try, complete, fail, be judged, and end up feeling guilty.

Because, overall, frustration is a better feeling then guilt, compared to frustration, guilt really sucks, and so must be avoided at all costs.

It's a game of which feeling feels marginally better.

So how does all this track with Self-Worth?

Well, once again, if we go back to the definition of the word, Self-worth is all about *doing*.

Self-Love is about *being*... it's the love you get from the Universe... for free... for just being alive.

But Self-Worth is something you create yourself, what you make for yourself whenever you flex your own doing muscles... try, complete and succeed... whenever you step outside of your Comfort Zone.

But it doesn't last forever... to maintain a good sense of Self-Worth, after you have conquered one mountain... rest, recharge... but after a while, you will need a new challenge to motivate you... a new far off mountain to dream of climbing. Something which gets you outside your Comfort Zone... because being trapped within the safety and boredom of your comfort zone is what, paradoxically, kills off your stock of Self-worth.

Hence the phrase, *don't rest on your laurels*.

Every now and then you need a new challenge, a new skill to learn, something to do to see if your muscles still work... and to recharge your Self-Worth.

Self-Love is there for the asking... Self-Worth is something you have to create for yourself.

But guilt can really screw-up our mental works... damage our internal mechanism... because if guilt is all about believing we have done something bad, and Self-Worth arises from a successful doing...

Well, if you suffer from guilt, then the last thing you will want to do, is actually **do**, because that might lead to more failure and greater guilt.

So the danger is that **Virgos** never step outside their Comfort Zones... unless there is something else, wild and crazy, going on in their chart, they seldom go off and have adventures (i.e. apart from Bilbo & Frodo, the majority of Hobbits must all be **Virgos**)... they let their sensible side (influenced by a fear of guilt) talk them out of ever travelling beyond their version of The Shire.

Which means they never give themselves the opportunity to accomplish great things (unless there is something else going on in their chart to compensate).

That's why guilt is so corrosive to our feelings of Self-Worth... and all of the above dramas are played out, almost every day, by someone who has a lot of **Virgo** planets in their chart.

It is natural for a small child to explore its world, its boundaries... and through doing so it makes mistakes, milk gets tipped over, the cat gets painted red, wall-paper gets drawn on... and boundaries do need to be set, and the child needs to know that certain actions are unacceptable in a civilized society.

But if the parent's response is too draconian, too harsh, then guilt sets in... and the child stops moving forwards... it becomes too afraid to try... and the guilt censor takes up permanent residence in its mind.

And if you get all that... then it will help you understand how the mind of a pure **Virgoan** works... and what emotional forces drive it.

Although, if a Virgo can get a handle on the whole guilt-shame thing, stop procrastinating, and avoid the need for everything to be perfect, then it's focus and attention to detail can make it it a very effective player on the Earth stage, with a good sense of Self-Worth, which is continually fuelled by all its successful doings.

Chapter 2-8: Libra & Heart Protector Meridian

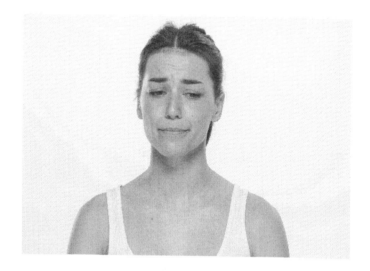

When you talk about **Libra**... you cannot *not* talk about...

Relationships and other people.

Because, for better or worse, other people and relationships lie at the core of what **Libra** is all about.

John Paul Satre once said... "*Hell is other people*"... which is true, but that automatically suggests that "*Heaven is other people*" as well... and as the gifted 20th Century psychic **Edgar Cayce** (aka the Sleeping Prophet) stated about his life:

LIBRA

The Astrological Glyph which the Ancient Astrologers associated
with the Sign of **Libra** was the Scales... and probably basic scales...
at least from our perspective... reliant on weight and gravity. Now...
Astrology was born in lands, such as Egypt and Mesopotamia...
and back then, scales were associated with trade and taxation...
and scales were used to ensure that people weren't cheating you...
or you weren't cheating someone else... that the gold which you
were being given was the real thing, and had not been diluted
down. So the glyph of the scales is associated with fairness, truth...
and fairness is one of the cornerstones of all Human relationships.
Remember, this was long before the invention of money, and so the
quality of the gold and silver you were being given for your goods
and services, and whether it had been diluted down or not, was
paramount to establishing a fair and equitable trading relationship.

* * * * * * * * * *

"If I ever get to heaven, it will be carried on the backs of all the
people I have helped."

Other people bring out the worst in us... and the best.., and vice
versa.

And in those two quotations is mapped out the whole territory for a
Libra.

Because, in a sense, Libra is an Astrological Sign caught between the
potential Heaven and Hell, which is to be found in our relationships
with other people.

Some people will treat us fairly, while others will try to cheat us.

And we must be able to deal effectively with each type of different
situation, if and when they occur.

Let me explain.

OK, the German astrologer **Reinhold Ebertin** originally made the
connection between Libra and the Heart Protector meridian, and
this link allows us to make a further association, drawing upon the
work of the kinesiologist, **John Diamond**, because in his energy
system/approach the Heart Protector Meridian is linked to the
positive quality of Relaxation, and the negative qualities of Regret &
Remorse...

And if I may, throwing in the Elemental Archetype for **Libra** from
Energy Astrology...*Mental Beauty*.

Now, if **Taurus** is concerned with Physical Beauty, **Pisces** with
Emotional Beauty, and **Leo** with Spiritual Beauty... then **Libra** is the
sign which focused on the need for... any guesses?... yes, Mental
Beauty.

But what is Mental Beauty? ... Well, in one direction... it is art,
poetry, fine writing... anything which awakens our mental, aesthetic
sense.

But the thing which all **Librans** elevate to a true art form is... *relationships*.

And if you think about it, relationships are mental creations.

OK, I know, there are species throughout the Animal kingdom which mate for life, and so engage in life-long relationships with the same partner, so humans are not special in that regard.

But it is only human beings who have taken relationships in a totally different direction, and elevated them to an art-form, and our use of language creates dimensions of harmony and conflict unknown by any other creature on land, sea or air.

And of the 12 Astrological Signs, **Librans** are the Sign whose purpose on Earth is to make their relationships the most beautiful they possibly can... the most harmonious... the most perfect...

And can anyone see the potential problem with that goal?

Yes... as **Satre** says... *Hell is other people.*

If there was a planet totally populated with **Librans**, then they might just stand a chance of achieving beauty and perfection... a planet of people living in perfect harmony... (as the old Coke advert used to say... "*I'd like to teach the world to sing in perfect harmony!*")

Unfortunately, and to quote **Duran Duran** here, this is Planet Earth... where the other 11 Astrology Signs roam around, unchecked by the Mental Beauty police.

And as soon as you throw in a **Virgo**, a **Capricorn**, a **Cancer**... or the worst imaginable for a **Libran**... a self-centred **Aries** into the mix... then beauty and harmony soon go out the window... and any **Libran** starts to struggle to hold on to their dream of a mentally perfect and beautiful relationship.

Unless they are in a relationship with another **Libran**, no other Sign has such an inner investment in trying to keep the beauty going in any relationship (although **Pisces** does come close in some areas, for different reasons)... and so **Librans** often feel let down, because they often feel they are doing all the work in the relationship.

And this is when we start to slide into the negative side of **Libra**, because so desperate are they to hold on to the beautiful relationship dream, that they start making compromises, they start to put the other's wants/needs first, ahead of their own, they start to bite their tongue when they should say *"No way"* or *"That's not for fair on me."*.

Imagine someone with lots of Planets in **Libra**, in a relationship with someone with lots of Planets in **Aries**... they must have bitten their tongue so many times down the years, they need a new one!

Librans will try to make the relationship work, even when it is at their own expense, long after they should have walked out the door.

They have a tough time letting go of a failed or failing relationship because they believe that if only they could compromise a little more, then they could make it work, they could make it all beautiful.

And divorce for a **Libran** must indeed be a total nightmare... especially if the intimate details of a relationship are brought out and discussed in open court.

Which brings us to the main negative emotion for **Libra**... Regret (and Remorse is really Regret on steroids)... Regret is when we continually re-work a scene or situation from the past, trying to find a way we could have made it better...

Librans will spend hours in their head, mentally re-playing failed relationship scenes, times which got ugly, times when the relationship fell from beauty, in the hope that they could find a way they could have said or done the right thing to have made it beautiful again... (sometimes long after the other person involved in the scene has married someone else... or even died, and is no longer around to answer back).

And always their focus is on them... what they did wrong... what they could have done differently.

If you want a sign that can match **Virgos** for beating themselves up, pick a **Libran**... because they often start out assuming they did something wrong... because at least then, they can change their behaviour to make the situation better. If it is the other person's fault, then a **Libran** is lost, because there is nothing they can change, and so the illusion of being able to change the relationship for the better is shattered, and the potential return to Mental Beauty is shattered too.

Also, **Librans** have an amazingly difficult time letting go of the past, especially in relation to failed relationships.

And, time and time again, during each mental re-play, they're looking for a way to re-establish a route back to the beautiful relationship they dreamed of.

"If only... If only... If only... If only... If only..."

However, the problem is that Regret leaves **Librans** open to attracting individuals who will manipulate them and take advantage of their good nature.

Why?

Because of their energetic resonance to the Heart Protector

Meridian.

There are 3 Meridians which are assigned the task of protecting the Heart from external influence or attack, and the most important of these three is... yes, you've guessed it... the Heart Protector Meridian... (and interestingly, they are all the meridians aligned to an aspect of beauty using the Elemental Archetype system).[1]

In life, we don't want to be too open, because then we just suck up all the psychic crap from other people, but neither do we want to be totally closed because then it is like being stuck in an emotional prison, which can be an isolating and lonely life.

So we are at risk if we are too open, and in emotional pain, if we are too closed.

In the real world, we, therefore, need some kind of protection that we can raise and lower, appropriate to the situation we find ourselves in.

This is where the Heart Protector Meridian comes in.

I always describe the Heart Protector Meridian as being like a drawbridge on a medieval castle, which we can raise and lower, as needs must. The innermost part of the castle represents the innermost part of our Heart, the juicy, warm, sacred bit.

We can raise the drawbridge (Heart Protector Meridian) whenever we sense that an enemy is close-at-hand, thus closing down access to our inner self.

We can also lower it when we feel that we are in the presence of people whom we love and trust so that we can share our love,

1   The other two protection Meridians are the Triple Warmer Meridian (aka Triple Burner, Triple Heater)... and the Small Intestine Meridian.

warmth and uniqueness with them (and vice versa).

But the problem for a **Libran** is, in their desperate and continual quest for a beautiful relationship, they remain open to people they should not be, who are out to manipulate them.

And really, that's the 3 life-lessons a **Libran** needs to learn:

- Let go of the past and regret so they can embrace a better future
- Attract nurturing relationships... and close down energetically to people who are out to manipulate them
- Have a flexible drawbridge... being open to the good people... closed to the bad people...

Once a **Libran** has got those three under its belt, they usually go on to live very successful lives, because they are experts at being sociable and working our their social connections for the better.

And as I had to explain to a 4-year old once, **Librans** have got nothing to do with **Librarians**... although a **Libran** would probably make a very good **Librarian**.

Chapter 2-9: Scorpio & Bladder Meridian

Imagine you have a friend, who is very, very **Scorpio**, and you both decide to take a trip to the ocean.

So you arrive at the ocean, and walk down across the sandy beach, to the edge of the ocean itself.

And it is a beautiful Summers day, and as you look out across the ocean, all is still and calm and peaceful.

And you say… *"Isn't the water nice and calm…"*

SCORPIO

*The Astrological Glyph which the Ancient Astrologers associated with the Sign of **Scorpio** s the Scorpion. Now... Astrology was born in lands such as Egypt and Mesopotamia, lands where Scorpions are known to live and thrive, in the hot and dry climate, and so people will have known all about them, and about their very real dangers. Scorpions are poisonous... Scorpions can kill... Scorpions are dangerous. So the Ancient Astrologers choose the image of a Scorpion because for someone with a great deal of **Scorpio** on their chart... they often have to deal with energies and emotions which are toxic, feelings in themselves or picked up from others. If handled the wrong way., these emotions are toxic.. but beneficial if handled in the right way... just like knowing the right way to handle a Scorpion.*

* * * * * * * * * *

To which your **Scorpio** friend replies... *"No, it isn't... look at all those waves!"*

You say... *"But there aren't any waves... the ocean is flat as a pancake?"*

Your **Scorpio** friend then replies... "*No, it isn't! Look... there... waves!*"

And as you look more carefully, you see that indeed your friend is correct, and on the surface of the ocean, even on this calm, Summers day, there are small waves, gentle ripples across the surface of the ocean.

Basically, your friend could see what you could not.

That's our first clue to the energy essence of **Scorpio**.

They are very, very sensitive to watery energies... to emotional energies... to the world of feeling... they can clearly sense and identify feelings and emotions which other people are mostly blind to.

Which is also why they have a reputation of being able to look into hidden places... secret places...

Because they can easily see and feel what other people just cannot.

Or they can see what other people are desperate to block or avoid seeing and can find themselves ostracised if they speak the truth about what is going on.

Let's include another story... and this one is from real life.

One day, a junior psychiatrist was working the graveyard shift on a psychiatric ward... i.e. Sunday afternoon... in Summer... and he was having to interview a woman who had been in and out of psychiatric wards for years, always complaining about the noises and voices in her head, and so had been diagnosed schizophrenic.

And his office was on a long corridor, and down the other end of the corridor, the only other person working was a secretary, typing, in the far distance.

And the woman was continually complaining about the noises in her head.

Suddenly the junior psychiatrist realized that her complaints about the inner noise perfectly fit the sounds of the secretaries' typewriter down the end of the long corridor... which he could just about hear in the distance... the noises stopped when the typewriter stopped... the noises started again when the secretary started typing again.

Any other day of the week, the offices along the corridor would have been full of people working... and so the typing would have been drowned out.

But not today... because everything was totally quiet... apart from the secretary typing, far down the corridor...

And so he ran a few experiments and discovered that this woman's hearing was super-super-super-sensitive, and she didn't have a mental condition as such.

She wasn't schizophrenic... she was just ultra-sensitive to the world around her.

When she was complaining about the noises and voices in her head... they were **real**.

But the psychiatric profession wasn't open to that possibility, and so they had classified her in accordance with the only box they could easily tick.

Schizophrenic.

So basically, what this woman needed wasn't another course in mind-numbing drugs… but a good set of earplugs.

OK, now what do you think the junior psychiatrist did next, now that he had discovered the truth about her condition?

Inform his senior colleagues, help to set her free from the condition which had plagued her for years?

Help others see that she wasn't mad?

What… and potentially be disbelieved, laughed at, and risk his promising career?

No, he kept quiet, told no one, left the institution a few months later, going on to greater things, and the woman stayed medicated for the rest of her life, and she probably died that way.

(So much for the Hippocratic oath, although he did write about it, years later, as an interesting story in his autobiography.)

Basically, that woman could hear what normal people could not, and her super-sensitivity made her life, a life in the modern world, which is so full of all kinds of noise and disturbance, practically unbearable.

The fact is that we all assume that we're all equally as sensitive as each other, but that's just not true, and when we're talking about **Scorpio**, the thing we need to understand, they're emotional and energy sensitivity is literally off the scale.

Their emotional sensitivity could detect the most subtle emotional tremor, which most people would be totally oblivious too (in fact, I will be brave and say that their emotional sensitivity/empathy merges into the full-blown psychic at times).

And yes, this emotional super-sensitivity can cause them a lot of problems.

Let me explain.

OK, the German astrologer **Reinhold Ebertin** originally made the connection between **Scorpio** and the Bladder Meridian, and this link allows us to make a further connection, drawing upon the work of the kinesiologist, **John Diamond**, because in his energy system/approach the Bladder Meridian is linked to the positive quality of Peace, and the negative quality of Frustration…

And if I may, throwing in the Elemental Archetype for **Scorpio** from **Energy Astrology**…*Spirit into Emotions*… (which basically means there is a lot of energy being poured into their emotional nature, super-charging it… making it very sensitive…).

People who live in a flat next to noisy neighbours, neighbours who keep their sound system on loud 24/7, live in a state of constant Frustration… because there is no silence… no moments of rest or Peace… there is no end to the noise.

Just like the poor woman living out her existence in the psychiatric ward, no way to stop the constant noise in her head.

And basically, **Scorpios** live their life that way, only for them, sound noise is replaced by emotional noise.

For a strong **Scorpio**, their emotional nature is so finely tuned, that they can feel the feelings, the emotions, of everyone around them… they are super-sensitive in that regard.

They are being continually bombarded by the emotional noise of the modern world.

And for your average **Scorpio**, they have no way to shut out this emotional noise, they are continually being bombarded by other people's emotional noise.

This is why they live in a state of Frustration and long for Peace and emotional silence.

But it doesn't end there.

There was a survey carried out, back along, asking people with chronic pain what the worse thing about their situation was, and their reply... the Frustration and Anger.

Apparently, they can block the physical pain, ignore it to some degree... but Anger and Frustration... their emotional reaction to their own pain, was the most difficult thing to take... and they said that they just longed to be able to switch off their own emotions at times... just to get some relief.

An **Uber-Scorpio** would probably say the same... only for them, it's a holiday from other people's emotional noise and their own emotions.

Therefore, for a **Scorpio**, it's not just other people's emotional noise which is the problem, but the continual wearing down, from within, from their own inner Frustration, in response to the external emotional noise.

Hence, they long deep down to escape to some far off island... to escape from the noise of other people... AND... from their own inner sense of Frustration...

They long for Peace, and for them Emotional Peace is deeply healing.

Also for a **Scorpio child**, unless surrounded by understanding + supportive adults, the early years can be quite frightening and confusing, because they are picking up adult emotions from the people around them which they lack the maturity and experience to understand.

Which is why sexuality for a **Scorpio** can be confusing.

Although sexuality is also a time when emotions are super-charged, and so **Scorpios** can also find it an attractive and appealing energy.

But when you are 3 years old... you just can't make sense of it all... adult noise... that makes no sense to your evolving mind.

There are times when life can feel tough and unwelcoming if you are an **Uber-Scorpio.**

However... there is a Catch-22 thing going on with **Scorpios.**

I have a friend who is very sensitive/psychic, and she used her abilities to keep her safe during her childhood.

Whenever her mother was in a foul mood, she would detect it early, knew what was coming, and so got out of the way, left the house, because she knew what would happen next if she stayed (enough said).

As a child, her super-sensitivity was her friend and protector, which is why she left her psychic radar fully open and switched on at all times.

But when she was an adult, and no longer needed to keep herself safe 24/7, she found it very difficult to switch off her psychic radar, even though it was wearing her energy down, not only because she associated it with keeping herself safe, but also because she liked the ability to tune into other people's energies... it was bit like watching a TV Soap Opera... very entertaining.

This is also why I believe **Scorpios** like the hidden, the secret, the mysterious.

Because when you are so psychically plugged in... yes, it can wear you down emotionally... all that Frustration... but also... it can provide you with lots of information... and it can be very dramatic and interesting too.

Hence, the double-sided nature of **Scorpio.**

Deep Frustration with all the emotional noise from those around them... and yet... they also love being plugged into the psychic internet.

They like being able to see into those secret, hidden places.

But now the BIG problem for **Uber Scorpios.**

If you are emotionally open and sensitive to the emotions of the people around you...

You just don't know what is going to hit you next.

The next person walking through the door... will they bring with them...

A wave of Anger...

A cloud of Depression...

A burst of Frustration...

Or something much worse, and much more toxic?

You just don't know what emotion you are going to pick up next.

If you are emotionally open to other people's energies, you just cannot control what is going to influence you next, which can be doubly Frustrating... not just the emotion, but the total openness, and lack of control.

* * * * * * * * * *

More Scorpio and Bladder Meridian... Why Frustration is SO Frustrating!

Over time, I have come to a much better... clearer... understanding of Frustration... and now see that it is a much bigger and deeper problem then I once thought.

Let me explain.

One of the things which I always find fascinating is when you track a feeling/emotion back to its source, through entomology say (i.e. the study of words), or back through different energy healing systems, and you discover that the feeling/emotion is different, works or is expressed differently, then how you would first have thought or figured.

And this is exactly what happened with Frustration.

The Dictionary definition of Frustration is usually something like:

"The feeling of being upset or annoyed as a result of being unable to change or achieve something."

And if you take that as your starting point, which would be many people's definition of what it is like to be Frustrated, and apply it to the Chinese Element system, then you would be looking at the Wood Element, and the Liver or Gallbladder Meridians.

Which are all about having a direction in life, being able to move forward, and feeling stuck/unhappy when your way is blocked.

And there is a certain truth in this. In fact, many energy healing systems, track Depression to the Wood Element and being blocked when you want to move forward in some area of your life which is super-important to you.

But the problem with Frustration, in many of these same energy healing systems, it is associated with the Water Element, and the Bladder Meridian (and with the positive energy/feeling of Peace).

So how does that work then, what has Frustration got to do with Peace?

How do we square this particular circle?

OK… well… if we move some of our mental furniture around a little… it does indeed work. We just need to step back, and re-look.

Now, one of the things which I have found is that to function well, to function at its optimum, our Conscious Mind needs the vibe of Love… and our Unconscious Mind needs the vibe of Peace, and Harmony helps too.

These are the two energy fuels which our two levels of Mind need to work at their best… and do the best for us.

And this is important, because our Conscious Mind sets our direction, steers the wheel on the car, but it's the Unconscious Mind that really does all the work, it's the engine for our life, providing the motion and momentum.

So we really want it working for us, in the best way possible.

When our Unconscious Mind is Peaceful and has overall inner Harmony… it literally purrs.

And it is like a car engine, running nicely, because it has been given the right fuel... the right vibration.

Warning... bad news coming up now...

But what do most people, especially when they are small kids and don't know better... or have any better solutions at hand... do?

How do we treat our Unconscious Mind, like a precious friend, or a dumping ground?

Well, unfortunately, we dump stuff in our Unconscious Minds, especially stuff we don't want to face, or deal with.

So our Unconscious Mind becomes the graveyard of bad and unpleasant memories, bad thoughts and feelings, which can also be lots of good stuff too (i.e. creativity, confidence, self-expression) but for some reason, we have defined them as being bad to us, or for us, so need to suppress them.

But, and here is the BIG problem, the more we dump stuff into our Unconscious Mind, the more cluttered and unstable it becomes, and the more it loses any inherent Peace / Harmony.

A bit like if you keep dumping waste and rubbish at a beautiful location in Nature, eventually it will turn into an ugly rubbish tip.

Or... another analogy...

It is like a waiter trying to carry far too many plates... or a car engine which is being run on the wrong type of fuel (i.e. diesel and not high-grade petrol)... eventually, the waiter/engine can no longer cope.

It means our Unconscious Mind becomes more and more Frustrated (which, remember, is the opposite of Peace and Harmony).

Now, you could say that Frustration is the way that our Unconscious Mind signals up to our Conscious Mind that... "*Hey, we've got a real problem down here... and we need to do something about it.*"

A bit like a luxury liner, where the Engine Room signals up to the Captain that there is big hole in the ship, and so they had better change course quick, do something about it fast.

But the question then becomes, is the Captain, or the rest of the 1st Class passengers up above, going to do anything about it?

Because as far as they are concerned the problem is down-below, so there is no reason why they can't carry on partying, no need to get their hands dirty, not when you are drinking a nice martini.

And that really is the central problem which many people alive now face.

The Conscious Mind has overloaded the Unconscious Mind with stuff that the Conscious Mind doesn't want to face.

Eventually the Unconscious Mind can no longer cope, and switches into Frustrated Mode, and starts generating the feeling of Frustration, partly in the hope that the Conscious Mind will take note and do something (because the Unconscious Mind can only act on the orders given to it by the Conscious Mind, only the Conscious Mind can change course).

But in the majority of cases, the Conscious Mind does nothing.

Either because it really doesn't know what is going on, has no idea that there even is an Unconscious Mind (and to be fair, until **Sigmund Freud**, for most of Human history, Humanity has struggled along without the notion of a deeper part to the Human mind, which literally does all the heavy lifting).

Or, because the Conscious Mind really doesn't want to deal with the stuff which it has suppressed from earlier in life, it does nothing, far too painful, especially if it means reliving some bad memories or unpleasent thoughts.

A bit like how a 1920s rich person really wouldn't want to go down into the ship's engine room and shovel coal, far too messy.

But the thing is, feelings like Frustration are like alarm bells, which says something is wrong, and require the Conscious Mind to enquire further, to work out what the sound of the bell really means.

But sometimes, and dropping the ship metaphor now, that's exactly what you need to do to fix your head.

And you have to ask the question... "*What does that loud, piercing sound means?*"

And then you have to step into the chaos for a while in order to bring it back into harmony.

Unfortunately, most people choose to live with Frustration, which is associated with the Bladder Meridian, throughout their lives. rather than look within, address the issues, and heal themselves.

Personally, I have a strong intuitive feeling that it is the healing of the Unconscious Mind, the transformation from Frustration back to Peace, which is really what changes an individual's core vibration and lifts them up to spiritual enlightenment.

It's not really the Conscious Mind going on a 2 day Yoga retreat, or visiting a sacred site, although they are nice.

What really makes the difference it appears, going down into the engine room, shovelling the coal, getting your hands dirty, creating some order and harmony, healing your Unconscious Mind.

But that's not what most people choose.

They choose to live with the Frustration rather then heal and grow, because for them, to change, to even consider the possibility of changing, is far too painful.

So do most people live with constant... 24/7... Frustration?

That would make life unbearable.

So what do the majority of people do, the only thing they can do... the counter-weight to Frustration?

Forget... find a way to numb their mind... they literally take the Unconscious Mind to the psychic dentist and choose to have the injection to dull the inner pain...

So the Frustration remains... but they choose to push the Frustration deep down inside as well.

We human beings (me included) are so weird at times.

Fortunately, we can also be wyrd if we choose, and that's what saves us.

In many ways, I have come to see that Peace / Frustration is the primary energy dynamic for our Unconscious Mind, and if we really want to get healed and whole at the deeper levels of our being, then we are going to have to face and deal with it at some point.

Chapter 2-10: Sagittarius & Spleen Meridian

When we talk about **Sagittarius**, and try to get under its skin, try to get to an understanding of its core, it's inevitable that we need to talk about Comfort Zones.

The key to understanding **Sagittarius** is… Comfort Zones.

Because **Sagittarius** needs to deal effectively with Worry & Anxiety in some way, if it is ever to expand outwards, embrace new ideas and new thinking.

In fact, some **Sagittarians** are searching for some grand philosophy, not just to give their life a higher meaning, but also, to keep their life-anxiety at a distance.

SAGITTARIUS

*The Astrological Glyph which the Ancient Astrologers associated with the Sign of **Sagittarius** was a Centaur, half-man and half-horse... and also an archer... which is a very complex symbol. Once again, we need to cast our minds back to Ancient Mesopotamia and Egypt to understand what this Glyph may mean in terms of the Sign of **Sagittarius**... and we must remember that for all these civilisations... horsemen and archers were cutting edge military technology... at the time, they were the best examples of people using their minds, and their ability to create and invent... and whenever something is invented and comes into form, someone, or a culture as a whole, has to step beyond its Comfort Zone... which is the essence of what **Sagittarius** is all about.*

* * * * * * * * * *

Two for the price of one... it is indeed possible.

OK, the German astrologer **Reinhold Ebertin** originally made the connection between **Sagittarius** and the Spleen Meridian, and this link allows us to make a further association, drawing upon the work of the kinesiologist, **John Diamond**, because in his energy system/approach the Spleen Meridian is linked to the positive quality of

Faith in the Future, and the negative quality of Worry & Anxiety...

And if I may, throwing in the Elemental Archetype for **Sagittarius** from **Energy Astrology**... *Grounding Spirit.*

So to start, what do we know about **Sagittarius** from Traditional Astrology?

Half-man, half horse... the philosopher of the Zodiac... opposite of **Gemini**... likes to dive deep into a subject and master it... etc... etc...

And all that is true.

But to begin our exploration, I would like to ask you a rather deep question.

How do you handle all the anxiety associated with just being alive?

I mean, you live on a big ball, hurtling through the void, on top of this molten ball of lava, with only a small tectonic crust between you and the fire below, and the tectonic plates move around, causing earthquakes and volcanos.

And one small twitch of Solar activity, intense Solar flares exploding out into space, and our whole civilization would be plunged into total anarchy.

And that's just thinking about some of the stuff happening *up there*, off-world, that could go wrong, because *down here*, there's lots of other stuff to be worried about, including... but also, closer to home...

Global warming, over-population, the fact the world economy is basically being run by mad-men and super-computers, and religious fundamentalism of every flavour you can imagine, and bio-diversity is under attack, and what happens if... ?

etc... etc... etc...

The point is that, when you step back, there are a lot of things in the Universe which could go wrong for us, both as a civilization, society, and as individuals.

Just driving to work each morning, could potentially open us up to danger from an unexpected direction... we just never know.

When you look at it from that perspective, getting out of bed in the morning requires a degree of Faith in the Future... Faith in Your Future... that things will turn out alright.

That we'll be OK and in one piece when we reach the end of the day and get back into our bed again.

And there's also the small stuff that we can also worry about if we were so inclined, whether we will have enough money to pay the bills next month, will we still have a job at the end of the year, how will we support our family going forwards?

Yes, all the small stuff... plus the Big stuff... and Universal scary stuff too.

When you stop to think, we all have so much to be anxious about, to worry over.

But the wonderful thing is, as individuals, 99.9% of the time we don't go around worrying about any of the above stuff, the stuff which could go wrong... we don't give it the time of day.

We have better things to do with our alotted time on this planet.

Partly, because we normally find a way of focusing on other stuff...

more positive stuff.

Just like the **Sagittarian** archer focuses on a target or goal.

Most people find a way of *coping* and *continuing*.... and so get on with their lives.

And this is very important, psychologists believe that the root of the cause of most mental imbalance, is anxiety, an inability of our Mind/ Unconscious to handle some element of the external world, so the worry continues to plague our Mind and eventually undermines our reason and sanity.

Anxiety undermines our ability to cope with the uncertain world us.

The way that I look at it... **Sagittarius** is the Astrological Sign specifically given the task of finding a way to cope with anxiety.

And to explain... once again, let's revisit our understanding of Comfort Zones.

Have you ever watched a one-year-old explore the world around them?

It is an interesting exercise because it also helps explain a great deal about how adults behave and navigate their way through adulthood.

Remember, the habits and patterns which we establish in our early childhood are the ones we tend to stick with throughout the rest of our lives.

A small child's exploration of the big world around them can be broken down into two distinct phases.

The first phase begins when the child gets bored with playing beside its mother and decides to set off and explore the exciting world which lies just beyond the horizon. So the child toddles off, for the moment putting any thought of mother and safety to one side, enticed by the prospect of all the adventure, freedom and newness that lies on the other side of the room or play-park.

But, as the child explores, at some point the thought suddenly enters his/her mind, "*Where has mother gone?*", and it looks around to find her. This is the start of the second phase.

If she is still nearby, in direct line of sight, then all is well, she isn't lost, and so the child is comforted and continues to explore.

However, if she appears to be far away, or even worse, can no longer be seen or located, then the child goes into full-blown panic mode, and frantically tries to find her again.

It either runs straight back to mother, or makes so much noise so that the mother is alerted to his/her plight, and so comes to the rescue.

Either way, the child returns to mother, and so feels safe and secure... their anxiety subsides for the moment... panic over.

Until, it gets bored, starts to wander off in search of newness and excitement... and the whole cycle repeats once again.

So the repeating pattern is fueled by boredom and the need for excitement on one side, and anxiety and the need for security on the other side.

What is important for all of us adults is to realize is that we do exactly the same thing, we repeat the same pattern in our lives, but often we do not even realise that this is what we're doing.

The point at which the child realizes that the mother is missing and starts to panic is what we can call the edge of our Comfort Zone. This is a psychological space that, while we are inside it we feel safe and secure, but when we venture outside of its apparent protection we start to experience panic and anxiety. The Comfort Zone that we mentally create as children we carry forward into our adult lives.

If **Sagittarius** is the sign given the task of handling our anxiety... then it needs a Comfort Zone... and it needs something to act as mother, and help it feel that the world is OK, the sky won't come crashing down on our heads, that basically everything will work out for the best.

But here's the thing...

... and I mean no disrespect here... because I do this myself.

The great journeys and quests which a **Sagittarian** goes on... the intellectual ivory towers they create, spending their whole lives researching the history of the Ottoman Empire, or saving the whale, or collecting driftwood from the beach and turning it into amazing artwork.

Are they activities designed to enrich the individual...

... or activities designed to keep the anxiety at bay?

Or both?

For me, my money is on **both**.

A **Sagittarian** needs something, an intellectual quest to give their life meaning, maybe even enrich the culture around them in some way.

But that intellectual quest also gives them something to do, and it also helps them deal with the nagging anxiety of life.

And to be honest, we all do it.

Our life-purpose has a dual nature, it is to find a meaning for our life, and also a meaning which will also help to keep the anxiety at arm's length.

It's as if we're distracting ourselves from the anxiety, while also giving ourselves a massive positive payoff.

All religions, all spiritual activity, can be seen from these two directions, these two perspectives.

They give great meaning, direction and purpose to our lives, and yet, also, they help us deal with the anxiety and uncertainty of life... why are we here, what is it all for, and how will I cope if the Sun explodes, the economy goes into meltdown... etc...

Personally, I think this is why the glyph for **Sagittarius** is half-man, half-horse... because whatever philosophy or belief system that is chosen, it has to satisfy the higher needs of the man, while dealing effectively with the animal anxiety which also resides in our brain.

So the arrow being fired by the centaur aims to, hopefully, satisfy both sides of our nature.

Our higher and lower natures...

Man and beast...

In an earlier chapter, I said there were 2 signs prone to depression... actually, from my experience, there is a 3rd:

Sagittarius.

Take away their intellectual comfy blanket, and a **Sagitarrian** will inevitably plunge into an anxiety attack, and possible lock-down depression, where they just won't get out of bed in the morning, because what is the point?

And a few times in my life, I have been standing outside the bedroom door of a **Sagittarian** saying...

"Are you sure you don't want to get up now... it's gone 11 o'clock... and it's a lovely day outside... and life isn't that bad?"

We all need to find some kind of meaning for our lives... whether it is a serious religion, whale-saving or stamp collecting... a reason to get up in the morning, but for an **Uber-Sagittarian** it is essential.

But when a **Sagittarian** have found an intellectual quest which motivates them, they throw back the bed covers, all systems firing, and pursue it with all the energies of man and beast.

So there is a Catch-22 inherent to being a **Sagittarean**.

They gaze out from their Comfort Zone, searching for a deeper meaning to life.

But leaving the safety of their Comfort Zone, even if only mentally, means they open up to the unknown... and to anxiety.

Feeling the anxiety, they increase their search for some belief-system or philosophy to keep the anxiety at bay.

And in search of such a protective belief-system... they often have to look beyond their Comfort Zone to find it... etc... etc...

That is the path of the **Uber-Sagittarean**.

Chapter 2-11: Capricorn & Gallbladder Meridian

If you check out the traditional Western Astrological record, you will find several themes arise, time and again, in relation to **Capricorn**:

- They're ambitious
- They make great entrepreneurs and can find a way to make the most of any situation
- They're not emotionally touchy-feelie

CAPRICORN

*The Astrological Glyph which the Ancient Astrologers associated with the Sign of **Capricorn** is the Goat. Once again, we need to cast our minds back to Ancient Mesopotamia and Egypt to understand what this Glyph may mean in terms of the Sign of **Capricorn**. Well... goats would have been one of the most common farm animals available since the dawn of time... and one of the most versatile. Goats have a reputation of being able to survive in a range of different environments and conditions, and able to feed off the most difficult land available. They are a creature designed to make the best use of the Earth plane... which is a bit like **Capricorns**... who, when focused, have the ability to make the best use of the world around them, and its resources, to achieve their dreams and goals.*

* * * * * * * * * *

This is why **Capricorns** like to climb mountains, not just the physical, rocky kind, but any kind of mountain associated with Human endeavours, such as political or corporate, and just like their associated Goat glyph, as they climb ever upwards, they are very sure-footed on uneven slopes.

And there is a story from my own life which brings all this
into greater clarity, while also pointing to the deeper nature of
Capricorn.

Back when I worked in I.T., I once had someone in my team who
was an **Uber-Capricorn**… including **Sun conjunct Mars**… and the
project he was passionate about had just been cancelled by senior
management.

And I was the one who had to tell him, because senior-management
make the decisions, and then most often leave it to middle-
management to do the dirty work… "*Sorry, the project's been
cancelled*"… in management-speak, disseminate the message.

Now, being a practical sort (or a cowardly manager, depending on
your point of view), I waited to tell him until Friday afternoon…
hoping the weekend would allow him to calm down, get his Rage
under control, although I wasn't looking forward to our Monday
morning discussion.

And as expected he was not pleased (actually that's an
understatement… he was *furious*), and left work at the end of the
week like a bull in a china shop.

But what happened next, totally surprised me. Because on Monday
morning he had taken all that Rage, all that potent energy, and
channelled it into creating a new website, and new business for
himself, and this event turned out to be a turning point in his life
(and he left the company, and set off in a new direction several
months later).

And this story tells you a lot about the essence of **Capricorn** energy.

Let me explain.

OK, the German astrologer **Reinhold Ebertin** originally made the connection between **Capricorn** and the Gallbladder Meridian, and this link allows us to make a further association, drawing upon the work of the kinesiologist, **John Diamond**, because in his energy system/approach the Gallbladder Meridian is linked to the positive quality of Reaching Out With Love & Forgiveness, and the negative quality of Rage...

Rage... which is probably the most destructive of all the emotions.

And if I may... throwing in the Elemental Archetype for **Capricorn** from Energy Astrology...*Energizing the Physical.*

Now, to start, what is the difference between Anger and Rage?

Well, when someone is Angry, they are still in control of their actions, but when someone is over-taken by Rage... Blind Rage... then they lose rational control, and their intense passion takes over (although they suddenly have tremendous energy resources/strength to call upon).

When enraged, a person is likely to destroy without thinking of the consequences, just because they can, because it makes them feel good.

They become like **The Incredible Hulk**... SMASH !!!

This is why most legal systems have the legal concept of manslaughter, or due to diminished responsibilities, to reflect that the individual was not functioning rationally at the time.

So Rage is intense, destructive energy without focused, rational control.

But as we have seen with the other Astrological Signs, the positive side of the pendulum shows some reflection of the negative side.

So the positive for a **Capricorn**… Reaching Out With Love & Forgiveness… is actually intense energy with focused, rational control.

And if one side is intensely destructive, the other side is capable of immense creativity.

And this is why **Capricorns** are so effective on the Earth Plane, why they can be effective entrepreneurs because they are so focused… and have all that energy of Rage *turned positive* to call upon.

Because what can destroy can also create.

It's just as a matter of knowing how to focus and channel the intense energy..

There is a belief in manifestation circles, you can have whatever you want, if you can keep your mind 100% focused on it, for long enough, which is actually very hard to do.

But of all the Astrological Signs, **Capricorns** find this the easiest to do.

When they set their mind on something, their mind becomes focused like a laser, and they will keep going until their goal is achieved.

Other Astrological Signs may give up, get distracted, but a focused, positive **Capricorn** doesn't get distracted.

They keep their eyes on the prize until it is won and theirs (and the prize money is in the bank, resting in a high interest account).

The other thing which we must mention, **Capricorns** find it very easy to make decisions and stick to them, which other Astrological Signs find difficult, and also to get the right balance between thought and emotion.

And this is very interesting thing in its own right.

The conventional wisdom has it that people make the best decisions when they are purely rational and not overly influenced by their emotions/feelings.

But neuroscientists have discovered when someone suffers certain types of damage to the pre-frontal cortex of the brain, that person becomes super-rational and can **never** make a decision, they spend hours upon hours going over the same facts, never settling on an outcome, because they can no longer connect with the feeling of which outcome they would prefer, which outcome they would like for the best.

A feeling is, therefore, all-important to decision-making and provides the foundation for our whole mental processes.

But feeling has to be kept in perspective, too much emotion also undermines the decision-making process.

And I think this is another area where **Capricorns** excel.

To other Astrological Signs, they may appear cold and without feeling, but I prefer to say they are very good at keeping their feelings in check, and using them to make the right decisions for themselves and the situation at hand.

Plus, they are hard-wired into two of the most extreme and intense emotions going... Rage & Reaching out with Love & Forgiveness.

However, the positive is Reaching Out With Love & Forgiveness, and that is something which I have found that **Capricorns** find hard... the whole Forgiveness thing. If you ever find a **Capricorn** who can easily forgive, then you will found one who has reached a high degree of personal evolution. Normally, it doesn't come easily to them, and it is something they need to work at.

So what is the downside of being a **Capricorn**?

Simple... it's the Rage.

If someone can be burnt up inside by their Anger, imagine what Rage can do to a person, especially if it is locked down inside them, and has no creative avenue of expression.

Because of its nature, Rage cannot be put under conscious, rational control, like Anger can, so it's not something which is easy to control, especially when you are a small kid, and your parents are pressuring you to control your inner nature. Which is why I was surprised when my employee, from the earlier story, was able to challenge his rage constructively and creatively.

In our Western rational societies, it is not an energy which we are usually comfortable with, although, interestingly, ancient and tribal cultures were, and knew how to channel it for the collective good.

But if an individual can connect with their **Capricorn** nature and channel it successfully, then they can indeed become a real force to be reckoned with.

Because, like I always say...

If they can master, control and focus their Rage... and turn it positive... Then they have all the energy they need to make a real difference in the world... to re-create and shape their world to be what they want it to be.

Capricorns are natural builders... they just need to focus their Minds on what they want to create.

Chapter 2-12: Aquarius & Lung Meridian

You can understand the more profound nature of **Aquarius** through understanding the weave which connects the following dates:

1997... and I am in a relationship with a Soul-mate who is **Uber-Aquarian**... and I find myself saying... "*What do you mean I am getting emotional again... and I should calm down and be rational... What's so wrong with having emotions? I am not* **Mr Spock** *from Star Trek, you know!*"

AQUARIUS

*The Astrological Glyph which the Ancient Astrologers associated with the Sign of **Aquarius** is the Water Carrier... someone carrying a jug of water, and pouring water from it. Once again, we need to cast our minds back to Ancient Mesopotamia and Egypt to understand what this Glyph may mean in terms of the Sign of **Aquarius**... and we must remember that these are all civilizations which grew up alongside major rivers... the Euphrates, Tigris, Nile... and water was channelled from these rivers to water the fields... and irrigate crops... which all requires social cohesion and co-operation to achieve. So this Glyph speaks of the social nature of **Aquarius**... social cohesion which leads to fertility and abundance.*

Plus, if you have ever watched women or young children, in Africa, carry water on their heads, from the nearest water source, maybe 10 miles or more from their village... That's when you realize that water carrying, for much of Human history, has been an act of love, family, tribe, caring, and social responsibility.

* * * * * * * * * *

1600... **Giordano Bruno** is being led out in Rome, about to be burnt at the stake, by the Catholic Inquisition, for his heresy of believing that all the stars in the sky are also Suns with their own planetary systems. His tongue has been bound so that he cannot spread any further heresy as he dies amidst the flames.

1939... **Adolf Hitler** and his chief architect **Alfred Speer** are in a vast room, with map tables, and miniature models of the cities and buildings they will build across Eastern Europe, once it has been conquered by the armies of the Third Reich.

There is an **Aquarian** thread woven throughout all of those events... along with...

1483... Eisleben, Germany, a friar called **Martin Luther** nails a proclamation to the wooden door of the cathedral (*The Ninety-Five Theses* against the financially lucrative indulgences)... and all hell breaks loose across Europe soon after.

You see, **Aquarius** often gets a bad press for being *emotionally remote*... which they can be...

But there are times when change is desperately needed, but being blocked by powerful vested forces.

And the only one who can say what needs to be said, who is fearless enough to speak the forbidden truth, is the person who is the cool and remote **Aquarian**, or someone with a big dose of **Aquarius** in their chart.

Let me explain.

OK, the German astrologer **Reinhold Ebertin** originally made the connection between **Aquarius** and the Lung Meridian, and this link allows us to make a further association, drawing upon the work of the kinesiologist, **John Diamond**, because in his energy system/

approach the Lung Meridian is linked to the positive quality of Tolerance, and the negative quality of Intolerance.

In Chinese medicine, the Lung Meridian is associated with our social and energy connections to other people, to our family, friends, and beyond...

And if I may, throwing in the Elemental Archetype for **Aquarius** from **Energy Astrology**... *Refining the Mind*... allowing us to update old and outdated thinking...

So first, let us identify the meaning of Tolerance, which Dictionaries usually define as:

"The ability or willingness to tolerate the existence of opinions or behaviour that one dislikes or disagrees with."

Which raises really quite an interesting dilemma...

For example, I like Star Wars while my friend likes Star Trek, but I am prepared to Tolerate his likes, just as he is prepared to Tolerate mine, we literally don't go to war over our differences of opinion.

Without Tolerance, human civilization would not be possible.

However, during the life of a society, and Human history, there are times when we need to Tolerate something, to allow society to function, and other times when Intolerance is the better option, and the need to kick out something which isn't working, or is just plain wrong and cruel, becomes paramount.

If a point hadn't come when society could no longer Tolerate slavery or the disenfranchisement of women, then the world would be a very different place.

The phrase... *I can no longer tolerate that kind of behaviour*... is not necessarily the wrong thing to say... it all depends upon the situation and context.

Human history often takes a turn in the right direction when an individual or group takes a stand and says... *I can no longer tolerate this, things need to change!*

Which is not to say that the catalyst person will be listened to, but change usually starts with the spark lit by a single individual...

Back in 1960s America, there was a Civil Rights movement long before **Rosa Parks**.

But her act of defiance on that bus in Montgomery, Alabama, in 1955, refusing to give up her seat to a white passenger, and move to the back of the bus, was the spark which lit the fire, which allowed so many others to say... *I can no longer tolerate this, things need to change!*

And also... *I am willing to stand and fight for those principles! Even if it costs me personally...*

And sometimes... even if it ends up costing me my life!

So I would argue that Tolerance/Intolerance are equally right and equally wrong, and it all depends on the context in which you and the society around you finds itself.

And the beliefs in your head, programming from your family, society and culture, that allows you to either Tolerate X or be Intolerant of Y.

And the weird thing is a member of the U.S. Civil Rights movement back in the 1950s and 60s, and a member of the Ku Klux Klan, are tolerant of some things, and intolerant of others.

Problem is... *they're just NOT tolerant or intolerant of the same things.*

But the whole Tolerance/Intolerance dynamic is how our society moves forward, why and how things get better, over time.

An **Aquarian**, on a good day, is finely tuned to this and knows the difference between what is good and what needs to change (but on a bad day… as we shall see… completely wide of the mark).

And if you look back through history, the majority of the great social reformers have been touched by **Aquarius/Uranus** in some way… the knowing that this is no longer acceptable… we can no longer tolerate this… things must change, and we're not going away until it does.

An **Uber-Aquarius** is finely-tuned to the subtle sea changes in society before they occur…

It's as if each **Uber-Aquarian** is someone from 20 to 30 years in the future, but having to live now, trying to tell us there is a better way, because their Heart has been to that better world, and it just *knows.*

Which then takes us to the next, interesting stage in our discussion.

In his book *The Wisdom of Psychopaths*, the psychologist **Kevin Dutton** argues that psychopaths do have a good side, and it can be quite useful to have them around the Human household.

Now, culturally, we tend to associate psychopaths all as unfeeling serial killers, but in reality, there are degrees of the psychopathic, and most psychopaths tend to go into big business, or politics, climbing the greasy pole to get to the top (and without much of a conscience, or emotional baggage to tie them down, they tend to do well at this, because they tend to allow nothing to limit them, they're not hindered by their own feelings, nor feelings for other people, they literally are all out for Number One).

Don't worry, I am not about to argue that **Aquarians** are psychopaths... even if they are the one Astrological Sign least likely to give you a great big bear hug on your birthday...

But if there is a spectrum of emotionality (made-up word, I know)... then **Cancer** will be at one extreme... with **Aquarius** at the other.

But **Dutton** argues that from an evolutionary point of view, Humanity producing the odd psychopath with each new generation is actually a huge advantage.

Who you going to call, when there's a sabre-tooth tiger terrorizing the village... who you gonna call... your tribal psychopath!

Because in a dangerous situation, the person who doesn't easily feel fear, who doesn't get over emotional, and can play it cool, has a distinct advantage, especially if they are handy with a sword or spear, flint, bronze, or otherwise...

There are times when being able to switch off your emotions is a very distinct advantage, and this is something which **Aquarius** can do to some degree, either switch them off, or tone them down.

And that's exactly the type of person you need to also speak the unspoken truth within a business, a family, or society at large.

Someone who isn't afraid to speak up and about what needs to change, and hang the consequences for themselves, the truth is far too important and needs to be said.

Like Greenpeace, back in the 1980s, when saving the planet wasn't trendy, people who were speaking the truth long before the majority of us caught on.

But who also created a foundation for others to build on in the last two decades...

1600... **Giordano Bruno** went to stake with his tongue bound because he was not afraid to speak the truth as he saw it (and it turns out he was right all along... and now Astronomers adore him...name spaceprobes after him)... during his life, even when the Catholic Church did everything in its power to silence him, his need to speak the truth was all-important.

And turns out, **The Sun** was indeed the centre of our Solar System, all along... and not **The Earth**... as many had believed.

All that fear, anger and rage pitted against him, by immense and powerful people and forces, and yet he didn't let it silence him, his truth, the truth, was more important.

1483... Eisleben, Germany, a friar called **Martin Luther** nails a proclamation to the wooden door of the cathedral.

Would **Luther** have gone ahead, with hammer and nail, if he was totally fixated on what would happen if the then Pope had got his hands on him?

Another bonfire, another burning of an unwanted truth..

And how many others were extinguished, out of sight, in forgotten times, centuries past, people who passionately believed in what they were saying, but who never made the history books, who were cut down before their words could set fire to the pages Human history.

You see...

The Big Powers tend to stay in power and get away with injustice because they frighten the average citizen into silence and inaction.

"Speak out and we'll burn you alive, prosecute you, put you in

prison, chains, persecute you and your family ...until you fade away to nothing and are forgotten... we have all the power, and you have none... be very, very afraid..."

And for 11 signs in the Zodiac that tends to work.

But there is one sign which replies, saying... *"I don't frighten that easily... and I will speak the truth regardless of what you try to do... or even do... to me... the truth I carry must be heard... it's too important..."*

Any ideas of who that Astrological Sign might be? ...

Yes... you're right...

Aquarius.

And they keep on going... relentless... fearless...

Until the slaves are freed... and women are given the vote... and minorities are legally empowered... and the truth is known... and the injustice is righted... and the page of Human history turns a little more towards the light...

Because, for them, their belief, their cause, is often bigger than their individual life, more important.

And their not caring, even for their own life at times, is their salvation, it helps them to continue on in the face of fear, threats and potential extinction, they don't allow fear and emotion to deflect them from doing what is right.

The Human race has always needed a few people in the tribe who aren't afraid of big, scary monsters.

But now we arrive at the big **Aquarian** fault. Intolerance of injustice is a good thing, but there are times when intolerance is also plain wrong, and when a lack of emotion prevents an **Aquarian** from caring, in the right way.

1939... **Adolf Hitler** and his chief architect **Alfred Speer** are in a vast room, with map tables, and miniature models of the cities and buildings they will build across Eastern Europe, once it has been conquered by the armies of the Third Reich.

But the thing was, *there were people already living in those locations...* in the cities and towns which would have been bulldozed to make **Hitler's** dream a reality... and millions of people would have been transported to Eastern Europe and Siberia (and many were)...

And there are real-stories of German families moving into beautiful houses, with wonderful furniture, all across Eastern Europe, in the early 1940s, when Nazi Germany was winning the war.

Not caring that the former owners, whole families, had been evicted by the Nazis, days or even hours before, forced out of their own homes, made homeless, to make *lebensraum* for the Arayan people of the Third Reich.

On the dark side of **Aquarius**... a beautiful idea often counts far more than emotions, counts far more than Human emotions and suffering.

If he had ever continued in power, and won the war, **Hitler** would have just marked it down as collateral damage, and a price worth paying for all those towering pillars of gleaming white marble all across Eastern Europe.

As I sometimes say... **Aquarius**... loves humanity... but doesn't always like sitting next to someone on the train.

On a good day, **Aquarius** understands what should and should not be tolerated... but on a bad day, when it's judgement is off, and its moral compass is misaligned, it tolerates the bad, and is intolerant of the good... (and it won't be told, it doesn't want to hear that its judgement is off)... it tends to ignore feelings and emotions because they are too messy and inconvenient while pursuing its own individual quest or struggle.

And if you are ever in a relationship with a Soul-mate who is **Uber-Aquarian**... you might find the following line useful... "*What do you mean I am getting emotional again... and I should calm down and be rational... What's so wrong with having emotions? I am not Mr Spock from Star Trek, you know!*"

Chapter 2-13: Pisces & Small Intestine Meridian

Pisces... that most mysterious... floating... mystic.... and downright ethereal of all Zodiac signs.

As has been said by many Astrologers, down across the ages.

Sometimes trying to understand **Pisces** is like trying to hold on to fog, or capture mist in your hand.

But if we are to have any real chance of understanding **Pisces**, and get to grips with its mysterious nature, then we must find answers to these two questions:

• Why is **Pisces** connected with Sadness, and why does it have a desperate need to avoid all the emotional ugliness in the world?

PISCES

*The Astrological Glyph which the Ancient Astrologers associated with the Sign of **Pisces** was an image of 2 Fish. Once again, we need to cast our minds back to Ancient Mesopotamia and Egypt to understand what this Glyph may mean in terms of the Sign of **Pisces**... and we must remember that these are all civilizations which grew up alongside major rivers... the Euphrates, Tigris, Nile... and so fish were another staple part of people's diet. But the interesting thing about fish... they live totally in another element... they live and can only exist within water. Which is a useful image for explaining how **Pisceans** are totally influenced by their emotions and emotional nature.*

* * * * * * * * * *

• Why is **Pisces** in a constant search for emotional beauty.

And let's be honest, just turn on the TV or Radio... and you soon get to see and hear of a lot of people behaving very badly to one another... all around the world... which **Pisceans** can't stand... it has them rushing to the door... any door... to another and more beautiful dimension that is... as we shall soon see.

Well, let's begin disentangling that by tracking the link between the

Zodiac sign of **Pisces** to the issue of Sadness, and their great need for *Emotional Beauty* to hold all this Sadness at bay.

OK, the German astrologer **Reinhold Ebertin** originally made the connection between **Pisces** and the Small Intestine meridian, and this link allows us to make a further association, drawing upon the work of the kinesiologist, **John Diamond**, because in his energy system/approach the Small Intestine is linked to the positive quality of Joy, and the negative quality of Sadness.

And if I may, throwing in the Elemental Archetype for **Pisces** from **Energy Astrology**... *Emotional Beauty* (and the desperate need to avoid emotional ugliness).

Now, how do all these elements weave together into a coherent, whole meaning?

The Dictionary definition of Joy is usually "*a vivid emotion of pleasure; extreme gladness*".

However, another, more energetic definition of Joy is that of Emotional Beauty.

When someone is experiencing Joy, then they are perceiving beauty within their own emotions, and this is somewhat similar to the Dictionary definition for Joy, where someone is taking pleasure in their own positive emotions.

This means that when someone is engaging in a Joyous experience... then they are also experiencing Emotional Beauty.

And, unfortunately, this can cause no end of problems, especially if you go looking for your fix of Emotional Beauty *out there*.

You see, the problem is that in our 3-Dimensional, physical world, Emotional Beauty isn't something which you can easily find, acquire or purchase on a regular or consistent basis.

And this ties in with the mysterious nature of **Pisces**... and with our inability to capture and hold mist in our hand...

You can't go down to your local shopping mall and buy a fresh portion of Emotional Beauty when you run out... and people can't be relied on to reflect back Emotional Beauty on demand.

In contrast, Physical Beauty is pretty easy to find... you can go for a walk in nature, have a nice meal, a warm bath, a relaxing massage, or even great sex... all of these things help the physical body to feel, to experience Physical Beauty (i.e. **Taurus**).

But when it comes to Emotional Beauty... it is a completely different story. **Pisceans** don't always find it so easy to acquire... and this is core to their problem with living on the Earth Plane.

Because if you get your Emotional Beauty from the external world, then you are largely dependent on other people, and so you are totally dependent on your relationships, and unfortunately, other people have a tendency to let you down, or become tired, so can't always deliver what you need, or when you need it.

Hence the inner Sadness, which always seems to be on tap, when the outer world lets the **Piscean** down, when the flow of Emotional Beauty fails and stops dead...

Now, to be honest, often they may not mean to let you down, you may indeed have found your one and only Soul-mate, the special person who *completes you*. But even then, they are also only Human, and they burp and fart in bed, and they have off days, and they get grumpy first thing in the morning, and they don't always like what you like, and so it is just not possible to keep the Emotional Beauty scenario running 24/7, no matter how much they do love you.

This is one reason why **Pisceans** like to escape into fantasy, romance, or sci-fi literature… to help them reimagine a better world, with them at the centre, as the Hero / Heroine.

If you ever meet a true **Piscean**, on the surface they may come across as perfectly capable and present, but in their heads, they are so somewhere else (and maybe not even be on the same planet, or even time or dimension).

I have a friend who holds down a high-powered management position… but loves Sci-Fi, and admits that often, in his head, he's somewhere else…

Unfortunately, there are times when Emotional Beauty comes crashing down to the ground (and you are left with an inner feeling of Sadness)…

Because other people aren't always reliable, or because a little rain pours into every life at some point, life isn't always sunshine and rainbows.

And this is why some people prefer animals/pets, who tend to be more reliable, more 24/7 loving and supportive.

Sadness is a hard word to track down definition wise, but one thread, it arises due to your relations to other people, the behaviour of other people, the world doesn't make you Sad, other people do, especially when they don't live up to your expectations.

So that fits with what we are saying here about Emotional Beauty.

When you are dependent on generating your Emotional Beauty from relationships, then other Human beings will let you down from time to time, just as you let them down, because no one can be someone else's fantasy, consistently, 24 hours a day, 7 days a week,

365 days a year, from now to the end of eternity.

It is just not possible.

Indeed, this is exactly why many **Pisceans** go off into fantasy land, because although any physical lover will be imperfect, any dream lover (or scenario) which they conjure up in their imaginations will be totally perfect, is completely under their mental control, and will never let them down.

And time and time again, **Pisceans** set their heart on finding that elusive Soul-Mate, perfect in all respects, who will complete them, and so remove them from all the drudgery and ugliness of their ordinary world...

But, unfortunately, fantasy cannot be a permanent solution to their problems, because it isn't real, and so is not emotionally fulfilling.

It's like eating food made out of cardboard. It might look like the real thing, but as soon as you take the first bite, you know that it isn't real and that you still feel hungry.

However, fortunately, there is another way to find true Emotional Beauty.

The traditional way of creating Emotional Beauty was/is through meditation or some other kind of spiritual practice.

Because if you can find a way to generate your own Emotional Beauty from within, then you are on much safer ground because you can create it whenever you need, and so you are not dependent on someone else, on any external relationship, although it is still beneficial to have them.

Chapter 2-14: The 4 Elements

The 4 Element system is one of the foundations of Western Astrology.

And one of the 1st things people are usually taught to check when reading an individual's Astrological Chart is...

*How many Planets are located in each of the **4 Elements**?*

Because each of the 4 Elements in Western Astrology is one of the 4 foundations upon which all personalities are based, energies which are being expressed *by* the personality... *through* the personality... and energies which are also *expressing* the personality.

The more Planets in an Element, the more dominant that Element is in an individual's psyche.

From a Western perspective, and the Western Mystery tradition, the 4 Elements are energies which create your personality, and once created, they are energies which you are also expressing through your personality.

Basically, you are the light, and you are also the lens.

So they are ultra-important, and your relationship to them also defines your life, and how successful you are... to a large degree.

Within an Astrological Chart, if there is one or more Planets in the **Earth Element** Signs:

- **Taurus**
- **Virgo**
- **Capricorn**

Then that individual is said to have a strong connection with their physical body, and a strong ability to manipulate the physical world around them, and they have a strong ability to get their physical needs met (unless there are other elements in their chart actively working against this).

Within an Astrological Chart, if there is one or more Planets in the **Fire Element** Signs:

- **Aries**
- **Leo**
- **Sagittarius**

Then that individual is said to have a strong connection with their core energy, with their inherent vitality, and they have a strong ability to motivate themselves and focus their energy towards achieving and manifesting desired goals (unless there are other elements in their chart actively working against this).

Within an Astrological Chart, if there is one or more Planets in the **Air Element** Signs:

- **Gemini**
- **Libra**
- **Aquarius**

Then that individual is said to have a strong connection with their mind and mental body, with their thoughts and imagination, and they have a strong ability create in and on the mental realm, and use their thoughts and words to influence other people and the world around them, and are able to communicate themselves effectively (unless there are other elements in their chart actively working against this).

Within an Astrological Chart, if there is one or more Planets in the **Water Element** Signs:

- **Cancer**
- **Scorpio**
- **Pisces**

Then that individual is said to have a strong connection with their emotional energy... with their feelings and emotions, they have a strong emotional intelligence, and are very good at reading and sensing the emotions of other people (unless there are other elements in their chart actively working against this).

The more Planets an individual has in one particular Element, the more proficient an individual becomes in that area of life, and the more dominated by that Element they also become.

And because there are only 10 Planets (11 if you count Chiron), it is impossible to have a Planet in each of the 12 Signs, and usually, you will find that one or two Elements are dominant in an individual's chart... thus swinging and focusing their personality in a certain elemental direction.

If someone has one of the above 4 Elements where there are **no** Planets in any of the associated Signs, then in traditional Astrology it is said that:

- For **Earth**, they are erratic with their connection to the physical world, one day they can be grounded and effective, and can manipulate the physical world well, and then the next day they can be ungrounded, and are impractical in the way they deal with the physical world around them.

- For **Fire**, they are erratic with their energy, one day they can motivate themselves well, and then the next day they seem to lack sufficient enough energy to do or focus on anything, and find it hard to motivate themselves to achieve their dreams and goals.

- For **Air**... they are erratic with their mind... one day they can express themselves well and think clearly, and then the next day they seem unable to think clearly or express themselves effectively...

- For **Water**, they are erratic with their emotions and feelings, one day they are emotionally balanced and in control of their feelings, and the next day they seem to be a prisoner of their emotions, and either their emotions are not flowing as they should, or they erupt in an uncontrolled way... there is no constant or steady flow.

For someone who lacks any Planets in a particular Element, then their lifetime task is to work towards gaining control and focus in that area of their life, gaining balance, gaining some control over that particular Element, so that their best day becomes their life every day.

So a missing Element in your Chart, an Element in whose Signs you have no Planets, is most often an area of your psyche where you need to do some work on yourself to achieve balance, to re-connect with, to strengthen that connection.

The energies are there, it's just that you need to plug back into those energies through Conscious effort.

For example, I have no Planets in Air, and early on in life, I could communicate well one day, and then be totally tongue-tied the next.

However, I have actively worked on this imbalance over the years... and now I write for a living, having bought my Air Element energies into balance.

So now, the good news.

Because **Energy Astrology** also has an energy component, a practical approach, it is possible to create Audio Essences which contain:

- The 3 Astrological Signs for the Earth Element... Taurus + Virgo + Capricorn.

- The 3 Astrological Signs for the Fire Element... Aries + Leo + Sagittarius.

- The 3 Astrological Signs for the Air Element... Gemini + Libra + Aquarius.

- The 3 Astrological Signs for the Water Element... Cancer + Scorpio + Pisces.

So... you can easily and effectively step into each of the 4 Elemental energies.

Earth... Fire... Air... or Water.

And feel them... and so work with them effectively.

Honest, it's a lot easier then you might think.

So if you have a problem with Air... or you are low on Earth... or if you find it hard to ignite your Fire to get moving... or are disconnected from your Water and emotions, and feel stuck and unflowing.

You can work with any of the 4 Elements on a *feeling level* with **Energy Astrology**, to bring balance back into your life.

Chapter 2-15: The Polarity Signs

One of the foundations of Chinese philosophy is the concept of **Yin** and **Yang**, that the Universe is based on, and created from, an underlying energetic polarity.

Like two ends of a Celestial magnet... with **Yin** at one end... and **Yang** at the other end.

And all things in Creation manifest due to the polarity and tension between **Yin** and **Yang**, so they are the foundation of our existence.

Nothing in existence can exist without it having some amount, or percentage, of **Yin**, and some amount, or percentage, of **Yang**, in its energetic composition, although as we shall see soon, that doesn't automatically mean it is always a 50/50 split between the two.

Being able to understand and accept this Universal polarity, is said to make our life so much easier, according to those Ancient Chinese sages, because we will be working with the Celestial flow and **not** against it.

And this concept of Polarity can also be found in an Astrological Chart.

In that half of the Signs are said to be **Yang** or Male, and the other half are said to be **Yin** or Female.

The **Yang Signs** are:

- **Aries**
- **Gemini**
- **Leo**
- **Libra**
- **Sagittarius**
- **Pisces**

The **Yin Signs** are:

- **Taurus**
- **Cancer**
- **Virgo**
- **Scorpio**
- **Capricorn**
- **Aquarius**

However, we do need to be careful at this point.

Because it is highly unlikely that the originators of what we call Western Astrology, the Ancient Babylonians and the Egyptians and the Greeks, had a concept which was 100% equivalent of Chinese **Yin** and **Yang**, as the Ancient Chinese perceived it.

Similar, yes... Male + Female... Sun + Moon... Night + Day.

But did the Ancient Astrologers, who created the foundation for Western Astrology, also come up with exactly the same concept as the Chinese?

Hard to say.

But doubtful... even if you take the knowledge and traffic travelling up and down the Silk Road, thousands of years ago, into account.

Although there was a sharing and exchange of information and wisdom up and down the Silk Road, for thousands of years, the ancient equivalent of the Internet... so maybe... who now knows?

But what we can say is that applying the concept of **Yin** and **Yang** to the 12 Astrological Signs does indeed *work*.

You see, according to the Ancient Chinese, the main difference between Yin and Yang is:

*   **Yin** is **holding** energy... it fixes and maintains
*   **Yang** is **flowing** energy... it moves and shifts

So the perfect example of **Yin** is a cup or bowl, whose function is to hold water, that is its primary function.

And the perfect example of **Yang** is a tube or funnel, whose function is to allow water to flow along its length, that is its primary function.

A cup with a hole in it would be less **Yin**, and a tube that was blocked up would be less **Yang**.

One would not be able to hold water (and so would become more **Yang**), while the other would not allow flow to occur (and so would become more **Yin**).

With **Yin** and **Yang**... holding and flow... it's all relative.

And when you stand back and look at the Universe, from an energy perspective, fundamentally, it's all about *holding* or *flow*...

And that is why some things are classified as more **Yin**, while others are classified as more **Yang**.

Take Men and Women as an example.

Women are classified as more **Yin**, mainly because they have a womb, which holds and protects new life for 9 months.

While Men are seen as having a penis, which spurts the new life into the womb, and then they flow on, so Man as classified as more **Yang**.

Summer is all about expansion and flow... (i.e. **Yang**)

Winter is all about holding the energy in the ground, to allow it to recharge, in preparation for a new season... (i.e. **Yin**)

And the same could be said about Day and Night.

The energies flow and expand during the Day, and they retreat at Night, recharging before the start of a new Day.

So when we say that each of the 12 Astrological Meridians is either **Yin** or **Yang**...

What we are really saying is that, in addition to being Male and Female...

The **Yin Signs** are all about *holding* and *nurturing* the energy they hold.

While the **Yang Signs** are all about allowing the energy they hold to *flow* and *expand*.

So when we look back at our list of **Yang Signs**:

- **Aries**
- **Gemini**
- **Leo**
- **Libra**
- **Sagittarius**
- **Pisces**

It is possible to say and see that these Signs are all about allowing energy to flow and expand in some way... but in relation to the Element assigned to that Sign.

- **Aries** is all about flowing and expanding Fire
- **Gemini** is all about flowing and expanding Air
- **Leo** is all about flowing and expanding Fire
- **Libra** is all about flowing and expanding Air
- **Sagittarius** is all about flowing and expanding Fire
- **Aquarius** is all about flowing and expanding Air

Wait a minute... where is Earth and Water?

Well... if we look at the **Yin Signs** we find:

- **Taurus**
- **Cancer**

- **Virgo**
- **Scorpio**
- **Capricorn**
- **Aquarius**

And when we conceive these in terms of holding and nurturing energies, we soon find that:

- **Taurus** is all about holding and nurturing Earth
- **Cancer** is all about holding and nurturing Water
- **Virgo** is all about holding and nurturing Earth
- **Scorpio** is all about holding and nurturing Water
- **Capricorn** is all about holding and nurturing Earth
- **Pisces** is all about holding and nurturing Water

So... that's where the Earth and Water Signs are hiding... they are all Yin in nature.

- **Yang** is Air and Fire, elements which flow and expand
- **Yin** is Earth and Water, elements which hold and contain

There is a mysterious, underlying symmetry to this stuff... if you choose to look deeper.

And remember, we're looking at this from the perspective of the Chinese energy system, not the traditional Western astrological system... and things stack up differently when viewed from the East.

So already we can see an obvious Universal demarcation line:

- Fire and Air are inherently **Yang**
- Earth and Water are inherently **Yin**

Which kind of makes sense, because you need the **Yang Elements** and **Signs** to flow, and you need the **Yin Elements** and **Signs** to hold and nurture.

And you can also see the truth of this when you consider the Physical Organs associated with the Meridians...

Some are more about flow, such as the Small and Large Intestines, and so are classified as **Yang**.

Some are more about holding, such as the Lungs and Heart, and so are classified as **Yin**.

You wouldn't want your digestive system to become blocked, and neither would you want your primary pump, the Heart, to spring a leak.

The right balance of **Yin** and **Yang** is vital to the correct function of these organs... and it isn't always about being 50 / 50.

Now, you could say... "*Isn't Water flowing... so shouldn't Water be Yang?*"

But the thing is... if you leave Water on its own... in a cup or a bowl... then it just says there... flat and unmoving.

Without energy input from outside... from the Wind or the Sun or Gravity... Water doesn't move... it just rests... and so Water is actually very **Yin**.

Someone else is probably thinking... "*Doesn't the blood also have to flow through the Heart... and the air flowing though our Lungs... so why are these organs classified as Yin?*"

Well... this is when we must return to one of the other fundamental principles of those Ancient Chinese Sages.

That on the Earth plane... nothing is **100% Yin** or **100% Yang**.

Everything must be a combination of both... in order to exist and function correctly.

True, something maybe more **Yin** than **Yang**.

And something maybe more **Yang** than **Yin**.

So the Small Intestine, to function correctly, needs to be more about flow then it is about holding.

And the Heart Meridian, to function correctly as our primary pump, needs to be more about holding then it is about flow.

Men are more **Yang**... but cannot exist without some **Yin**.

Women are more about **Yin**... but cannot exist without some **Yang**.

And, because Nature is wyrd and mysterious and complex at times, in their individual makeup, some Women are more **Yang** then your average Male.

While some Men are more **Yin** then your average Woman.

It's not always Black and White... the Universe is full of so many shades of Grey.

The Universe does like to mix it up occasionally, especially on the individual level.

Which you can discover through an individual's natal chart, and counting up the Signs in which the Planets fall at their moment of birth.

If there are more Planets in **Yin Signs**, then **Yang**, that individual will have more of a holding and nurturing personality.

And if there are more Planets in **Yang Signs**, then **Yin**, that individual will have more of a flowing and expansive personality.

But having said that... a lot will depend on what those Planets are.

Mars in a **Yin Sign** may still have more of a kick to it then the Moon in a **Yang Sign**.

It all depends... it is all relative.

And there is always culture and karma that has to be thrown into the mix too.

So things are always so... individual... and you can never be 100% sure how things will turn out.

OK... there is more to **Yin & Yang** then we have time to cover here... especially in relation to **Meridian Yin & Yang**, that we will be covering in another book.

But for now... for **Energy Astrology**... that is sufficient for our needs.

Chapter 2-16:
The 3 Modalities

The **3 Modalities** of Astrology are:

- **Cardinal**
- **Fixed**
- **Mutable**

And the 4 Astrological Signs which relate to each of these 3 Modalities are a bit like the following 3 Olympic Athletic events:

- The 100 Metre Sprint
- The Marathon
- The Decathlon

Because they all relate to the use and application of energy, to achieve an outcome or goal, over different lengths of time and/or distance.

An Athlete engaged in winning the 100 Metre Sprint must move very fast, and very quickly, over a short distance, although that consumes up his energy resources very quickly, and so they would be unable to keep up that speed for long. Which is very **Cardinal**. A short burst of high energy, hopefully, to get things started, to get things moving, to win, as long as winning can be achieved in a short period of time.

An Athlete engaged in winning the Marathon, over a distance of 28 miles, must pace themselves, find a constant rhythm and speed, which will allow them to expend their energy consistently, over the entire distance, so that they can make it to the finish line, without burning up or becoming tired and exhausted too soon. Which is very **Fixed**. A sustained outpouring of energy over the distance you need to cover so that you can reach your desired goal. Winning can only be achieved by lasting the full distance.

Sports in the Decathlon include: 100-metre dash, running, long (broad) jump, shot put, high jump, and 400-metre run, 110-metre hurdles, discus throw, pole vault, javelin throw, and 1,500-metre run. So the Decathlon is a mixture of short distance and long-distance running, plus jumping and throwing disciplines. To win outright in the Decathlon requires an Athlete to be good in the majority of these sports, not just one, and be able to shift their focus and energy from one event on to the next, and then the next. Which is very **Mutable**. Flexibility and openness so that an individual can turn their energy towards a new challenge or goal, letting go of the old, as and when appropriate.

You can see the truth of this if you look at the main picture above, where you have 5 different kinds and styles of running, with a sprinter on the left, a long-distance marathon runner on the right, and a middle-distance runner in the middle. Notice how the

Sprinter is leaning more into their run, to maximize their speed, while the Marathon runner is more upright, to maximize their endurance and stamina. Each is adopting the body posture best suited for the type of race they are engaged in.

Because each athletic discipline is carried out over a different length/distance, it requires each individual to use their energy in a different way, and so adopt the appropriate body posture, along with the necessary mental attitude and approach.

And this is also true for any Human activity, whether in sport, business or just going through our daily life, where needs and circumstances are changing all the time.

Some activities are short in duration, but require a burst of energy to get us started. This is where **Cardinal** energy helps.

Some activities are longer in duration and take time, focus and concentration to achieve, and we need stamina, and the ability not to exhaust, overuse or overextend our energy. This is where **Fixed** energy comes into its own.

And when any task has come to an end, we need to be able to shift and change our focus, move on to the next task, the next priority, and so we need to be able to let go and change inner gear. This is where **Mutable** energy is needed.

The problems occur when an individual's Astrological chart, and so their personality, is leaning more towards 1 of the **3 Modalities** at the expense of the others, and this creates an imbalance, where an individual is trying to approach all their life situations with one primary energy strategy.

As if someone was trying to sprint their way through a 28 Mile Marathon, or set out at the speed of a long-distance runner, slow and steady, in an attempt to win a 100 Metre Sprint.

So if you have someone who is too **Cardinal**, you have someone who is always starting projects, but who quickly runs out of energy, out of stamina and enthusiasm, and so moves on to the next thing, giving up on the old. Yes, they are great at starting projects but hopeless at finishing them, which can lead to a very frustrating existence. This person may have a great deal of energy and can make a lot of noise perhaps, but if you look around them, they have very little to show for it, before their life eventually comes to its end.

But, in contrast, if you have someone who is too **Fixed**, you have someone who finds it hard to start a project, but when they have started one, they become so focused and committed that they find it hard to let go, and so are continually focused on continuing, and they never know when to stop, they never know when enough is enough. And their constant tinkering as time goes on may even make things worse, like overcooking a meal, which can lead to a very frustrating existence. They find it very hard to get moving, but once they are engaged, like a super-tanker, they find it hard to come to a complete stop, and so find it hard to change and adapt.

And if you have someone who is too **Mutable**, you have someone who is always changing their Mind, always deciding to shelve one project, just after starting it, because they believe the next idea which has just entered their Mind will be much better to work on. So they are continually chopping and changing, and nothing ever gets done, nothing ever gets finished or completed. So, like the **Cardinal** individual, they have very little to show for all their efforts, although they can always talk to you about what might have been.

The **3 Modalities** are like the gears on a car, which are designed to work together. Your car was never designed to work well only in 1st, 2nd, 3rd or 4th gear, and driving around in reverse all the time would be plain madness.

So the Human personality was never designed to function well with just one **Modality** dominant.

But if someone is too **Cardinal, Fixed,** or **Mutable**, that is what they try to do as their default, they're trying to make their life work with one basic approach, as either a Sprinter, Marathon runner, or Decathlete.

The **4 Cardinal Signs** are:

- **Aries (Fire)**
- **Cancer (Water)**
- **Libra (Air)**
- **Capricorn (Earth)**

And these 4 Signs are like a 100 Metre Sprint because they relate to the application of an immense amount of energy over a very short and focused period of time. So whenever a Planet lands in any of these 4 Signs, it's own energy is given a **Cardinal twist**, and so becomes more energized in its expression, although its core energy remains the same. Each of the 4 Signs shows the **Cardinal energy** being expressed through a different Elemental Energy – Fire, Water, Air or Earth.

The **4 Fixed Signs** are:

- **Taurus (Earth)**
- **Leo (Fire)**
- **Scorpio (Water)**
- **Aquarius (Air)**

And these 4 Signs are like a Marathon Runner because they relate to the application of an immense amount of energy over a much longer period of time, over a much greater distance, and so stamina and the ability to pace become important. So whenever a Planet lands in any of these 4 Signs it's own energy is given a **Fixed twist**, and so becomes more focused and dogmatic in its expression, although its core energy remains the same. Each of the 4 Signs shows the **Fixed energy** being expressed through a different Elemental Energy – Earth, Fire, Water, or Air.

The **4 Mutable Signs** are:

- **Gemini (Air)**
- **Virgo (Earth)**
- **Sagittarius (Fire)**
- **Pisces (Water)**

And these 4 Signs are like a Decathlon Athlete because they relate to the application of energy to different tasks and activities, and the ability to effectively re-focus on the task in hand. So whenever a Planet lands in any of these 4 Signs it's own energy is given a **Mutable** twist, and so becomes more fluid in its expression, although its core energy remains the same. Each of the 4 Signs shows the **Mutable** energy being expressed through a different Elemental Energy – Air, Earth, Fire or Water.

There are two problems when it comes to Astrology and the **3 Modalities**.

The first problem is that an individual can never find a perfect balance. It's a question of mathematics really. There are only 10 primary Planets, and only 12 Astrological Signs, so even during those rare times when the Planets are spread evenly around the Solar System, and so the Natal chart, it is impossible to have a Planet in each of the 12 Signs, and sometimes they are clustered and bunched up in a certain area of the chart, and so put the emphasis on a particular Modality or two... leaning that individual to a certain approach or attitude in their life.

It's as if they have mastered a hammer, and so approach each problem in terms of hammering.

OK, if you need to knock in a nail, then a hammer is good. But if you are trying to cut a piece of wood, less so, and a saw is a much better choice.

This means that most personalities are built around one or two **Modalities**. They are either too **Cardinal**, too **Fixed**, or too **Mutable**, and so must consciously work to bring themselves back into balance. Which is possible, but something which an individual has to work at consciously.

The second problem, some planets thrive and prosper in some **Modalities**, while for other planets, it is much less the case.

For example, **Mars** loves **Cardinal**, loves the explosion of energy, isn't too bad at working with **Fixed**, but isn't too comfortable with **Mutable**, because it's not so keen on the let go and change aspect.

In contrast, **Neptune** is not so keen on **Cardinal** and **Fixed** but loves **Mutable**, and the whole emphasis on change and flow.

So when a Planet lands in a **Modality** it is not fully in harmony with, this can present problems for the individual with that set-up in their natal chart. But as with most things Astrological, no energy is ever a dead-end, there are always ways to find of working with, and positively expressing that energy.

Chapter 2-17: The Uniqueness of Astrological Signs

Going through each of the **12 Astrological Signs**... and defining them in terms of their **Element**... their **Polarity**... and the **Modality**... is a beneficial exercise for many reasons.

Because, firstly, it helps us to understand what each of the 12 Signs does, what its main energy focus is within our psyche.

But is also helps us to understand that each of the 12 Astrological Signs is... *unique.*

Because in the pantheon of the **12 Astrological Signs**...

There is only one Yang + Fire + Cardinal Sign... and that's **Aries**.

There is only one Yin + Earth + Fixed Sign... and that's **Taurus**.

There is only one Yang + Air + Mutable Sign... and that's **Gemini**.

There is only one Yin + Water + Cardinal Sign... and that's **Cancer**.

There is only one Yang + Fire + Fixed Sign... and that's **Leo**.

There is only one Yin + Earth + Mutable Sign... and that's **Virgo**.

There is only one Yang + Air + Cardinal Sign... and that's **Libra**.

There is only one Yin + Water + Fixed Sign... and that's **Scorpio**.

There is only one Yang + Fire + Mutable Sign... and that's **Sagittarius**.

There is only one Yin + Earth + Cardinal Sign... and that's **Capricorn**.

There is only one Yang + Air + Fixed Sign... and that's **Aquarius**.

There is only one Yin + Water + Mutable Sign... and that's **Pisces**.

So when you look at it that way... you soon see that each of the **12 Astrological Signs** is not only different... it is indeed *unique*.

It takes our energy... it takes our Consciousness... and focuses and shapes it in a way that *none* of the other **11 Astrological Signs** can do.

OK, so each of the **12 Astrological Signs** has its drawbacks... its disadvantage... its weakness.

And sometimes this is because we are approaching it in a way it was never intended to be used because what is a weakness in one context is a strength in another.

But in our life... we will still need ALL 12 of them.

Because, once again, each one does something that none of the other 11 Signs can do.

Because each one is a different type of light or energy when you compare it to the others in the line (as our chapter image shows).

Each one has a different function, and working together, they make a whole.

A bit like a car engine... the starter motor... the spark plugs... the pistons... all are needed to work together for the engine to work overall... they cannot function in isolation.

In the same way, for a Human individual, each **Astrological Sign** only has meaning and purpose in relation to all the other elements it is working alongside.

Because when we are living our life, we encounter so many different situations, on so many different levels, that we need our full Astrological team to have any chance of success in this fluid and ever-changing world of ours.

So they are indeed very much a team, all working together.

If you are trying to fix something on to the Earth plane... manifesting it through and down, so that it is stable and here... then there is only one Sign that is totally up to the job... and that's **Taurus**... Yin + Earth + Fixed.

And if you are trying to get your emotions flowing... then there is only one Sign that is best for that job... and that is **Cancer**... Yin +

Water + Cardinal.

And if you want to start thinking in new ways... then there is one Sign that probably supports this the best... and that's **Libra**... Yang + Air + Cardinal... (and not **Aquarius**, which is close... but has a different function within the Astrological Pantheon... Yang + Air + Fixed... **Aquarius** is more about focusing and sticking with an idea once you have it in mind).

But I always find it interesting to note that all the Earth and Water Signs are always Yin, while all the Fire and Air Signs are always Yang.

But if you stop to think about it, Earth has to be Yin... because it is a stabilizing and holding energy, while Fire has to be Yang, because it is reactive and expanding.

So the Elements are either Yin or Yang... and what makes the real difference between them is the Modality, the Cardinal, Fixed or Mutable, that appears to be what mixes things up.

It is why Astrologers always say... even when you don't have a Planet in a particular Sign, and on your natal chart that Sign is seen to be empty, that doesn't mean it isn't doing anything, that doesn't mean it is empty and inactive in your psyche.

If, as **Energy Astrology** suggests, each Sign is associated with a Meridian, then it is always doing something in your energy anatomy.

No Sign or Meridian is ever idle.

In fact, you could argue the complete opposite.

For a Sign that has no Planets, it can do it's thing easier then if a Planet was present because it is unencombered by the influence and weight of that Planet.

Sometimes having a Planet in a Sign complicates the activity of that Sign/Meridian, makes it harder for it to do its thing.

Although the paradox is...

A Planet in a Sign makes it harder to work that Astrological Sign.

Because the weight of that Planet on that Sign / Meridian automatically switches it into the negative mode.

But also, it also makes it easier to work with the energies of that Astrological Sign.

Because you are far more familiar with the energy... good and bad... flowing and non-flowing... and so you are more plugged into those energies... they are more familiar to you.

Now... the uniqueness of each Sign... which we have explored in this chapter is made even more unique when we add the Elemental Archetype for each of the 12 Signs... but as said, we will be covering all that in a lot more depth in a later volume of this Energy Astrology series.

Chapter 2-18: Other Possible Combinations

Once you have established the link between the **12 Astrological Signs** and the 12 Meridians... then you can really start to *think outside of the box...*

Because there is a whole range of other possible Meridian-Sign combinations which were never considered possible by traditional Western Astrology...

But they *are* possible if you take the time to look through the eyes of Chinese and Eastern astrology and energy approaches.

For example... the Meridian-Sign combinations based on Chinese **5 Element Theory**... which gives us:

Wood:

Liver Meridian & Gallbladder Meridian = **Gemini + Capricorn**

Fire 1:

Heart Meridian & Small Intestine Meridian = **Leo + Pisces**

Fire 2:

Heart Protector Meridian & Triple Warmer Meridian = **Libra + Taurus**

Earth:

Spleen Meridian & Stomach Meridian = **Sagittarius + Cancer**

Metal:

Lung Meridian & Large Intestine Meridian = **Aquarius + Virgo**

Water:

Kidney Meridian & Bladder Meridian = **Aries + Scorpio**

So... if you look at each of the above through the eyes of Western Astrology, the above associations are only possible if there are two or more Planets forming an aspect between them in an astrological chart...

But... from the perspective of **Energy Astrology**... it is indeed possible to bring these particular energies together in a direct and focused way... and experience what unique doors they might open for you.

But it doesn't end there... in some Chinese energy traditions, which work with Meridian combinations outside of the normal 5 Element associations... there is a system called **Division Points**... different associations between the 12 Meridians... which if we translate across into the **12 Astrological Signs** gives us:

Division Points 1: Greater Yang

Bladder Meridian + Small Intestine Meridian = **Scorpio + Pisces**

Division Points 2: Lesser Yang

Triple Warmer Meridian + Gallbladder Meridian = **Taurus + Capricorn**

Division Points 3: Shining Yang

Stomach Meridian + Large Intestine Meridian = **Cancer + Virgo**

Division Points 4: Greater Yin

Lung Meridian + Spleen Meridian = **Aquarius + Sagittarius**

Division Points 5: Lesser Yin

Heart Meridian + Kidney Meridian = **Leo + Aries**

Division Points 6: Terminal Yin

Heart Protector Meridian + Liver Meridian = **Libra + Gemini**

Now... the 5 Element associations are said to control the flow of our energy *within* our energy system and anatomy... whereas Division Points are said to control the flow of energy *between* our individual energy system and the world around us... with our environment.

Both of which are ultra important to us, because...

Yes, we need to ensure that our energy flows well within our energy anatomy... that there are no blocks or leakages in our energy... which is the main focus of the 5 Element set-up...

But also...

We need to ensure we are taking in the right energy... and the right amount of energy... from our surrounding environment... a kind of energy breathing... which is the focus of Division Points.

And without this breathing in of energy... or Chi... from our immediate environment, then we cannot continue to function in a balanced and integrated way.

In her book, *The Invisible Mind*, **Valerie Hunt** writes about an experiment which shows what happens when people are cut off from the electromagnetic field of their environment... and I have also discussed that same experiment in my book *Energy Boundaries - Volume 1*.

So if you think of it this way...

Astrological Sign Elements connect us to the wider Celestial energies...

Division Points connect us to the energies of our environment...

The 5 Elements integrate our own energies internally...

Kind of like a 3-dimensional lattice of energy.

Finally, there is another way to approach the 12 Meridian and Astrological Sign energies... a way which turns them into **Elemental Archetypes**, which go to the core of what each Astrological Sign is searching for... but we will be covering that in a different volume in this **Energy Astrology** series.

PAGE THREE: THE ASTROLOGICAL PLANETS

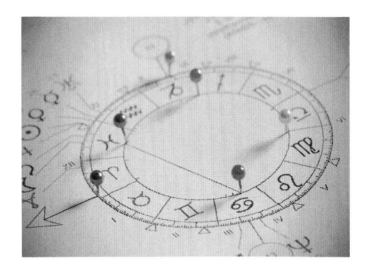

Chapter 3-1: The Astrological Planets

Now, in this Section, we are moving on to an exploration of the Astrological Planets.

As we discussed earlier, in **Energy Astrology**, the Planets relate to Chakras, and the other Astrological elements in the Chart, such as the Nodal Axis, also relate to aspects in an individual's energy anatomy, in accordance with the following list:

- **The Sun** = The Heart Chakra
- **The Moon** = The Sacral Chakra
- **Mercury** = The Hand & Feet Chakras
- **Venus** = The Throat Chakra
- **Mars** = The Solar Plexus Chakra
- **Jupiter** = The Base Chakra
- **Saturn** = The Knee & Elbow Chakras
- **Chiron** = The Thymus Chakra
- **Uranus** = The Brown Chakra

- **Neptune** = The Crown Chakra
- **Pluto** = The Soma Chakra
- **The South Node** = The meeting of the Ida & Pingala Nadis at the Base Chakra
- **The North Node** = The meeting of the Ida & Pingala Nadis at the Brow Chakra
- **The Midheaven** = Where the Sushumna Nadi merges back into the Kunda field at the Crown Chakra
- **Imum Coeli** = Where the Sushumna Nadi emerges from the Kunda field at the Base Chakra

The Astrological Glyphs for the Planets
(Top Row - Sun, Moon, Mercury, Mars...
Middle Row - Venus, Jupiter, Saturn, Uranus...
Bottom Row - Neptune, Pluto, Chiron, North Node.)

And we will be exploring each of these Planet/energy anatomy combinations in more depth in the following Chapters in this Section.

But first, there is something else which all the Planets share, according to **Energy Astrology**.

They all relate to an aspect of our psychological **Comfort Zone**.

Where the usual Dictionary definition of Comfort Zone is something like:

A situation, place or state where one feels safe or at ease.

How does that relate to Astrology?

Let me explain.

Have you ever watched a two-year-old explore the world around them?

It is an interesting exercise because it also helps explain a great deal about how adults behave and navigate their way through adulthood.

Remember, the habits and patterns which we establish in our early Childhood are the ones we tend to stick with throughout the rest of our lives.

A small Child's exploration of the BIG world around them can be broken down into two distinct phases.

The first phase begins when the Child gets bored with playing beside its Mother, and decides to set off and explore the exciting world which lies just beyond the horizon. So the Child toddles off, for the moment putting any thought of Mother and safety to one side, enticed by the prospect of all the adventure, freedom and newness that lies on the other side of the room or play-park.

But, as the Child explores, at some point, the thought suddenly enters his/her Mind, *'Where has Mother gone?'*, and it looks around to find her. This is the start of the second phase.

If she is still nearby, in direct line of sight, then all is well, she isn't lost, and so the Child is comforted and continues to explore.

However, if she appears to be far away, or even worse, can no longer be seen or located, then the Child goes into full-blown panic mode, and frantically tries to find her again.

It either runs straight back to Mother, or makes so much noise so that the Mother is alerted to his/her plight, and so comes to the rescue.

Either way, the Child returns to Mother, and so feels safe and secure. Panic over. Until… the Child gets bored… starts to wander off in search of newness and excitement, and the whole cycle repeats once again.

So the repeating pattern is fueled by boredom and the need for excitement on one side, and anxiety and the need for security on the other side.

And this pattern is old… I mean, really, really old… it is threaded through all life on Earth across 1 billion-plus years.

Evolution has dictated that animals that stay within their Comfort Zone… stay within the boundaries for which their nature and body is best designed, have a much greater chance of survival.

Polar bears which go wandering off into the Sahara, or Lions which decide to live up in a tree in a jungle, animals which move outside of the environment for which they are best suited have much less chance of surviving and passing on their genes to the next generation.

Now, the differences when this strategy of Comfort Zones reaches us Human Beings is that:

a) We have a Brain and Mind that is capable of conscious, self-awareness, which can create a number of difficulties and complications. Our conscious thinking can sometimes get in the way, and we end up tripping over our own evolutionary shoelaces.

b) Our Human Brain/Mind also allows us to develop and respond to different circumstances, and so we are the one creature on the Planet which the option of expanding beyond our pre-programmed Comfort Zone. This is the reason why we are able to inhabit every landmass on Earth, hot or cold, wet or arid.

Because Humans can step outside of individual and collective Comfort Zones, Humans can try out new ideas faster, and then pass them on to others if they prove to be beneficial. Individuals, working together, can evolve faster if we share our experiences.

But in terms of Human Beings as individuals...

What is important for all of us adults is to realise is that we do exactly the same thing. We repeat the same Comfort Zone pattern in our lives, but often we do not even realise that this is what we're doing.

The point at which the Child realises that the Mother is missing and starts to panic is what we can call the edge of our Comfort Zone. This is a psychological space that, while we are inside it we feel safe and secure, but when we venture outside of its apparent protection, we start to experience panic and anxiety. The Comfort Zone that we mentally create as Children we carry forward into our adult lives, it's our adult mental safety blanket.

For the Child, their Comfort Zone is initially represented by the Mother, but for adults, our Comfort Zones comprise a whole host of different things, both real and metaphorical, and Comfort Zones vary considerably from individual to individual. Comfort Zones also come in different shapes and sizes, some are quite large, while others are quite small.

COMFORT ZONE

INSIDE:

Safe
Comfortable
Predictable
Existing Skills
Known
Unexciting
Boring

OUTISDE:

Unsafe
Unknown
Unpredictable
New Skills
Exciting
Adventure

Comfort Zones - Inside & Out

My Comfort Zone will be very different from your Comfort Zone, and your Comfort Zone will be very different from your brother or sister, or your friends. After all, we are all unique individuals, even if we are created from repeating archetypal patterns. That's what Humans bring to Evolution, our Comfort Zones are multi-dimensional and full of colour.

Apart from the real protection which you Mother/Father can provide, along with any tangible skills that you acquire during your life (like flint-napping, weaving, or computer programming), the remainder of your Comfort Zone is built from mental constructs, your own ideas and beliefs about how the world works, which may not have any real roots in objective reality. Whether these beliefs and ideas would be able to protect you, if ever put to the test, is debatable. However, their magic lies in the fact that you think they would, and so your anxiety is kept at bay.

Modern psychological techniques, the ones which actually do work, to some degree, such as NLP or CBT, are partly designed to update your Comfort Zone, and give you a better set of beliefs and ideas, ones which will improve your ability to interact with your external world. Interestingly, Special Forces training is also about giving their personnel a set of attitudes and beliefs that allows them to deal effectively with the situations they may encounter (although their version of reality is a bit more violent than yours or mine).

As an adult, whenever you step outside of your Comfort Zone – i.e. to learn a new skill, meet new people, or travel to a different country – then you immediately trigger a burst of anxiety. You cannot prevent this anxiety from occurring, it happens automatically whenever you cross the boundary of your Comfort Zone. In a sense, anxiety is a warning signal designed to alert you to the fact you are wandering into uncharted territory, and so need to pay attention. Your Subconscious Mind, which usually runs much of your life for you on auto-pilot, cannot help if the Conscious Mind decides to go any further, so as a warning you experience a sense of anxiety.

Comfort Zones & Anxiety

But when this anxiety naturally arises, people respond in either one of two ways:

• They manage the anxiety, develop strategies to prevent it overwhelming them, and they keep moving forward towards their goal.

• They panic, turn around, and rush back to the perceived safety and security of their Comfort Zone, and look for ways to justify why they have given up on obtaining their goal (and they look for something or someone to blame for defeating them).

Because once again, when we are small Children, our parents and other adults either teach us a) how to successfully handle our anxiety and go after our goals, or b) how to play it safe and live within our psychological means.

Also, have you noticed that some people, when they step outside their Comfort Zone or are forced outside by external circumstances, create a lot of unnecessary psychological noise and activity? This is their Inner Child, hoping that if they make a lot of noise, someone, Mother perhaps, will come and save them. Unfortunately, for these adults, help seldom comes (because as an adult, you're meant to be able to look after yourself).

And, sad to say, all Mothers eventually grow old and pass on, so each Child is left on their own at some point in their life... left to their own devices and inner-strength.

If you choose to live out your life completely encased within the security of your Comfort Zone, then you will learn nothing new, go nowhere unusual, and boredom will be your constant companion. But for many people, this is the lesser of two evils. When asked to choose between anxiety and boredom, unfortunately, many, many people would rather choose a life of boredom and sameness then suffer the anxiety and uncertainty of setting out along a new and different life-path.

Many people like to believe they would have the nerve to walk down the path less travelled, as the American poet **Robert Frost** writes, but how many of us would take this path if actually given the opportunity?

And what if there was no path, and we had to forge a fresh one through an unknown forest, clearing a way for others to follow? How many people would be brave and happy to do that?

For many people, staying within the safety of their own Comfort Zone, and the collective Comfort Zone of their family, group, and the culture/society they are a part of is the much safer option.

Because, and this is an important point, we don't just have one Comfort Zone, we also share in the collective Comfort Zones of all the groups we belong to, which in turn influence our own Comfort Zone. In fact, you could say that our individual Comfort Zone is also a patchwork created from all the collective Comfort Zones we belong to.

We will touch upon this more when we come to explore the Social and Transpersonal Planets.

For example, I have my own individual Comfort Zone, but I also share and am plugged into my family's Comfort Zone, my local community, and my country's, as well as any other company, or organisation or social group I am a member of. These all possess collective tribal Comfort Zones, which can influence and control my behaviour, especially if I am not striving to be conscious of my thoughts and actions. The fact that my parents are in their mid-80s means that their Comfort Zones, which evolved back in the 1930s, have also been woven into my own at some level, and so influence me from the side.

You can easily prove the truth of this by seeing what happens to people when they are made redundant, or thrown out of their local club, or their family/teenage gang totally ostracises them for some reason. Their world is often shaken to its core, and they are plagued by a sense of overwhelming anxiety. For many, it's the same as the Child no longer being able to find the Mother. A total meltdown occurs.

This is why many of us will go to great pains to stay acceptable to the groups we belong to... why people go to great lengths to make unworkable and unfulfilling relationships work. But there are potential dangers with this strategy of social acceptance.

But there is a force within each Comfort Zone that fights to maintain the status quo, no matter what horrors lurk within.

We can see this in dysfunctional families, where the collective Comfort Zone can only continue to function as long as everyone ignores the obvious, the elephant in the room. The Father who is violent or the Mother who drinks... everything feels safe and secure as long as no one brings the truth out into the light of day. Anxiety is kept at bay through ignoring reality.

This can also occur on an individual level.

For example, a man, in his late 40s, can see that his factory is going to eventually close down with the loss of his job, however, there is currently very little opportunities in his local area for his particular skill set.

In the time left, before the factory closes, does he:

• Retrain in a new set of skills, which employers in his area actively require?

• Look to move to another area, one where his current skill set is in demand?

• Do nothing, and hope that after the factory closes, he will be able to find a job in his local area for his current skill set?

Now, putting other factors and considerations to one side, how he responds to this situation will depend greatly on how he handles anxiety in his life. His Comfort Zone contains his current job and skill set. To learn a new skill set, or move to a new area, will mean stepping outside of his Comfort Zone.

If he is someone who is good at positively dealing with anxiety, then it is possible he might opt for the first or second options. However, if he is someone who actively avoids anxiety, then it is far more likely that he will opt for the third option and do nothing, and hope everything will turn out for the best. But as soon as he goes for option 3 then his fate is in the hands of the Gods, and his anxiety can only be kept at bay through ignoring what might happen.

Unfortunately, reality catches up with everyone in the end, and sometimes we have to face our worst fears.

Once again, we need to understand that people will go to enormous lengths to avoid the feeling of anxiety, and modern psychology believes that anxiety is the root cause of much mental illness. The Mind becomes so desperate to avoid feeling the anxiety that it literally ties itself up in knots, which is the cause of mental imbalance.

And sometimes, to escape a burst of unwelcome anxiety, people will do and act in ways that, later, they regret.

In terms of our Subtle Anatomy, anxiety is associated with our Base Chakra, along with fear, and in Chinese Energy Medicine anxiety is also associated with our Spleen Meridian. Both the Base Chakra and Spleen Meridian are associated with the Earth Element, and so when we experience anxiety it depletes our Earth Element and ungrounds us, it literally knocks the ground out from underneath our feet.

But what then is the difference between anxiety and fear?

Well, put simply, the way I would describe it is that fear hits us physically, while anxiety hits us mentally.

When we experience fear it is our physical body that goes into overload, but with anxiety, it is our Mind that goes into mental overload. If you have ever had to spend time with some who is anxious, you will know that their Mind is constantly thinking, but that thinking never gets them anywhere.

When we experience fear, our body just wants to run, but with anxiety, our Mind goes into overdrive, trying to think our way out of a bad situation, even though when anxious we are in no position to think rationally about anything, and we definitely can't think outside the box. Anxiety undermines our ability to think straight and realistically. But unfortunately, when you are anxious, you can't switch the Mind off and all you seem to be able to do is think... non-stop... which can be exhausting.

And, of course, the bad news is that if someone can figure out what presses our anxiety buttons, then they can use that to influence and control us. If they can make us anxious then a) not only will we automatically do anything to reduce the anxiety, but also b) we won't be thinking straight or rationally, and so we may go along with any plan the other person proposes, and c) our constant worrying makes us even more ungrounded.

If you examine how cult leaders control their members, one of the ways is to keep them in a constant state of anxiety. Then they are less likely to question the orders they are given, they are much less likely to engage in rational thought at all. If the leader can also provide their group with an external enemy to worry about and focus on, who is continually at the gates, then so much the better.

But now, the good news... what can we do practically to prevent this from happening to us?

Well, there are two things that I can practically suggest. The first is an understanding of The Psychology of Flow, and the second is an understanding of your Astrological Moon sign... which we will cover deeper in our Sun & Moon Chapter.

Understanding the Psychology of Flow:

The best way to expand your Comfort Zone, while not also being overwhelmed by a great tsunami of anxiety, is to expand it at a rate and speed where you can comfortably deal with the anxiety generated by the expansion... so that it never overwhelms you.

This advice comes from the psychologist **Mihaly Csikszentmihalyi**, whose life's work has been the investigation of people's Comfort

Zones, all of which helped him to formulate his influential book *Happiness: The Psychology of Flow.*

As we saw earlier, if we stay totally within our Comfort Zone, then we not only experience a feeling of security but also one of boredom, because after a while we are experiencing nothing new. But if we leave our Comfort Zone, then not only do we experience anxiety but also potentially feelings of freedom and excitement as we encounter new information and sensations. There are forces that try to keep us within our Comfort Zone (security and anxiety), but there are also forces that are enticing us to leave and expand our horizons (boredom, freedom and excitement).

Now the trick, according to **Csikszentmihalyi**, is to move out of your Comfort Zone at a rate and speed that allows you to experience enough freedom and excitement to motivate you to keep going, but not enough to create sufficient anxiety to discourage or stop you in your tracks.

In addition, your Comfort Zone also represents the skills that you have acquired and mastered to date. So if you can use your existing skills to master new ones, it is also possible to find the balance point between boredom and anxiety, between security and excitement.

If you do all this, then you spontaneously enter a psychological state which **Csikszentmihalyi** refers to as Flow.

According to **Csikszentmihalyi**:

"When all a person's relevant skills are needed to cope with the challenges of a situation, that person's attention is completely absorbed by the activity. There is no excess psychic energy left over to process information about what the activity offers. All the attention is concentrated on the relevant stimuli."

As a result, one of the universal and distinctive features of optimal experience takes place: people become so involved in what they are doing that the activity becomes spontaneous, almost automatic; they stop being aware of themselves as separate from the actions they are performing.

Csikszentmihalyi explains that when a dancer starts to dance then they often get caught up in their experience, they forget themselves, and in this forgetting, they experience a state of Flow, a state of happiness, joy, and exhilaration. He goes on to quote similar experiences from a rock climber, a Mother reading to her small daughter, a chess player... all of whom describe this feeling of Flow in terms of their own activities, different contexts, but the same basic experience.

The dancer does become the dance... for a short while, but that is why the creative can be so addictive.

Whenever an individual is totally immersed in the Flow experience, they really don't have the spare mental capacity for worry and anxiety or boredom, all their concentration and mental bandwidth is taken up with an experience of being in the moment.

Csikszentmihalyi goes on to state that although the Flow experience appears on the surface to be effortless, it can only be sustained through mental or physical effort, or through ability and acquired skills, and is held together through concentration and focus. This means that fear, worry or doubt can break the magic spell which sustains the Flow and bring us crashing back to our normal stuck reality.

The Ancient Greeks defined ecstasy as the ability to stand outside of yourself, outside of your fears, your worries, and your concerns, and if you can do that then you are automatically in a state of Flow... a state of self-absorbing ecstasy... because for a moment you have forgotten all the things that limit you, you literally forget yourself, which in the Indian mystic tradition is known as the state of samadhi.

Based on **Csikszentmihalyi** observations:

• When we remain in our Comfort Zone, we cannot enter a state of Flow.

• When we allow ourselves to be overwhelmed by anxiety, we cannot enter a state of Flow.

• When we do not develop skills that we can enhance, master and take pride in, we cannot enter a state of Flow.

To create Flow, we need to be brave and venture out from our Comfort Zone, just as a small Child bravely sets out to explore the world around them. In fact, you could argue that a Child is naturally in a state of Flow when they are exploring and playing. It is only anxiety that crashes their party.

But, often, we adults have lost that ability to play naturally like a Child, and are lousy at locating that exact balance point between boredom and anxiety, and so end up being either tipped into total boredom or total anxiety in our personal lives.

You also come across this phenomenon in large companies and organisations, especially ones that have stagnated, and need to change fast in order to survive.

Usually, a young and dynamic manager, or management consultant, is brought in to create change, to whip the organisation back into shape, and their motto is something like *"Everyone has to get out of their Comfort Zones if we are to survive"*.

Comfort Zones & Success

I'm going to sound a little bit cynical here, but usually, the young and dynamic manager has negotiated a bonus scheme that ensures they will be rewarded no matter what happens, whether the organisation eventually succeeds or fails, and so their words about *"We're all in this together"* ring a little hollow. They didn't get to the top without knowing how to look after Number 1.

Their analysis of the situation is usually quite correct, the organisation has become stuck in its ways, and everyone has to be challenged to move out of their collective Comfort Zones if it is to survive.

But then what happens next:

• Does the manager try to find the balance point, so that the employees can move forward with excitement and with minimal anxiety?

• Does the manager totally trash the collective Comfort Zone, so that all the employees are plunged into a state of uncertainty and anxiety?

Yes, you've guessed it, what's the point of being a senior manager if you can't trash something when the mood takes you.

To be fair to these senior managers, when faced with a change in their own lives, they are usually very good at dealing with their own anxiety, so don't really understand how other people could be crippled by theirs. These types of manager usually end up creating the very situation that they should desperately have been trying to avoid.

As well as having to deal with all the organisational changes and new skills necessary for the organisation to survive and prosper, the employees have to do so while also wading through their collective sea of anxiety. And when people are anxious, what do they do? They desperately try to hang on to their Comfort Zones, resist any new ideas, and this makes the whole situation worse.

Now I admit, there are times when things are so bad that a manager has no other option but to push people out of their Comfort Zones, and hope for the best. But I have also seen so many bad managers who, with little or no understanding of how people function, have made a bad situation worse through their pathetic attempts at social engineering.

From my own experience, those managers who do succeed in these extreme situations are usually either the inspirational, high-energy types or managers who can establish strong inter-personal bonds with their employees, so that either way, the work-force decides that, despite their fears and anxiety, they want to follow the manager of their own free-will.

So what if you are an employee caught up in such a situation, or you are involved in any situation where someone is trying to trash your Comfort Zone, and you are becoming more and more anxious, what should you do?

Well, it all comes down to how good you are at controlling your own anxiety levels. If someone else has effectively blown up your Comfort Zone, and thrown you into the sea of anxiety, then the only person who can counter these feelings is you.

So knowing what makes you anxious… and knowing what reduces your anxiety are essential skills during these anxious times.

For example, if you are someone who knows that:

• Gardening and being close to nature can reduce your anxiety,

• Reading and intellectual stimulation can reduce your anxiety.

• Physical fitness and training can reduce your anxiety.

• Spending time with friends and family can reduce your anxiety.

• Tidying and clearing clutter can reduce your anxiety.

Then ensure you make time for those activities in your personal life to counter-balance any stress you are feeling in your work-life (or potentially even vice-versa, I know of one person who was so stressed at home, that they came to see work as being relaxing).

We will explore this further and deeper in our Chapter on **The Sun & The Moon**.

Think of your Comfort Zone as your castle. You can't stay inside forever, you will only get stale and bored if you try, and you may need to extend it from time to time. But it is also your primary defence against anxiety and uncertainty in this unpredictable world, and so it is worth defending.

Energy Astrology & Comfort Zones... The Surprising Truth:

Now, when I started this journey, exploring and developing **Energy Astrology**, which was as much to do with my own personal healing as it was about developing an energy system which other people could use and benefit from.

When I started, I was working under the assumption that our psychological Comfort Zone only related to 2 Planets, **The Moon** and **The Sun**.

Our **Astrological Moon** is the Planet responsible for maintaining and protecting our Comfort Zone, which is why it is associated with the tribe and family, and the feeling of safety and security.

And our **Astrological Sun** is the Planet responsible for expanding our Comfort Zone, if we want it to, so we can reach for, and achieve, our goals and dreams.

However, over the years, I have come to realise that this is too narrow a view.

That ALL the Planets... and other the Astrological elements, each one relates to our psychological Comfort Zone in some way.

Organising it... structuring it... making it work well (or not).

They all have a part to play in the structure and correct function of our psychological Comfort Zone.

And in the Chapters which follow in this Section, I will be exploring in much more depth how each of the Planets relate to our Comfort Zone, the role each of them plays in our psyche, as well as how they relate to our Chakras.

Which also expands out from the individual out to the collective too, as we move from the Personal Planets to the Social Planets, and out to the Transpersonal Planets.

And as you understand these relationships, and their exact function, it does make understanding your Astrological Chart a lot easier, and making it work for you a lot easier too.

Final Thoughts:

Consider the picture below, which does encapsulate much of the current business thought around Comfort Zones.

Stepping Out of Your Comfort Zone

Which is...

Comfort Zones are bad and will keep you trapped and unhappy
Stepping outside of your Comfort Zone is good and always lead to

success

So the girl standing outside of the Comfort Zone is looking happy and excited.

While everyone else, who is standing and remaining inside the collective Comfort Zone, is looking unhappy, and positively miserable in comparison.

So the message of this picture simply is:

- Comfort Zones are bad
- Stepping outside of your Comfort Zone is good

But is this always the truth?

Is that how it always plays out in the real world?

And also, just stepping outside of your Comfort Zone, is that always a guarantee of rewards and success?

Is that all it takes to succeed at every endeavour?

Unfortunately... No... it isn't... because there are always other factors at play in any situation...

Like resources, timing, connections, planning, communication, competition... to name a few...

Basically, Evolution wouldn't have stuck with hardwiring Comfort Zones into the brains of every creature that ever lived, over a billion-plus years, if there wasn't a real benefit to be had, and that is still true for Humans, no matter how evolved we like to think ourselves to be.

Which is... Comfort Zones can keep us safe... they help us to avoid unnecessarily dangerous situations...

And if we do need to go into such a situation, for whatever reason, they make us be on our guard, pay extra attention.

Plus, if you step out too far from your Comfort Zone... too soon... then not only is there a tsunami of anxiety to deal with.

But you are also drawing further away from your existing skill-sets, which you may also need to successfully handle the new situation.

Sometimes success isn't just about learning a new skill but also about using your existing skills in a new way... change + modification + re-learning...

But, in the above picture, the girl is standing quite far away from the collective Comfort Zone, and so should/will be experiencing anxiety, having probably gone out too far, too soon.

That far out, it's not all smiles and Yah-hoo!

Plus, if she had indeed mastered the new skill, she was seeking, then automatically, she will be drawn back into her individual Comfort Zone, because once you have learnt and mastered a new skill, it becomes part of your Comfort Zone, the foundation on which you build for the next stage of your life.

Like when someone learns to drive a car... it requires conscious thought and effort at first, and then over time, it becomes automatic, no thought required, it becomes integrated into their Comfort Zone.

So the only way that the Girl could stay where she is, permanently, would be to continually learn new skills 24/7, which isn't possible, it would be a life of constant anxiety, and the Human Brain isn't built to handle that kind of uncertainty.

In life, we all need periods of certainty, rest and recuperation.

So there is a 2nd insight with regards to the Flow experience.

Over time, as we learn and grow, we all need to flow in and out of our Comfort Zone, and there is no one fixed position that works for all circumstances we encounter in our life.

Not trying to continually live within your Comfort Zone.

Because then you will end up living an uninspired life of boredom.

Nor trying to continually exist outside of your Comfort Zone.

Because then you live an anxious life of uncertainty.

In life, any life, there are times when you do need to step outside of the Comfort Zone.

Either to learn a new skill or to deal with an unexpected and unknown circumstance.

But there are also times when you need to step back into your Comfort Zone... to rest on your laurels... to re-charge for your next adventure.

So life is about flow... flowing in... and flowing out.

The Yin and Yang of Comfort Zones.

The Yin and Yang of being fully alive.

And we shall now explore how each of the Astrological Planets supports our Comfort Zone... and this continual life-flow.

Chapter 3-2: The Sun & The Moon

From the perspective of **Energy Astrology**, it's very hard to talk about our Astrological **Inner Sun** and **Inner Moon** without also talking about our energetic, individual Comfort Zone.

And the reason why it is hard is that an understanding of Comfort Zones goes to the heart of what **The Sun** and **The Moon** are all about.

*In this Chapter, there are two sections, one for **The Sun**, the other for **The Moon**, and we focus on each one separately. However, because there is so much crossover between the two, it is hard to focus on one totally without bringing in the other occasionally, although hopefully, the difference between the two will be clear and concise as we proceed.*

In the movie, *War of the Worlds (2005)*, directed by **Steven**

Spielberg, there is a scene where the alien invaders are fighting the U.S. military, and an all-mighty battle is taking place... on the other side of a large hill... where the civilians on one side of the hill cannot see the battle which is taking place on the other side... unless they go to the very top of the hill, and so put themselves in great danger.

Tom Cruises' character doesn't want to see what is happening on the other side of the hill. He is too scared, and he is desperate to protect his young daughter, and so wants to get away from the battle as soon as they can.

But his son, played by **Justin Chatwin**, is desperate to see the battle with his own eyes, and so leaves his father and sister, venturing off on his own adventure and quest (although they are all reunited, safe and alive, at the end of the movie).

You can watch that scene in this particular YouTube video clip: https://www.youtube.com/watch?v=X7rfWPbEufo

Basically, for me, this scene highlights the fundamental difference between our **Inner Sun** and **Inner Moon**.

Our archetypal **Inner Sun** is desperate to see what is on the other side of the hill, even if that puts us in personal danger. While our **Inner Moon** is always trying to keep us safe and puts our need for personal protection ahead of any cravings for curiosity and newness, we may have.

As a master filmmaker, **Steven Spielberg** knows this, and so is playing with these two psychological forces within his audience, as they watch the scene. Part of us wants to run away with the Father, while another part wants to follow the Son to the top of the hill... to see what is on the other side... to step beyond their Comfort Zone.

THE SUN

And it is that dynamic between our **Inner Sun** and **Inner Moon**, which defines the majority of Human life, whether as a species, culture, or an individual.

For Traditional Astrology, the **Astrological Sun** is paradoxical, in many ways.

It's the one Planet which isn't really a Planet, it's a Star, the centre and creator of our Solar System. But it's just one of millions and millions of other stars in our Galaxy, so it is not really unique.

It's the only **real** source of light within our Solar System.

As our **Sun** formed, all those billions of years ago (4.751 to be exact), its growing and immense gravitational pull formed the rest of the Planets around it, creating our Solar System out of the dust, gas, and space debris that didn't fall into **The Sun**.

The Sun is mentioned daily in Astrological newspaper column, it's the one where most people know their Sign... *I'm a **Taurus**, I'm a **Scorpio**, I'm an **Aquarian**... what Sign are you?*

But it's also the one Planet where people tend to have a tenuous understanding of its function, at best, even amongst some people who study Astrology.

*"Oh, your **natal Sun**, all that's to do with individuation or inspiration... I think?"*

Part of the problem, our **natal Sun** is it is not 100% *who we are*, it's *who we aspire to become*, an inner force driving us onwards to do or make something out of our life, to give it some kind of shape and meaning, and that is a different thing entirely.

Our **natal Moon**, that is our beginning state, our foundation, the who we start out as, while our **natal Sun** is the process and route to get to somewhere else entirely, to literally make something else of ourselves, even if it is different to what our family and tribe would prefer our life to be, or have been.

*Our **Moon** is who we are now... and our **Sun** is who we could become... if we put in the effort.*

Just as the Solar Sun originally pulled in material from Outer Space in order to create our Solar System, so our **natal Sun** tries to pull in situations, people, resources, skills to help us build a larger life for ourselves.

Our **Inner Sun** aspires to become something more, better, or higher.

And as we will soon see, when you put it into the context of an understanding of Comfort Zones, all that confusion and un-clarity just disappears.

Remember back in school, during the Physics class, where you learnt about those two primary forces, centrifugal and centripetal.

- **Centrifugal** = a force, arising from the body's inertia, which

appears to act on a body moving in a circular path and is
directed away from the centre around which the body is
moving.

- **Centripetal** = a force which acts on a body moving in a circular
path and is directed towards the centre around which the body
is moving.

And how you probably got to demonstrate those 2 forces in action
by swinging a bucket full of water around your head, and how as
the bucket swung around, and there was tension on the rope, the
water stayed put in the bucket, how these 2 forces worked together
to create a static situation, until either the rope broke, or the circular
motion lessened, and someone got wet.

(*What do you mean you never did that experiment? But it was so
much fun!*)

Well, in a similar way, our Comfort Zone is composed of 2 distinct
and opposing Astrological/Psychological internal forces, each one
pulling in a different direction, and sometimes they balance and
cancel each other out, while at other times one force is greater
than the other and wins out, and so the individual is locked into a
particular direction in their life.

In Astrological language, these two forces are known as our **Inner
Sun** and **Inner Moon**.

These two forces are the principal forces organising our
psychological Comfort Zone, although ALL the Planets are at play in
some way or other, as we shall see later in this Section.

But to begin with, let's revisit our basic understanding of Comfort
Zones.

Remember? About the two-year-old Child exploring the world
around them, and how the process can be broken down into two

distinct phases?

Once again, quickly (and it is worth going through it again because it is important and fundamental to most of our Human behaviour.)

The first phase begins when the Child gets bored with playing beside its Mother and decides to set off and explore the exciting world which lies just beyond the horizon. So the Child toddles off, for the moment putting any thought of Mother and safety to one side, enticed by the prospect of all the adventure, freedom and newness that lies on the other side of the room or play-park.

But, as the Child explores, at some point the thought suddenly enters his/her mind, "*Where has Mother gone?*", and it looks around to find her. This is the start of the second phase.

If she is still nearby, in direct line of sight, then all is well, she isn't lost, and so the Child is comforted and continues to explore.

However, if she appears to be far away, or even worse, can no longer be seen or located, then the Child goes into full-blown panic mode, and frantically tries to find her again, making a lot of noise.

It either runs straight back to Mother, or makes so much noise that the Mother is alerted to his/her plight, and so comes to the rescue.

Either way, the Child returns to Mother, and so feels safe and secure. Panic over.

Until it gets bored, starts to wander off in search of newness and excitement, and the whole cycle repeats once again.

So the repeating pattern is fueled by boredom and the need for excitement on one side, and anxiety and the need for security on the other side.

What is important for all of us adults is to realize is that we do exactly the same thing, we repeat the same pattern in our lives, but often we do not even realise that this is what we're doing.

The point at which the Child realizes that the Mother is missing and starts to panic is what we can call the edge of our Comfort Zone. This is a psychological space that, while we are inside it we feel safe and secure, but when we venture outside of its apparent protection, we start to experience panic and anxiety. The Comfort Zone that we mentally create as children we carry forward into our adult lives.

OK, got all that back in your Brain again?

Now that we have revisited our basic understanding of Comfort Zones, it is now perhaps easy to see that they are created from 2 internal, psychological forces... centrifugal and centripetal.

There is a centrifugal psychological force which wants to push us out of our Comfort Zone, and there is a centripetal psychological force that wants to pull us inside, keep us locked inside, and so keep us safe.

And all Human Beings who have ever lived are, to some extent, locked within the tidal pull of those 2 psychological forces.

And in Astrological terms, the centrifugal force = our **Inner Sun**... and the centripetal force = our **Inner Moon**.

So our **Inner Sun** wants to push us out, eject us from our Comfort Zone, wants us to grow and expand, and when you understand that, all the stuff which is said about the **Astrological Sun** starts to make total and coherent sense.

Inspiration... Individuality... Uniqueness...

All of which require someone to step outside of their known, cultural or family or tribal Comfort Zone, and walk down the path of being different (i.e. being an individual).

Whenever an individual steps outside of their Comfort Zone, they do so as that, as an individual, because they are stepping outside of their existing knowledge base, their tribal programming, all the skills and knowledge they have gathered to date, they are going it alone as an individual, hoping that they will be able to figure out this new situation. They are embarking on the Hero's Quest, their individual Hero Quest.

Yes, whenever an individual steps outside of their Comfort Zone, they are anxious, even afraid perhaps because they are stepping into unexplored territory. They are stepping into the unknown. But also, there is excitement and an adrenaline rush, and inspiration, and a wonderful newness to life, the chance for exploration.

And all that good stuff is fuelled by our **Astrological Sun**.

But it is important to realise that certain Zodiac Signs tip the balance of our **Inner Sun**, one way or the other, where it comes to our confidence and ability to venture beyond our Comfort Zones:

- **Sun in Aries**... can't wait to pack up and leave for a new adventure.
- **Sun in Cancer**... will feel great anxiety taking the first step beyond the known, and usually prefers to play things safe.

But also... our **Sun Sign** defines, to a large degree, that which will entice us to leave:

- **Sun in Taurus**... will more willingly leave the Comfort Zone on a quest for physical beauty
- **Sun in Pisces**... will more willingly leave the Comfort Zone on a quest for emotional beauty

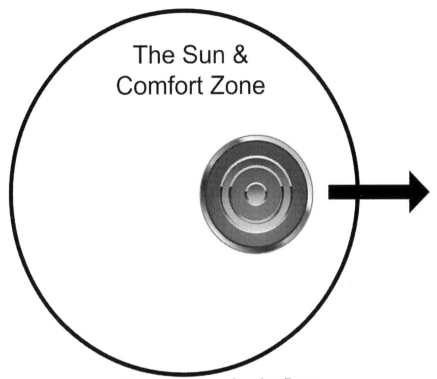

The Sun and our Comfort Zones

- **Sun in Libra**... will more willingly leave the Comfort Zone on a quest for mental beauty
- **Sun in Capricorn**... will more willingly leave the Comfort Zone on a quest for building an empire
- **Sun in Scorpio**... will more willingly leave the Comfort Zone on a quest for inner meaning and inner peace

Each of these is the carrot which motivates that particular **Sun Sign** to move outwards and explore.

Now, in Traditional Astrology, both **The Sun** and **The Moon** are known as the 2 Luminaries, because they are the brightest points of light in the sky, night and day.

Of course, being Modern Men, we know now that the light of **The Moon** is really a reflection of **The Sun**, and that **The Sun** is really the only source of light in our Solar System.

But whatever the source, light is very important in our Solar System.

It is essential to life on Earth, for whole hosts of chemical and biological processes which are essential for life to continue.

And the same is true for our Astrological Charts and the workings of our inner psyche.

Inner light and warmth are ultra-important to how our personality works.

Let me explain…

Imagine your **natal Moon** standing in the centre of your Comfort Zone.

That is when your **natal Moon** is at its brightest, where it has the most light.

Because that is when it feels the most comfortable, and so when you also feel the safest and most secure, which is what **The Moon** is all about, its primary task and goal, to keep you safe.

However, as **The Moon** leaves the centre of the Zone, and moves slowly out to the edges of the Comfort Zone, the light of **The Moon** gets less, starts to fade, becomes weaker and weaker.

Until a point comes when stepping beyond the Comfort Zone, the light of **The Moon** is at its weakest, maybe even totally extinguished, and so **The Moon** starts to panic.

Because **The Moon**, and our Comfort Zone, is all about feeling safe and secure, to keep our anxiety levels as low as possible.

All Lunar strategies for survival are designed to ensure that **The Moon** remains in the centre of the Comfort Zone.

*However, our **Natal Sun** is the complete opposite.*

If our **Astrological Sun** were to stand in the centre of the Comfort Zone, in the exact centre of the circle, the light of **The Sun** is weak, practically non-existent, dark.

But the closer **The Sun** goes towards the edge of our Comfort Zone, the brighter it becomes.

And when it steps out, over and beyond the outer line demarcating the edge of our Comfort Zone, **The Sun** suddenly bursts into even more light.

It goes positively Super-Nova.

And through this process, we can see the difference between our two Astrological Luminaries.

The Moon is brightest at the centre of the Comfort Zone and grows weaker as it travels towards the edge, while **The Sun** is weak or dark in the centre, but it's light increases as it moves out towards the edge, and even more when it crosses the line and heads out into Unknown territory. **The Sun** becomes brightest as it starts to move into the Unknown.

So focusing on the **Astrological Sun** now.

Why should that be?

Well, when you explore the meaning of **The Sun** in Traditional Astrology, you find that it is linked to things like inspiration, and individuality.

Remember...

The Moon is who you already are, while The Sun is who you are trying to become... and inspiration is the juicy fruit that hopefully gets you there... or at least makes you want to try...

Or rather, perhaps we should say, who the Universe would like you to become (whether you are up for the challenge is an entirely different matter, and it will depend on the make-up of the rest of your Astrological natal chart to show whether you are up for the journey).

The Moon doesn't have to do anything or go anywhere, in order to remain safe, secure and intact. But if **The Sun** remains still and doesn't move, then life becomes stagnant, dull and boring.

So **The Sun** is really all about movement, the journey, and we can see this when we return to our metaphor of the Comfort Zone.

OK, if we stay inside our Comfort Zone, yes, it is safe, it is secure, but it is totally composed of what we already know, the known, which can quickly become stale and boring.

And because, as Humans, we have evolved way beyond our animal past, our Brains and our Soul also needs newness and excitement.

We need to be inspired, we need fresh information, new discoveries, we need to discover what is over the horizon.

All of which exist on the edge of the known, and out into the unknown, beyond the edge of our Comfort Zone.

And this is where we get to tie into the Archetype of **The Astrological Sun**, and what it is really all about.

From a Universal perspective, if Humans were all **The Moon**, 100% dominated by Lunar forces, then there would be no Conscious Evolution.

We would be like all other mammals, and the dinosaurs before them. Evolution would be driven by a stray chromosome, an accident of DNA, taking place slowly, over thousands of years.

But with Man, because we are Conscious and because we can think, and reason, because we are self-reflective, because we know there is an edge to our Comfort Zone, and have the imagination to wonder what is beyond its edge, we're less dependent on Unconscious Evolution, either as a species or as individuals, and we, therefore, have more control over our own destiny to some degree.

Humans are animals which know that there is such a thing as a Comfort Zone, whereas the rest of the animal kingdom has no idea what motivates them.

Before Mankind, Evolution occurred at the species level, but with Mankind, each individual has the potential to grow and evolve, if they so choose.

Now, don't get me wrong, there are Lunar forces within us trying to keep as safe, saying bored is better than anxiety, or dead.

But as a species, there is a **Christopher Columbus** born every now and then, who will think and say, "*No, I don't believe the Earth is flat, I am going to sail out beyond the horizon, to see what is there, who knows what I might discover.*"

Now, OK, **Columbus** thought he was going to discover a new sea route to China, which would open up new, lucrative trade routes. He didn't reckon that North and South America would stand in his way and that the World was larger, stranger and more different, and richer, then he could ever have thought.

So his ability to press ahead, into the unknown, on a quest to see what was out there, led to the World becoming larger, in many, many different ways (although the local, indigenous populations and cultures, he helped discover, and eventually decimate, often say they wish he hadn't bothered. Their own discovery of Europe and the Old World was probably somthing they could have done without).

Which then begs the question, if **The Sun** is a force which propels us to venture beyond our Comfort Zone, what do the 12 different Astrological Signs add to the energetic equation?

Well, for different individuals, the Sign in which their **Sun** is located denotes the emotions, feelings, thoughts and beliefs which, in a positive sense, help them to take the step beyond their Comfort Zone, and in a negative sense, keep them, trapped and stale, inside.

Safety vs Adventure.

But now, let's go back to the Traditional Associations for Astrology for **The Sun**, which are:

- Individuality
- Inspiration
- Uniqueness

How does that track?

Well, with our Comfort Zone approach, it tracks very well.

You see, if we say that our Comfort Zone is **The Moon**, and originally, is composed with all the beliefs and ideas which have been passed down to us from our family and society and culture, all we have inherited from other people, ***then it isn't really ours***.

It is something which we have acquired, inherited, or borrowed.

But 99% of the time, it isn't anything which we have actively and consciously chosen for ourselves, or thought about, or made a decision to cultivate within ourselves. Just something our infant brain got programmed with when we were young.

And there is no guarantee that the knowledge we inherit in childhood is accurate or correct. A lot of people in history didn't travel too far from home because they believed that the Earth was flat, and they would fall off the edge if they ventured too far from home. Because they were told that the Earth was flat, that was the truth, and, unlike **Christopher Columbus**, they didn't question those in authority, people who often make up a truth to keep themselves in power.

But when we are brave, and we choose to step BEYOND our Comfort Zone in some way, whether it is to go climbing in the Himalayas, or learn a new language, do what others say is impossible, or not for people like us… whatever.

That is a Conscious choice on our part, it is an individual choice.

And when you win, the win is all yours (plus all those who have helped you along the way, obviously… as per any good Oscar acceptance speech).

And it is through choices like that that we create our Solar individuality, we expand and feed our Natal Sun, as it moves towards the edge of our Comfort Zone and becomes brighter.

There are 3 Great 20th Century Thinkers who we need to touch upon at this point, all giants in the field of personal and spiritual development.

G I Gurdjieff and **C J Jung**… and **Joseph Campbell**.

Now, **G I Gurdjieff** (1866 to 1949) used to say, and this infuriated many people:

"Man isn't born with a Soul… he has to create one."

So all those people who think they can get into heaven without any work or effort, think again.

According to **Gurdjieff**, you have to work and evolve and grow to get into heaven.

Which is the same as saying, you have to step out beyond your Comfort Zone, on all possible levels.

You see, your **Moon Sign** defines where you start out in life. But if you leave it at that, if you go no further, from the point of the Universe, what then is the difference between a Man and a lion, or a dormouse, or any other animal who dies in the same state of Consciousness as the one they were born into?

The whole point of the Human Race, from the perspective of the Universe, Humans are creatures that can change, that can be different at the end of their life then from their beginning, they can grow and evolve into something else (and something higher up the Evolutionary scale, hopefully).

And it is that change, that growth, that the Universe is most interested in, and it is hard-wired into our psyche via our **Astrological Sun & Sun Sign**.

Our need to grow and expand in some way.

But only if we can overcome the status quo within us, the inertia of our **Moon Sign**, which is trying to keep us safe and secure, and while also feeling comfortable working and expanding our **Sun Sign**.

Our **Inner Moon** is programmed to protect our physical body, but can get in the way of our higher purpose, while our **Inner Sun** can help us achieve that, but can take risks which may put our safety and security in jeopardy.

And most individuals are walking the tightrope between the two.

The next great 20th Century thinker is **C J Jung**, who put forward the assertion that the point of being alive, for each and every man, was to achieve a state he called Individuality:

"*By individuality, I mean the peculiarity and singularity of the individual in every psychological respect. Everything that is not collective is individual, everything in fact that pertains only to one individual and not to a larger group of individuals.*" (Definitions, CW 6, par. 756.)

Or as **Jung** also said:

"*A consciousness of differentiation, or individuation, is needed to bring individuality to consciousness.*" (CW6, par. 755.)

Which is another way of saying you need to step outside of your Comfort Zone, individual, family, tribal and collective... occasionally, once in a while, if you ever want to become more then you think you are, or what others have told you are, in order to achieve this state of Individuality, where you are the one deciding the path and fate of your life, to a large degree, and you are not just being pushed around by family, tribal and social forces.

Because out beyond the Comfort Zone, your Comfort Zone, our Comfort Zone, that's where all the gold and treasure lies (and we will definitely explore this further when we come to our **natal Pluto**).

All their dreams and aspirations lie, for the majority of people, outside of their Comfort Zones, and if they successfully pursue them, if they master and achieve what they need, then those skills will then become woven into their new and expanding Comfort Zone.

But the individual achieved it all for themselves, and often by themselves. Hence the term, Individuality.

That is an ongoing process. But only if you are prepared to live out your Solar energies, and engage in the process, and have a high anxiety threshold.

It is interesting that one of the qualities which the majority of self-made millionaires share... not just the ability to have amazing and lucrative ideas, and the ability to act on them... but a high anxiety threshold. They are able to withstand the anxiety which occurs when they step out beyond their Comfort Zone, when they are going after their business dreams and aspirations, much more than the majority of people, who are happy to just exchange their time and skills for a steady but fixed paycheck... without having any of the anxiety of asking where their next meal is coming from.

But to do that, to get that which we really want out of life, we need to go on a quest, we need to face our fears and anxieties as best we can, and move beyond them.

Which brings us to **Joseph Campbell**, and his work on the Hero Quest. (He's the academic who inspired **George Lucas** to create Star

Wars as a mythic story.)

- The Hero lives in a tribe
- The Hero + tribe is suffering, and they desperately need something magic to save them from a terrible situation
- The Hero leaves the tribe to get that magic something, which will put things right
- The Hero undergoes many trials and tests on their way to achieving that magic something, facing their fears and anxieties head on, and they are fundamentally changed in some way
- In the final stages, they win, they are successful, the magic is obtained
- They return to their tribe with that magic something, the world is put right, end of story

But is that really the end?

Some tales end with the Hero unable to fit back into their tribe because they have become too changed, and so need to move on, having tasted the excitement of the quest, they now desire new adventures.

Some times the tribe doesn't want what the Hero returns with, they cannot see its true value for them, and they may even ridicule the Hero upon his return.

Not every inventor or artist is recognised in their time.

As Vincent Van Gogh and Nikola Tesla would testify too.

Not every tribe or society can see the potential of the cool, new invention on offer.

But the problem is, once you have stepped beyond your Comfort Zone, you cannot easily step back into the old ways, there is no return to the past tribal Consciousness you once easily inhabited.

There is no forgetting. There is no going back.

You cannot undo or take back the shift in your own Consciousness.

Plus, why would you? Why go back to boredom after you have tasted excitement?

And often, the Archetypal Hero has to leave their old tribe behind because they cannot think in that small way ever again.

So in terms of **Energy Astrology**, our **Inner Sun** is the psychological, archetypal force which tries, and wants, to propel us out of our Comfort Zone, to become all that we can be, in our lifetime, to achieve all our gifts and potential.

And within **Energy Astrology**, our **Inner Sun**, is associated with our Heart Chakra… our ability to allow our inner light to shine out, to be recognised… and is associated with an inner psychological force that wants to blast us out of our Comfort Zone… and off on another adventure!

THE MOON

Put simply, in Traditional Astrology, your **Moon Sign** represents your Comfort Zone. It is the container which holds it all together.

And in **Energy Astrology** that tracks across to our Sacral Chakra, the seat of our sensuality, emotions, feelings, and physical creativity.

The Moon is associated with all the things which normally are associated with your Comfort Zone, your Body, your Mother, your Family, your Tribe, and your Home. All the things which are meant to make you feel safe and secure, inside and outside.

Or, to put it this way, your **Moon IS** your psychological Comfort Zone, and your **Moon Sign** is also the colour and weave of your Comfort Zone.

The Sign and House in which your **Moon** is located is what defines how your particular Comfort Zone, at the core, is different from 11 in 12 other people.

The Moon and our Comfort Zone

So if your **Moon** is your Comfort Zone, which is associated with Body, Mother, Family, Tribe, and Home, then how you perceive each of these is coloured by the Astrological Sign in which your **Moon** is located.

For example, **The Moon** and its respective Sign is seen as representing how you perceived your Mother when you were an infant (i.e. both your relationship with the archetype of the Mother and your relationship with your real/physical Mother), along with also representing how you perceive your Family, your Tribe, and your Physical Body.

In fact, there are 12 different flavours of Comfort Zone available, each one based on one of the 12 Astrological Signs.

So if you have **Moon in Sagittarius**, then you will have seen your Mother as being more **Sagittarian** in how she looked after you, and if you had **Moon in Cancer**, then her style of caring would have been more **Cancerian**.

Moon + Sign also represents how successful you were at exploring the world around you as a Child, and so how successful you are now, as an adult, in dealing with your anxiety.

Your **Moon Sign** is therefore associated with the type of anxiety that you experience, as an adult, whenever you choose or are forced, to leave the safety and security of your Comfort Zone.

However, in **Energy Astrology**, the Astrological Sign in which your **Moon** resides also shows you:

- Which negative feeling automatically undermines your psychological Comfort Zone
- Which positive quality automatically strengthens your psychological Comfort Zone

These are the negative feelings which, whenever you feel them, also help to trigger the feeling of anxiety within you, plus the positive feelings which help you to cope in a stressful situation, help you to turn things around.

Basically, for you, these associated feelings have become so interlinked, you cannot feel 'X' without also feeling anxiety.

For example, if you have **Moon in Libra**, then the feeling of regret will also trigger the feeling of anxiety, for someone with **Moon in Capricorn** the trigger feeling will be rage, and for someone with their

Moon in Pisces the trigger feeling will be sadness.

As you can see from the list below, **Sagittarius** is the odd one out, because its negative quality is worry as well as anxiety. So whenever a **Sagittarius Moon** feels anxiety, it gets double the dose.

However, the good news is that if a **Moon in Sagittarius** person can find a way to stabilise and transform their anxiety, then they become emotionally grounded and a very effective emotional operator. But this does take some serious inner work to achieve.

Because individuals desperately try to avoid the feeling of anxiety wherever possible, they will also go out of their way to avoid these associated trigger feelings.

This means someone with **Moon in Virgo** will try to avoid feeling guilty, because this will trigger their feelings of anxiety, and **Moon in Libra** will actively avoid the feeling of regret wherever possible.

Now, in some weird and spooky way, most birth Mothers are usually very good at knowing exactly which trigger feeling switches on their child's brand of anxiety and so can use this to control you from a very early age.

The Mother who wants their **Moon in Virgo** child to tidy their room will make them feel guilty. But if the child's **Moon is in Leo**, she will probably get angry with them, because they hate the thought of anger directed at them, and so are likely to back down and tidy their room.

Now, if our Mothers can do this mind-manipulation thing on us, then the same is also true for anyone else who would seek to influence us using anxiety until we take the power back into our own hands and break the connection between anxiety and our trigger emotion.

So, whenever you are starting to feel anxious, for whatever reason, then all you need to do is use the **Crystal Antidote/Audio Essence** that is associated with your particular **Moon Sign**, and this will help you to reduce the associated trigger feeling.

In addition, anyone can use the primary **Anxiety Antidote**, as it is not just reserved for **Moon in Sagittarius**, and this can also help to reduce your levels of anxiety overall.

So the list is:

- **Moon in Aries** – Fear
- **Moon in Taurus** – Hopelessness
- **Moon in Gemini** – Unhappiness
- **Moon in Cancer** – Emptiness
- **Moon in Leo** – Anger
- **Moon in Virgo** – Guilt
- **Moon in Libra** – Regret
- **Moon in Scorpio** – Frustration
- **Moon in Sagittarius** – Worry & Anxiety
- **Moon in Capricorn** – Rage
- **Moon in Aquarius** – Intolerance
- **Moon in Pisces** – Sadness

OK, unfortunately, from an Astrological perspective, there is a small problem with finding the sign for your **natal Moon**. You see the Moon travels 14 degrees during a single day, and because each Zodiac Sign is only 30 degrees across, it only takes **The Moon** under 48 hours to cross in and out of each Sign. So the bad news is that unless you know your exact time of birth, then it will be impossible to identify the exact position of the **Moon Sign** in your natal chart.

Normally, when I am trying to identify someone's **Moon Sign**, and I don't know exactly when they were born, I set the time to Noon, find out where **The Moon** was located at that moment, and then look to see what Signs fall seven degrees on either side of **The Moon**.

Occasionally, **The Moon** will fall right in the middle of a Sign, and so there is no question of that person's **Moon Sign**.

However, when it isn't so clear cut, the good news is that on the day you were born, there are only two options possible, and if you know what those two Signs are, most people are able to identify, from the issue list above, which negative quality most undermines their Comfort Zone, and so fuels their feelings of worry and anxiety.

For example, if you were born on a day when **The Moon** was in **Cancer** for the first part of the day and **Leo** in the second part, then your choice is between Emptiness and Anger. So is it Anger that creates anxiety within you, or a feeling of Emptiness? I have found that most people are easily able to work out which trigger emotion turns on their anxiety.

Although you may not know your exact time of birth, this shouldn't stop you from roughly identifying your **natal Moon** placement, and so also identifying the associated emotional trigger for your anxiety. And once you know that then it is easy to start working out counter-measures to your issue.

If you can muscle-test, or have a friend who can do it for you, then you can also use muscle testing to identify which negative quality most weakens your Comfort Zone, and this then helps you identify which **Crystal Antidote** you need to use, the issue you are trying to resolve.

Crystal Antidotes are covered in a later Chapter... and they're really cool.

If you don't have the right **Crystal Antidote** to hand, or not able to easily obtain one, then you can also use the Meridian Affirmations developed by the Kinesiologist **John Diamond**, to ease feelings of anxiety.

These Meridian Affirmations are given in the list below.

- **Aries Moon** = Kidney = *I am sexually secure. My sexual energies are balanced.*
- **Taurus Moon** = Triple Warmer = *I am light and buoyant. I am buoyed up with hope.*
- **Gemini Moon** = Liver = *I am happy. I have good fortune. I am cheerful.*
- **Cancer Moon** = Stomach = *I am content. I am tranquil.*
- **Leo Moon** = Heart = *I love. I forgive. There is forgiveness in my heart.*
- **Virgo Moon** = Large Intestine = *I am basically clean and good. I am worthy of being loved.*
- **Libra Moon** = Heart Protector = *I renounce the past. I am relaxed. My body is relaxed. I am generous.*
- **Scorpio Moon** = Bladder = *I am at peace. I am in harmony. Dissonances and conflicts within me have been resolved. I am balanced.*
- **Sagittarius Moon** = Spleen = *I have faith and confidence in my future. I am secure. My future is secure.*
- **Capricorn Moon** = Gallbladder = *I reach out with love. I reach out with forgiveness.*
- **Aquarius Moon** = Lung = *I am humble. I am tolerant. I am modest.*
- **Pisces Moon** = Small Intestine = *I am full of joy. I am jumping with joy.*

These Affirmations can be used to reduce the level of anxiety experienced by your **Moon Sign**, through relieving the stress of your trigger emotion, and so helping to balance and harmonize the energy of the associated meridian.

I also suggest, regardless of your **Moon Sign**, you can also use the affirmation associated with the Spleen Meridian / Sagittarius to reduce your level of anxiety overall.

- **Sagittarius Moon** = Spleen = *I have faith and confidence in my future. I am secure. My future is secure.*

The great thing about using these Meridian Affirmations is that they are free, easy to use, and once memorized, or written down on a small piece of card and carried in your purse or wallet, can be used anytime and anywhere.

But remember, when you are repeating these Affirmations, also allow yourself to initially feel your anxiety, and don't try to suppress it… and then allow it to gently fade. As you repeat the words, your Unconscious Mind will gently transform your anxiety into positive feelings… just as freshwater will clear a muddy pond of dirt if it is allowed to flow into and through the pond.

But the thing about anxiety, it is a warning message from your Unconscious Mind, it is trying to tell you something about your life, which is usually that you are about to leave the safety of your Comfort Zone in some way, that maybe you are going too fast in some area, or that you need to equip yourself with new skills to cope with what lies ahead.

But the important thing to remember is that, if there were no other Planets in our Inner Sky, only **The Moon**, there would be little or no change or growth going on because **The Moon** isn't really interested in that kind of thing.

The Moon is quite happy to put up with boredom and same old, same old if that is what it takes to maintain the status quo, and keep anxiety at bay. And what's so amazing about excitement and interest anyway?

But then… to be fair… **The Moon** does try and keep you safe.

Chapter 3-3: Mercury

Now, in **Energy Astrology**, all the planets can be, and are related to, a different aspect of our personal and energetic Comfort Zone, and **Mercury** is no exception to this.

However, what makes **Mercury** unique, with the exception of **Chiron** to some degree, it is the only Planet which does not work in some kind of energetic pairing with another Planet.

Sun & **Moon**... **Venus** has **Mars**... **Jupiter** is linked up with **Saturn**... **Uranus**, **Neptune** and **Pluto** all work together in a similar transpersonal way.

But **Mercury** is a loner... is *the* loner... it doesn't have another set Planet to play with and bounce off of in a paired relationship.

MERCURY

OK, **Uranus** is often considered to be the higher octave of **Mercury**, but in terms of our Astrological Comfort Zone metaphor, as we shall now see, that doesn't really track very far.

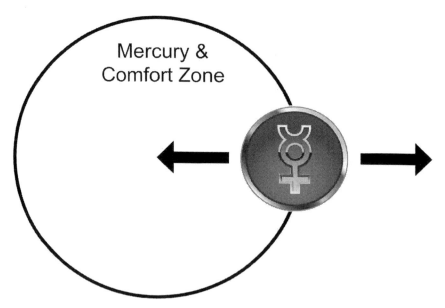

Mercury and our Comfort Zone

And this lack of dynamic tension with another Planet goes to the heart of what **Mercury** is all about, as is shown in the above diagram.

Because in relation to our Comfort Zone, **Mercury** can go *anywhere*.

Because **Mercury** is our Mind, or at least, the Mind associated with the personality self, with the Conscious self.

And so our Mind, our inner **Mercury** can travel fully within our Comfort Zone, and it can travel easily outside of our Zone too.

And the outside of our Comfort Zone, any Comfort Zone, no matter how big, the outside is always infinite in comparison.

Which totally fits with the role of **Hermes/Mercury** as Messenger of the Gods in Greek and Roman Mythology, who was the only God, apart from **Hades/Pluto**, and **Persephone** for 6 months of the year... who could go in and out of the Underworld.

Mercury can go anywhere in the Universe, can imagine anything (if given sufficient information, and it isn't being blocked), it can even conjure up ideas and concepts that couldn't possibly exist in our real world.

For example...

5 Questions.

Can you imagine what it is like at the bottom of an active volcano, or at the centre of the Earth?

Can you imagine what it may be like to live in a different country... one you have never visited before?

Can you imagine what it is like being on **The Moon**?

Can you imagine what it is like at the bottom of the deepest ocean?

Can you imagine what it is like living in Narnia?

If you can, if your imagination had sufficient information to conjure up an image, an idea, however vague and incomplete, then in your Mind, you went there, even if we all know that that would be impossible.

That is the important thing about our Mind, our **Inner Mercury**, if we can think it, imagine it, if we can hold it within our Mind, then we can go there and explore the possibilities.

And draw up plans to make our imaginations into a tangible reality.

Even if it something we have never physically experienced before.

What has fuelled Human civilization the most, and still does, is the ability of our Mind, our inner Mercury, to travel beyond the known, and consider the question… What If?

In the 16th Century Italy, the Franciscan Friar **Giordano Bruno**… *"What if all the stars in the sky are like our own Sun, with planets revolving around them like our Solar System?"*

1903… two brothers… **Orville** and **Wilbur Wright**… find a practical answer to the question *"What if men could fly?"*

1908… **Henry Ford**… *"What if we make things differently… on a kind of production line… that will speed up manufacture time and so reduce costs… we could make automobiles that the common man could afford."*

1928... **Alexander Flemming**... *"What if the mould in this Petrie dish, which has killed off all the bacteria, could be used as medicine?"*

For each of the above examples, the individuals involved had to allow their Minds to travel beyond the known for their time, to travel outside of their own mental Comfort Zone, but also that of their society, culture, and tribe, which told people that such a thought and thing was **not** possible.

They had to allow their Minds to roam free and unhindered in order to make and recognise the important connections.

In 1928, a different scientist might have thrown the mould Penicillin away as being nothing more than a contaminant in their experiment. Not all scientists have the eyes to see, even when they are following the scientific method to the letter.

Now, 3 of the 4 above got celebrated and/or rich in their lifetime, the 4th got ridiculed and finally was burnt at the stake for heresy by the Catholic Church back in 1600.

The ability to think outside of our current reality, allows us to be creative and explore other possibilities for our life and society.

But one of the dangers for any Human Being has been... is... and will probably continue to be...

If you think too far ahead, beyond what your fellow Man and society are comfortable with, and they cannot see the benefit of what you have found, what you are saying, they are likely to ridicule you, or worse.

Just because your Mind can journey there, and appreciate the discovery, doesn't mean that other Minds can, or will.

But the ability to do so does lie dormant within each Human… we all have **Mercury** within us, we are all dreamers at Heart, although some of us prefer to slumber on through our lifetime, or prefer to let others think for us.

Mercury is our Mind's ability to think and go to other places and spaces, even when we have physically never been there before, or can physically never go there in reality, because it is either too dangerous to do so, or because it only exists in the world of fantasy and imagination.

But, remember, as **Dumbledore** says to **Harry Potter** in the last novel in the famous series, *"Of course it is all in your head, but that doesn't make in any less real."*

Our World is continually changed and made new, and sometimes for the better, by ideas which start off in someone's head.

And that ability, to think outside of any kind of box or container, goes to the core of what it is to be Human.

OK, most of the time, for the majority of people, our **Inner Mercury** is solely tasked with helping us navigate our known world, the territory we have already mapped out, applying the knowledge and skills we have already acquired, or which has been mapped out for us.

And for some, that is all they want and desire, and they and their culture/tribe may actively punish any **Mercury** which seeks to explore further afield, as happened to **Giordano Bruno** back in the 16th Century.

But as our diagram above shows, to just use **Mercury** inside our Comfort Zone is like driving a car with only 1 gear.

Because **Mercury** can do so much more.

Yes, we are programmed by Nature, just like any other animal walking the planet, but for some wyrd reason, our programming also contains the option to evolve and grow beyond our programming, to step outside of our Comfort Zone, if we choose.

In fact, any new Human learning is reliant on **Mercury's** ability to step outside of our Comfort Zone, individual, cultural, or tribal, and initially show us what is possible.

For example, let us suppose someone who had never flown before, is about to take their first flight on a plane, and they are experiencing a degree of anxiety ahead of boarding.

Now, to someone who has flown before, regularly, they don't experience any such anxiety, the experience is a known, because to them, flying is part of their Comfort Zone, it is a definite known, and so located within their Zone.

But to our novice, who has never flown before, flying is an experience they have never had before, and so exists outside of their Comfort Zone, because it is an experience which is totally new to them.

But here is the important thing.

Suppose they also have a pet dog who is also booked to go on the same flight as their owner, the individual who has never flown before.

For both the dog and the owner, the experience of flying is outside of their Comfort Zones.

But the dog cannot think about flying, ahead of time, they can only encounter the experience as it happens. In fact, the dog probably doesn't even realise that it is about to go on a long journey, at high altitude, until it starts to happen.

From the dogs perspective, it is driven to someplace called an airport in the owner's car, which is loud and noisy, then put in a metal box, then loaded on to this large thing with flat wings... and then there was a lot of noise and vibration, which lasted for several hours, and then it was taken off the thing with wings, removed from the metal box, and then reunited with its owner.

So the dog may become anxious as it is loaded on to the plane, and the plane takes off, because this is all new to it, but it won't become anxious *ahead of time*, because it is unconscious about what is about to happen to it, the anxiety starts when it steps outside of its Comfort Zone and starts to experience the total unknown (i.e. being put inside the metal box). For the dog, anxiety is in the moment, because it lacks a Mind which can look fully ahead in time.

And to be honest, if it wasn't locked inside a metal box, it would probably run off the plane and escape, animals are programmed not to step outside of their Comfort Zone given the choice, they are programmed to stick to their programming, unless a Human gets involved and makes them do the opposite.

However, in total contrast, the Human owner can contemplate the whole experience ahead of time, and feel anxiety when they contemplate what is about to happen.

Anxiety a week before the flight, anxiety the day before the flight... anxiety as they are about to step on board the plane, anxiety as the plane takes off, as well as thinking about all the good things which will happen when they finally arrive at their destination.

Which means 4 BIG things:

1. A Human can experience anxiety ahead of the experience itself, as well as during the experience.

2. A Human can think about, and contemplate the experience, not only in terms of the anxiety, but also in terms of the benefits which may arise from learning the new skill, experience or knowledge, the potential excitement.
3. A Human can potentially decide to over-ride its feelings of anxiety and press-on, thus becoming successful, and integrating the new skill, experience or knowledge into its Comfort Zone.
4. A Human can use anxiety to its advantage, contemplating dangers and what may go wrong, prepare for them in advance, so maximizing the chances of success.

Animals can experience the anxiety, but none of the other stuff above, that is all part of the Human domain.

But none of those advantages is possible without a healthy and active **Mercury**.

Hermes/Mercury was Messenger of the Gods in Greek and Roman Mythology, who was the only God who could go in and out of the Underworld, fly up to the highest heaven, and dive down into the deepest ocean. **Mercury** spanned the realms of all the other Olympians.

But to really understand the energy archetype and template behind astrological **Mercury**, we also need to travel back in time... 3 million years.

Which is something we can only do thanks to our **Inner Mercury**... yep, it can travel in time as well as space.

To the plains of the Serengeti in Africa... somewhere around the Great Rift Valley perhaps.

To a point in time, when and where our Great Ape Ancestors came down from the trees, moved out of the forests, and started to walk, upright, out into the grasslands beyond.

And so started the process of evolving into proto-Humans.

During this period, at the dawn of Human Evolution, Mankind started to eat meat (probably first through scavenging, later through killing small animals, and later, bringing down bigger prey), and so started to evolve a bigger Brain, leading to greater intelligence.

But... how do we know if any of the above is in the correct sequence?

Because that is something which scientists still can't be sure of.

Did the eating of meat lead to the development of our bigger Brain... Or did the development of bigger Brains lead to the act of eating meat?

Did living in large social Groups lead to the development of social skills... Or did the development of better social skills... and language... support the ability to live in larger Groups, and co-operate more effectively?

Or did it all happen side-by-side... one influencing the other over time... so there was no easy cause and effect which could be detected?

Who can tell now, because fossilized bones can only tell us so much, which is really very little when you come to think about it.

Animals don't need to know what happened, they live totally in the moment, but Human Beings, we are super curious about everything... past, present, and future.

But if we were able to travel back in time, what we might discover... at key points in Human Evolution... something like...

"When I strike these 2 pieces of flint against each other, it creates a very sharp edge... and I cut myself on that edge and drew blood. I wonder... what if we used these sharp edges to skin prey... or on the tips of spears or arrows?"

Or:

"When I strike these two pieces of Flint together, it gave off yellow sparks... which fell on the dry grass and caused a fire to be born... just as when the lightning from the sky sometimes causes new fire when it strikes the dry grass. This fire keeps us warm... this fire keeps us safe from other predators at night... and allows us to see when there is no Moon in the sky. So striking stones together can create fire."

Or:

"I dropped raw meat from the last kill into the fire, and when I pulled it out with a stick, it tasted better... and my fellow tribesmen don't seem to suffer sickness the same after the meat has been first burnt... so we have started to drop all our meat in the fire now... although some say it tastes even better it the meat is held just over the fire with a stick."

Moments in history... accidents in time... which would have been lost, would have gone nowhere, led to nothing...

Except, there was a Human Being present, with a **Mercury Mind**, capable of seeing a deeper pattern emerging, capable of putting two and two together, capable of seeing the new possibilities on offer, leading to a more efficient, healthier and productive life for the tribe.

Now, in **Energy Astrology**, **Mercury** is linked to the Chakras in the centre of our Hands and in the soles of our Feet.

Energy Astrology

So how does that work, why that particular association?

Well, as modern science has shown, our right hand is connected with our left brain, which is connected with reason and rational thought.

While our left hand is connected with our right brain, which is connected with intuition, our ability to consider the bigger picture and pattern and think in new and original ways.

And so, when you bring these two hemispheres together, left and right, you create a Whole Brain, which is capable of moving in time and space.

Between words of fantasy and reality.

Between the real and the imagined.

Between the inside of our Comfort Zone and the outside.

In fact, it's perhaps not too much to claim that the whole of Mankind's success is due to our ever curious and versatile **Inner Mercury**...And what makes **Mercury** unique... with the exception of **Chiron** to some degree... it is the only Planet which does not work in some kind of energetic pairing with another Planet.

Because **Mercury** does not need any other Planet to limit it, or define it.

Mercury does some of its best work when it can roam and soar... unlimited.

Because **Mercury** is our Mind, or at least, the Mind associated with the personality self, with the Conscious self.

In fact, in the remainder of our 21st Century, **Mercury** may very well dethrone **Zeus/Jupiter**, and be crowned King of the Gods.

Chapter 3-4: Venus & Mars

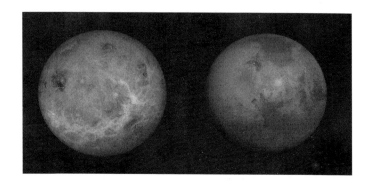

In Traditional Astrology, **Mars** and **Venus** are often seen as clear polar opposites.

Mars is male; **Venus** is female.

Mars is the warrior; **Venus** is the lover.

Mars is our motivating and assertive side; **Venus** is our receptive and sensual side.

Mars is strength and assertiveness; **Venus** is beauty and harmony.

Apparently, all Men come from **Mars**, and all Women come from **Venus**, or so we have been told.

But the thing is when we step across into the perspective of these two planets from **Energy Astrology**, it's not so clear cut, as we will now see.

MARS

In Traditional Astrology, **Mars** is often described as the Warrior for **The Sun**, or the **Sun's Solider**.

And in **Energy Astrology**, **Mars** is associated with our Solar Plexus Chakra, which lies just below our Heart Chakra, our **Inner Sun**, and is the centre from which we assert ourselves, our wants and needs.

And so this is very true, our **Mars** is the planet which fights for what our **Sun** wants or needs (if things are set-up right).

So if **The Sun** is trying to move out from the centre of our Comfort Zone, out towards the edge, and hopefully beyond, then we can visualise **Mars** walking ahead of it, with a big sharp metal machete, clearing the way, tackling the obstacles in our path, like someone hacking their way through a dense jungle.

One of the main purposes of **Mars** is, therefore, to help our **Sun** handle the obstacles which may be standing in our way, during our lifetime, obstacles which are blocking our ability to achieve our dreams and goals, or even just from getting our primary survival needs met, and the Sign in which **Mars** is located will indicate how our Inner Warrior goes about doing that.

The flavour of our particular kind of assertiveness.

In many ways, **Mars** is one of the most important Planets out there, especially if we are committed to living out a life down on the Earth Plane.

Some Signs, like **Mars in Aries**, will try and totally obliterate any obstacles, maybe even going for the nuclear option, others like **Mars in Libra** will try to sweet talk those obstacles into moving aside.

Just as there are different kinds of Solider on the battlefield, with different approaches and temperaments and weapons, so there are 12 different kinds of **Martian Warriors**, who go about fighting for our **Sun** in different ways.

So **Mars in Scorpio** is more your Special Forces type, who will want to get all the intel on the enemy before making their move, while **Mars in Cancer** is also prepared to consider emotional blackmail as a possible and valid strategy for getting its own way.

Each of these **12 Mars** has its advantages and disadvantages, and overall, for **Mars**, sometimes attack is the best form of defence.

Plus, have you ever watched emergency aid workers, on the TV news, distribute food and water in a war zone or some poor area of the World which has been struck by famine or a natural disaster? Often, the starving people are so desperate, that the distribution turns into a riot, with people desperately fighting for each sack of grain coming off the aid truck, with the strong winning, and the weak getting little or no food.

But each person who is fighting for that food is empowered by an

Inner Mars, that is trying to do the best for that individual, and their family and clan. And so it is usually the young men who fare the best, the strongest and fittest, the ones who are prepared to unleash the rough and tough side of their **Inner Mars**.

Although, there is an interesting side observation to be made here, drawing upon the archaeological evidence from sites such as Pompeii.

It is has been observed by modern science that when a natural disaster strikes, our Brains lock into the famous fight, flight or freeze mode, and logic and rational thought gets put on hold, our primitive survival brain kicks in, and so we put our individual needs first, ahead of everyone else. And young men are no different here, and they are the fittest and strongest and can run fastest, and so it is not uncommon to find them at the front of a fleeing pack of scared Humans (with the frail, old and weak at the back). Not always, but very, very often.

However, once the initial danger has passed, then the young men look around as they power down, and their social ties and obligations start to re-assert themselves, and they start trying to protect other people, especially the other members of their tribe. Not always, but very, very often.

This is why, when archaeologists started to excavate the physical remains in Pompeii, down on what was back then the coast, they found the bodies of the women, old men and children located inside places of apparent safety, and the bodies of the younger men were all outside, trying to protect their kinsfolk.

Initially, **Mars** fights for the individual, but it can also fight for others if needed, which is a very **Mars in Cancer** thing to do... although many of the other Mars Signs will also get up and fight for others too.

Energy Astrology

The Astrological Signs in which **The Sun** and **Mars** are located, along with any aspects between them, will also indicate how well these two Planets are in alignment, how good they are at communicating with each other. For **The Sun** to get to where it needs to go, then it really helps for **Mars** to also be moving in the right and same direction, or turning up on the right battlefield, on time, and with the right equipment to fight the required battle.

Because if **Mars** is not in the right alignment with **The Sun**, it is quite common for people to feel frustrated, impotent even, that nothing in their life works out as they expect or want, and they don't understand why their life is much more of a struggle then other people.

Basically, it's as if their **Sun** is trapped inside a dense jungle, with little chance of escape, and **Mars** has wandered off, taking with it the only sharp machete.

But to really understand **Mars**, we first need to ask the question:

Where can we find our Inner Warrior?

Are they hiding under the bed?

Are they hiding in the closest?

Have they taken a leave of absence?

No, there would be no point in a Warrior who was hiding, or just not there when needed, absent without leave.

The Secret Service Protection must be there, in place, every time the US President leaves The Whitehouse.

Or when the Queen leaves Buckingham Palace in London.

No excuses, that is their role and function, to protect and defend.

To stand between the VIP and harm's way, to protect them from the big bad World out there, which can be a dangerous place, especially if someone doesn't agree with you, and wishes to do you harm.

Plus, the US Secret Service have guns, martial arts training, and can always fight back if needed, they're not just there to take a bullet. Just like our **Inner Mars** can also fight back if needed (and within our Astrological chart, there is no Planet more VIP then our **natal Sun**).

Or fight when you need to feed yourself and your family, and you need to hustle and fight to get one of the last food sacks on the emergency aid truck.

A good example of why we need our **Natal Mars** can be also seen in the movie Serenity where the crew of said spaceship travel to the distant and mysteriously forgotten planet of Miranda, where the evil Parliament have added a chemical to the water to hopefully make the planetary population docile and compliant to their wishes and dictats.

That has been the dream of every king, ruler, and dictator since the dawn of history, a population of Humans who will do what they are told, who are subservient, and who won't question or answer back.

But adding the chemical doesn't have the effect which the Parliament wants or expects.

Under the influence of said chemical, 20% of the population turn ultra-violent and highly aggressive, and become the feared Reevers (**Mars** gone mad), while the remaining 80% just lie down on the ground, give up on their life, and allowed themselves to starve to death (**Mars** gone totally absent).

Either way, it's an example of **Mars** gone bad.

Mars is our ability to motivate ourselves, so that we can get up and do things, such as found a business empire or just get out of bed in the morning.

Without our **Inner Mars**, what's the point of getting up in the morning, what's the point in going to work, what's the point in trying to get a job, what's the point in even continuing?

If you have ever spent time around someone who is a state of full-on depression, you will know that they suffer from a total lack of motivation. What is the point of anything? They close down inside and have come to the conclusion that doing nothing is the best alternative, because everything they do ends up in pain and disappointment in some way, and so they might as well lie down on the ground (or in their bed, or on a sofa), and give up on life completely.

This is also known as learned helplessness within the context of Positive Psychology.

The field of Positive Psychology, most often associated with the work of **Martin Seligman**, was born during the 1960s, and is most often associated with the following famous experiment.

Basically, in this experiment, dogs were locked in a cage, where the floor was electrified. Or rather certain areas of the floor were, and when the dogs found themselves on a section of a floor which was hot-wired, they quickly jumped up and found and moved to an area of the floor which was safe, because the scientists had just switched on the electricity in that piece of floor.

They moved to an area which appeared to be safe at the time.

However, over time, the scientists started to increase the amount of floor which was electrified, until the point was reached when there was no longer any safe area, and the dogs continued to receive electric shocks no matter what they did.

So what did the dogs do?

Well, eventually they just lied down on the floor, gave up... and allowed themselves to be electrocuted, even if, in reality, if they had only tried some more, they would have found that the scientists had subsequently reduced the electrified floor area, and there were now new safe spaces they could have lied in without becoming electrocuted.

But they gave up trying to find a solution. What was the point?

This psychological phenomenon was termed *learned helplessness*. The dogs had learned that their situation was hopeless, and had given up; they just laid down on the ground and allowed themselves to be electrocuted. They had decided that life = pain. They no longer tried to find a better solution to their plight, and so missed the fact that the situation around them had changed, and the electrified floor area was now only limited to the small piece they were currently lying on.

So, basically, when those poor dogs lost all hope, they just gave up, their energy crashed, and they entered a state of apathy, they just lied down on the floor, even though they were continuing to be shocked because they had given up all hope of a better life.

Guess what; the exact same thing can happen to Human Beings.

In normal circumstances, our **Inner Mars** will keep trying for a better situation or outcome for our life.

But if someone has been broken within, usually during a traumatic or abusive childhood, and been taught that no better solution is possible, they are without hope; then they will have been taught to be helpless. Which is the same as saying their **Inner Mars** has been crushed within them.

OK, they may not lay down on the floor and give up, as the dogs did.

But they often give up on aspiring for something better, give up on their personal hopes and dreams, and they allow themselves to become numb inside. What's the point in dreaming for something better?

A crushed and stamped on **Mars** can't lead **The Sun** to a better life... because it has had all the fight beaten out of it.

Which means, in terms of our Comfort Zone analogy, **Natal Mars** has crawled up into a tight ball on the floor, through all that is has suffered and is no longer moving, the **Natal Sun** can't move without **Mars**, so is therefore trapped too, and has given up on its dreams, and the **Natal Moon** is left in total charge… saying *"We need to play it safe; we mustn't rock the boat, we don't want to get hurt again!"*

To be an effective Warrior for us, our **Mars** must be up and about, out there, facing the enemy, ready to do battle; otherwise, we lose our prime motivator on the Earth plane. The gas that should go in our gas tank.

We need our **Natal Mars** to empower our **Natal Sun**, help it to get to where it wants and needs to go.

But the problem with the Traditional Astrological approach of **Mars** being the Warrior of the Sun is simply that:

Our Astrological Mars can also be the Warrior for The Moon too.

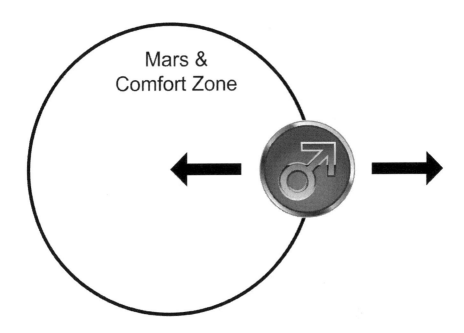

Mars and our Comfort Zone

Mars works for both **The Sun** and **The Moon**.

Although which of the two our **Mars** tends to favour depends a great deal on which side of the fence our personality leans. Are we more play it safe, or do we love a good adventure, in our overall approach to life?

Our Mars can fight to help us step beyond our Comfort Zone, just as much as it can help fight to defend it.

That's one of the reasons why someone simply saying *"Step outside your Comfort Zone!"* doesn't always meet with the positive response they were expecting, especially in the realm of Big Business.

For example, if someone is trying to drag our **Moon** out from our Comfort Zone, our place of normal safety and security, who do you think comes to the rescue?

Mars.

Mars is capable of fighting for **The Sun** or **The Moon**, equally, depending on the dynamics and focus of our individual chart.

Mars can be a Warrior for **The Sun** or **The Moon**, depending.

So if an individual's psyche is more risk-averse, and they don't like going on quests, they are far more the stay at home type, then the balance in their psyche is more towards **Mars** fighting for **The Moon**, fighting more to maintain the psychic status quo.

But if an individual's psyche is more adventurous, loves to live dangerously, hates being bored or becoming stale, then the balance in their psyche is more towards **Mars** fighting for **The Sun**, fighting more to expand and grow beyond their Comfort Zone.

And the Sign in which **Mars** can be found, and its relationship to **The Moon** and **Sun Signs**, can also tell you a great deal about whether someone has a default setting lurking in their Astrological chart.

Is **Mars** more a Warrior for **The Sun** or **The Moon**?

However, we need to be careful not to paint ourselves into a corner here. Because no one is **100% Sun** or **Moon**, never 100% Yin or Yang.

And in any life, there are times when **Mars** is capable of switching sides, moving from defending **The Moon** to fighting for **The Sun**, or vice versa, if the conditions are right.

So change is always possible.

But one of the interesting things about **Mars** in relation to **The Moon**.

If our Comfort Zone can be said to be like a castle, then **Mars** can be seen as a Warrior defending that castle.

And if our Comfort Zone is a psychological construct, made up of all the ideas and beliefs and feelings which we rely on to keep us safe and secure, then **Mars** will also be fighting to defend those too. Even in the face of the truth, **Mars** can and will continue to fight to defend the indefensible.

Especially when those beliefs are under attack, or are perceived to be, even if those beliefs are no longer relevant, out-dated, are no longer serving our own best interests, or have been shown to be plain wrong by hard evidence.

"The World is round and not flat? Yeah, right. I would like to see you walk up to the edge and not fall off. I bet you wouldn't have the guts to do that!"

So the trick to effective change, in these circumstances is to get your **Inner Mars** to switch sides, to fight for **The Sun**, and the new life you want to activate, and not for **The Moon**, and the old habits and patterns you need to let go of. And often, there is a way to do that via each Astrological chart, via personality re-wiring.

Although, once again, sometimes, a lot easier said than done for many people. Lunar habits are hard to give up.

Plus, unfortunately, we need to understand that **Mars** can also fight on behalf of an unjust cause.

A lot of good men fought for the Nazis during WW2, because they believed in the wrong thing, although at the time, they believed in the rightness of their cause.

Our **Mars** can often be like a soldier for hire, a soldier of fortune.

Normal army training is to condition men (and now women in some countries) so that they act under orders, keep fighting under fire, and never question what they have been ordered to do.

You fight, you don't think.

And our **Inner Mars** is a bit like that, sometimes, it often just does what the other Planets tell it.

It's the other Planets which decide upon the rightness or wrongness of any cause.

That's not the realm of **Mars**. If you track back to **Mars/Ares** in the Greek and Roman Myths, you will find that the God of War wasn't a great thinker, not a God to think deeply about anything.

Mars' function is to fight for what we want and need. But our Ego can always get in the way, override the wishes of our Heart, and go after stuff and situations that are not good for our Soul, Heart or life-purpose.

But now we come to the BIG downside for the **Mars** and our Solar Plexus Chakra... Shame.

The definition of Shame is when you come to believe that you are a bad person.

(In comparison, Guilt is when you are a good person but have done a bad thing.)

If you believe you are a bad person, because of Shame, then everything you do, everything you touch, must also be bad as well.

So with Shame, your badness is toxic, your badness is like an acid, which burns into everything and anything it touches.

Including your own psyche, your core sense of Self.

Which means your Inner Warrior, unfortunately, is no longer too great at fighting battles on your behalf.

Because your **Mars** is bad, You are bad, your dreams and goals are bad, your life is bad, your relationships are bad, your situation is bad... etc... etc.

You get the picture, there is no escape from this tsunami of Shame and badness.

In fact, on the battlefield of life, your Inner Warrior, your **Mars** has probably fallen to the ground under the sheer weight of Shame, is crippled with self-doubt and terrible self-worth issues.

Often the only way people can deal with this Shame is to project it out on to other people or things, which often need to then be destroyed – i.e. the zeal to destroy of many religious and political fanatics.

And so it's no wonder that a Shame influenced **Mars** gets beaten up... repeatedly... by the other **Mars Warriors**, out to get what they want for themselves, because Shame influenced **Mars** has become ineffective as a fighter, while others are not carrying the same weight and issues, and so aren't pulling their punches.

Often due to poor Self-Worth, these weak **Mars** types are destroyed by Guilt and Shame.

"No! You can't have what you want and desire in life. Because you are a BAD person, and so don't deserve it. Ever!"

But what exactly is Self-Worth?

Well, back in the 1980s, psychologists and personal development teachers used to go around using the words Self-Love and Self-Worth as if they were interchangeable.

Back then, it was believed that Self-Love and Self-Worth... well... they were the same thing really.

But all that stopped rather abruptly when a psychologist happened to give a Self-Worth questionnaire to a group of Mafia Hoods who were locked up in prison, and if memory serves, I think it was a prison somewhere in New York State.

You see, according to the theory at the time, the Mafia Hoods were meant to score LOW, thus showing that they did what they did because of Low Self-worth.

But actually, they all scored HIGH, which showed they enjoyed doing what they did, which was loan-sharking, protection rackets, pimping and physical violence to people who got in their way.

Ouch!

Science is full of examples when people don't behave how the theory says they should.

The question then becomes is Science open-minded enough to pursue the new direction, or will it stick its fingers in its ears, going *"We're not listening... La-La-La... we're still not listening!"*

Well, they did listen, and because of this unexpected result, the whole 1980s Self-Worth personal development industry was thrown into a total spin.

How could they possibly square this circle?

How could bad people have high levels of Self-Worth?

Actually, it's very easy to square this circle, if you recognize first that Self-Love and Self-Worth are not the same things.

In fact, they are quite separate and so need to be approached differently.

And that Self-Love is a Being thing, while Self-Worth is a Doing thing.

And seeing that **Mars** is our ultimate Doing and Action Planet, it means that **Mars** is plugged into our Self-Worth, for better or worse.

Self-Love is what you get from the Universe just for being born, just for turning up, it's your birthright, and there is nothing you need to do to earn it.

OK, it often it gets lost and buried and forgotten, and there are many, many people who don't love themselves, but Self-Love is always there, buried in their psyche, all they need to do is reach down, dig down, and re-connect to the flow.

However, Self-Worth is something you have to make for yourself, a fuel you have to refine, and you do so through your actions and achievements.

So **Mars** goes out, performs all the actions and steps to help **The Sun** move beyond our Comfort Zone, and when we can do that, it fuels our sense of Self-Worth. When our Comfort Zone expands, so our Self-Worth also expands with it.

You create Self-Worth Club points for yourself whenever you step outside of your Comfort Zone, go on a quest and conquer, whenever you are successful in some area of life, or just get off the metaphorical sofa and try.

Which is why it is important for a parent to support their kids, and help them to succeed in some area of life (… and those parents who have to win at everything, even if it means crushing their kid's fragile sense of Self-Worth in doing so, in the end, not cool parents).

And sometimes, you don't even need to totally succeed to feed your Self-Worth, the very act of trying, even if you fall short of your end goal, is enough to feed your Self-Worth.

To paraphrase the poet **Tennyson**, it's better to have tried and failed than not have tried at all.

And the Doings will vary from person to person because what motivates each person to step outside of their individual Comfort Zone will vary, but we all need to strive in some way to build our sense of Self-Worth. It's part of being Human, it's hot-wired into us.

But it's the people who sit at home, who don't strive, who don't try, those are the ones who have Low Self-Worth.

So going back to the prison and the Mafia hoods. They were probably all psychopaths, totally disconnected from any love and compassion, but they got a kick out of doing what they did, and the very doing, even if it was anti-social, it still fed their sense of Self-Worth.

And this is the thing, it's also what made them successful in life (although, I must admit, ending up in prison, with a lifetime sentence, isn't that great an indication of success).

But there are many psychopaths who never get caught, and who end up at the top of the social ladder, running companies, or political parties.

And it's their High Self-Worth which propels them forward in life.

You see, Self-Worth isn't always about being a nice person, it's your inner connection to Self-Love which secures that.

Which is also why **Mars** needs to be seen as a soldier for hire, it can work for the good guys or the bad guys.

Ultimately, it is down to other forces, and Planets, to decide whether **Mars** is used for good or not.

You have to do something to create a feeling of Self-Worth, and then that feeling then propels you forward, to greater success, which creates even more feelings of Self-Worth... and on... and on...

In fact, the whole thing can get quite addictive, and you can't rest on your laurels forever (to quote the Ancient Greek phrase). The Self-Worth fuel will only last so long, and then you need to engage on another quest to top up the tank again.

Although, the eagle-eyed among you might have spotted the loophole. Maybe you could jump-start the process with the feeling... having the feeling first? Yep, that is entirely possible.

Which is something you can do with personal development, find a way to create the appropriate feelings to kick-start your inner engine, and once you are motoring forwards, the sheer momentum with keeping your Self-worth tank topped up.

Yes, you can jump-start your **Mars** engine to some degree.

But to do that, you first need to want to, which is another Doing, which brings us back to Mars again.

We need to Do to get the fuel to fill up our Doing tank, so we can go out and do more Doings, and so get more fuel for our Doing tank, so we can go out and do even more Doings.

Now, didn't I say Mars was important?

VENUS

Imagine that you are travelling on a boat, crossing the Atlantic or Pacific Oceans perhaps, and you stare out over the side.

What do you see?

Water, water, everywhere...

Energy Astrology

Water... all the way around the boat... yes, there is a lot of water...

Anything else?

Water... and waves...

Yes, you see the waves moving across the surface of the ocean, all around the boat.

But that's only a small part of the picture.

Because the ocean which you are travelling across literally goes down beneath you and the boat for miles.

So your observations are just of the surface of the water, and you are forgetting everything which exists below you.

True, that is all you can see, everything else is hidden from your sight, deep down below you, below the boat.

But beneath the surface is a whole other world of motion and action, and the majority of what moves the surface world is sourced by actions above or below.

The surface waves are mostly created through the action of wind across the surface of the water.

But below, there are water currents, and deeper currents still, which move the oceans across the surface of our Planet, and also control the weather-systems on our Planet to a large degree.

And these ocean currents are also driven by Solar and Lunar forces, although we never register this with our senses.

(Warning: Apt metaphor coming over the horizon soon.)

So any ocean is far more then you can or will ever see on the surface.

And the same is true for our Mind.

Our Conscious Mind exists at the surface, but below that are deeper levels, which **Sigmund Freud** termed the Unconscious Mind, and there are even deeper levels below that, where our sense of Individuality and separateness merges into the Collective and Universal.

There are deeper and deeper levels to us all, each one of us, and **Venus** is the Planet which controls, influences and organises all the levels of our Mind, from the surface right down to the deeper levels, of which we are not normally conscious.

Remember, in Greek Mythology, **Aphrodite/Venus** arose from the sea of the coast of Cyprus, the Goddess came out of the ocean, she arose out of those depths, and she was given form by the remains of **Uranus**, who was the original Celestial God, and she had no Mother. So she has a strong connection to the deep and the formless. She cannot be said to be completely of this World.

But **Venus** influences our Mind in a way which may not be readily apparent, especially if we have been conditioned to assume that our Mind is like a Big computer, being run by complex algorithms and software, and that we are all thoughts and thinking.

Because **Venus** works through *vibration* and *harmony*.

You see, we tend to assume that our Mind is just organised along the lines of rational thought. How our Mind thinks tends to be what most people assume they are, all they are.

But that's like a dirty glass of water assuming that it is the dirt, forgetting all about the clear water which is hiding behind all the dust and sand.

And as Brain scientists have discovered over recent decades, there is more to us then just reason and words.

OK, close to the surface, close to everyday Consciousness, it looks like we use rational thought to navigate our way through life.

But that really isn't the case, and there are levels of Mind which are more intuitive, more feeling orientated, more visually orientated, and I have found that some deeper parts that work and function using vibration, just like the ancient wisdom teachings suggest.

It's just that our existence as social creatures, with a high reliance on language to communicate with our fellow Humans, means our Conscious Mind puts great store in reason and the rational.

But that is not necessarily true for the deeper levels of Self below our Rational Mind, in the deeper levels of our Self, which the majority of people are oblivious to, occasionally accessing these levels through a half-remembered dream upon waking.

Now, it has been said in Traditional Astrology that if **Mars** is the Warrior of the Sun, then **Venus** is the Lover for the Sun, and there is a certain truth in this statement.

But as per usual, with this statement and approach, we are only dealing with the surface level of the truth, and there are much deeper levels to explore, just as there is a whole ocean beneath the surface waves.

Venus = Harmony = Tidy

Like if we are to say that **Venus** is the Cleaning Maid of **The Sun** & **The Moon**.

… Yes, I am being serious here, just hear me out.

Because, once again, it goes back to our understanding of Comfort Zones, and what **Venus** brings to the Comfort Zone party.

Whenever we learn a new skill, we need to venture out beyond our Comfort Zone to acquire it, and **The Sun** and our **Mars** help us to achieve that.

But then once learned; eventually, that skill becomes known and is integrated into our Comfort Zone. Into the realm of **The Moon**. It is woven into our Comfort Zone, and so becomes known and workable.

It becomes part of our existing skillset, something which we have integrated so well that we no longer need to think about it, like learning to drive a car. Difficult at first, but after ten years as a driver, something which the majority of people do on automatic.

But when that skill, that knowledge, those gifts are first brought into our Comfort Zone, initially, is it all done in a neat and orderly way?

Does **The Moon** integrate the knowledge inside in an orderly and structured way, carefully placing the information on the right shelf in our Bio-Brain library?

Not really.

Our **Moon** isn't really cut out to be a librarian. Our **Moon** is not a neat and tidy kind of celestial deity.

It is the task of **The Moon** to bring the knowledge and skills within, to integrate them into our Comfort Zone.

When that is accomplished, then job done, from **The Moon's** perspective.

Lunar integration only means they are brought into our Comfort Zone, that they become tagged as known, but after that is achieved, they are left there, just inside the door of the library, left for others to correctly file and store.

It's a bit like saying that a library is a place to store books, but if those books are just dumped in the library in a disorderly way, with no system for cataloguing them, no way of filing or finding them easily on the shelf, as if the Dewey system had never been invented, then it would be all but impossible to find the information you needed in the future. Which could put you at a distinct disadvantage when you were desperately trying to remember the correct, winning answer to the $1 million dollar question on *Who Wants To Be A Millionaire*?

For our Brain, and also for our Comfort Zone, to be effective, we need to classify, order and structure the information stored in our head.

We need to bring some order to the informational chaos.

We need to tidy up our Mental Space.

And that's where our inner **Venus** comes in because **Venus** is the equivalent of our librarian.

OK, we are used to thinking of **Venus** as being all glamorous, beautiful and sexy, which is also correct, so the idea of **Venus** also being a librarian can be a little odd at first. Maybe see **Venus** as being a super-sexy librarian if that helps.

Venus provides order, structure, and harmony, even beauty to our internal space so that we not only make sense to ourselves, but we can find the information we need within us, quickly and easily, which helps us to make sense of our external World, and so better navigate said external World.

When **Inner Venus** is weak for some reason, that individual suffers from an inability to know themselves, because their inner world is chaotic, disordered, and so that individual finds it hard to locate the sense and meaning inside their own head. Because it is so chaotic up there, they often prefer to not even look within and try to find a reason for their behaviour and actions. That is why, occasionally, a psychologist or counsellor can be useful, because they are looking into our disorderly head with a Mind which, hopefully, has achieved a degree of order and harmony, and so can see through our inner mess.

And the Sign in which **Venus** is located will highlight which kind of inner harmony, and classification system, we prefer to use or should be using, because there are 12 basic types.

Do we classify our Mind in a **Scorpio** way, and so look out at the World with **Scorpio** tinged glasses, or are our filters more **Capricorn**?

So **The Moon** dumps the new stuff into our Comfort Zone, but it is **Venus** which stores and organizes the new stuff in a way which is most useful for that individual, weaving the information in with the old, so that a sense of inner harmony is achieved.

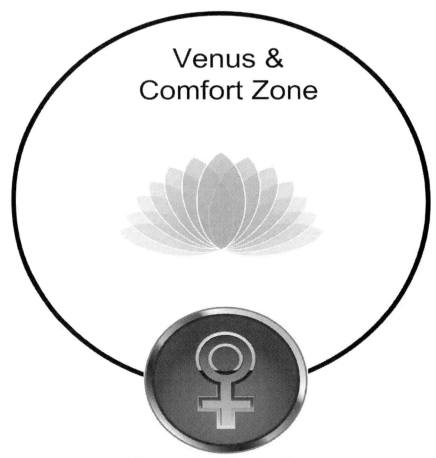

Venus and our Comfort Zone

Which is why **Venus** is often associated with the quality of harmony, because an active **Venus** brings harmony and structure into our Mind.

Venus tidies up behind **The Moon**.

Venus brings harmony into our inner Mind library, helps us to understand ourselves and the World around us, helps us to fit in.

Which brings us to our next point, which is **Venus** helps us to build strong and effective social skills.

We can always tell a lot about the workings of a Planet by the marriage made in Greek and Roman mythology. **Aphrodite/Venus** was married to **Hephestian/Vulcan**, who was the inventor and blacksmith of the Gods, who was the one who forged the thunderbolts for **Zeus/Jupiter**, but who never once thought about using them for himself.

A problematic marriage perhaps, but basically, with this marriage, **Venus** has got the whole skill thing sown up, on multiple levels. The skills we express with our hands and the skills we express with our Mind.

Now, it was in one of **Robert Gladwell's** books, *Outliers: The Story of Success*, where he tells the story of a very intelligent man, who was probably a genius on many levels, but who had failed at their single attempt at going to University.

Because he had been born to lower-class parents in the United States, who weren't able to teach him the social skills to fit in with a mostly middle-class US University system and population, so when he attended the said University under a scholarship, he didn't feel accepted, he felt alienated by the middle-class kids and professors around, he didn't know how to speak their language or fit into their academic World, and so he eventually dropped out, and people felt he had never lived up to his true potential.

Now, there is a continual debate about how to raise up the lower classes, and socialist politicians usually state its because of poor education, and that the lower classes should be given easy access to higher education to re-balance the injustice, and there may be some truth in this.

But, as **Gladwell** suggests, a big chunk of the problem is really down to the gap in social skills.

It's not just a matter of more and better information. To fit in, people need to know and understand the social game which is being played around them, and shown how to play the game well.

OK, you may have the most amazing ideas going around in your head, but if you are not shown how to take those ideas and structure them into a coherent argument, and then how to structure them into an accepted academic essay format, which follows all the rules, if you are not shown how to do that, it's going to be hard for you to play the University game well or be successful.

The thing is, middle-class kids, know these social rules and conventions well before they go to University, or when they are going in to see a Bank Manager to ask for a loan to fund their new business. They are polite, know what to wear, speak when spoken to, laugh at all the right jokes, make a good impression.

So they fit in, and the middle-class Professor or Bank Manager sees them as one of their own, they are not intimidated by them, because they speak the correct tribal language.

A young person from a lower-class background can, therefore, be at a distinct disadvantage here, because they have never been greatly exposed to that social and tribal culture (and the reverse is also true if a single middle-class kid is trying and fit in with a lower class family. It's understanding the rules of the social game which help someone fit in, using the right words in the right context, along with knowing when to use a fork, spoon or knife).

And it is interesting that over the past couple of years, there has been a re-focusing of effort, and a number of the more socially aware companies have started to take disadvantaged kids into the workplace before they go to University, exactly so they can learn the social skills and etiquette they will need to survive and prosper later on in life.

That's not to say that middle is better than working or upper class, just that you need to know the rules of the social game you are currently in and play those social cards to the best or your ability if you want to prosper in said social environment. That's the same as when a social anthropologist is approaching an undiscovered tribe in the Amazon or in Borneo. Learn the language fast, along with what to do in polite tribal society, and what is considered socially unacceptable behaviour, which could get you killed... or worse.

Whether there has been a re-balancing of the social divide now that Banks are closing down on the high street, going virtual, and loan applications are being processed more online, by computers, and so playing the social games is perhaps less of a factor... who knows?

But **Venus** is the Planet which is known for its good graces, etiquette and social skills, and this is down to its ability to take in the social rules from the people around us, understand the rules of the social game which is being played, and so figure out how to play that game well.

And in that regard, **Venus** is just as important as **Mars** for getting our needs met.

Sometimes in life, we need to go out and grab what we want or need, fight for it, and so **Mars** is important when those situations arise. But there are other times when we need to liaise with other people, win them around to our point of view, talk them into giving us what we want.

And that's when our **Inner Venus** becomes super-important.

In the modern world, it is currently very rare that we can achieve something big without the input and support of other people. Very few of us are blacksmiths, spending days in the forge alone, doing our own thing. And even a blacksmith often has to have spoken to the Bank for a loan to set-up their smithy, or got the loan from their family perhaps, to begin with, and they will also need to be polite to their customer base to stay in business. No one likes a bad-tempered, foul-mouthed, socially inept blacksmith.

In the modern world, Humans need other Humans, and so need to know how to best communicate and interact with them within a social context.

But, going back to **Venus**, our ability to establish harmony and social skills in our outer world is wholly dependent on their being a high degree of harmony within our inner world, within our Mind.

Having said that, about **Venus** and social skills, what about the whole **Venus** and values thing which you sometimes get in Traditional Astrology?

Well, let's return to your metaphor of the Comfort Zone for a possible explanation of values.

The usual dictionary definition of values goes something like:

(noun) the regard that something is held to deserve; the importance, worth, or usefulness of something:
(noun) a person's principles or standards of behaviour; one's

judgment of what is important in life:
(verb) estimate the monetary worth of (something):
(verb) consider (someone or something) to be important or
beneficial; have a high opinion of:

But if we drill down, the fundamental thing is, if we value something, then in our personal opinion, we consider it to be important to us.

It may be because it has a practical or material value... or financial value... or social value... or a purely personal value... but it is important, and we will act in some way to retain or defend it. Because it means something to us.

If you are trying to fight your way through a dense jungle then a machete has a high value, and you would be willing to pay a high price for one if you didn't have it, as it would make your life easier.

If you have ever watched any programmes on antiques, you will know that an old photograph album of family pictures, maybe from the turn of the century, has little or no value in an auction room. But to the people who had those photos taken, a century ago, they were of immense personal value (just as the photograph of my deceased father in the room I am typing this has a real personal value to me) because it helps us to maintain a connection to those individuals who have passed on. There is nothing as sad as when you can no longer remember what your loved one looked like, the memory of their face is starting to fade.

So value is relative. It shifts and changes from person to person, from circumstance to circumstance.

But the first important thing for us to realise here is that if something has a value to us, especially a personal value, it is because **Venus** has woven it into our Comfort Zone. It has become part of the fabric of our life-stream for some reason, and to remove it would cause us pain, discomfort, or unease. Or the other word we could use here anxiety. And that's why people have been known to run into a burning building to save a family photograph album because furniture can be replaced, but the connection to their past cannot.

Now, as we have said, if **The Sun** is in the centre of our Comfort Zone, then it is relatively dark, non-bright (if there is such a word).

And as it travels out to the edges of the Comfort Zone, it gets brighter and brighter, and when it crosses over the boundary, it becomes positively incandescent with light.

So if **Mars** is the one, with the machete, clearing the path for **The Sun**, what is the role of **Venus** in helping **The Sun** to expand outwards?

Back in the 1970s, if you lived in the United Kingdom, and stayed up late then you could watch Open University programmes on BBC2, programmes which were broadcast in support of educational courses which the Open University put out for its students (it's now all online, I believe).

And in one such programme, which I can always remember, on behavioural psychology, there was a Beatle following a line of light.

No, not John, Paul, George or Ringo... a real-life insect Beatle.

A Beatle is programmed by Nature to always head towards the light, because that is the Beatle's best chance for food and safety, and so it always walks along the path of light to its source.

But then, those naughty behavioural scientists back in the 1970s, who loved to torture creatures less evolved than themselves, they would suddenly switch off the light beam the Beatle was following... and switch on a 2nd one, heading in a different direction.

And so the Beatle would suddenly have to re-orientate itself.

And start to walk down the 2nd light-beam, heading towards its source.

Until the scientists switched that off too and switched on the 3rd beam of light.

And the Beatle would re-orientate itself again, and set off in a different direction.

So, apart from demonstrating the Universal truth, if in doubt, *head towards the light...* and hope it isn't a Vampire with a spotlight.

What does this help to tell us about **Venus** and its relation to our Comfort Zone?

Well, if our **Sun** is in the centre of our Comfort Zone, trying to move out, then from the centre of the Zone, radiating out, are a hundred or so different beams of light, shining out towards the edge and beyond, and our **Sun** chooses one or two of those light beams to follow, the ones which look the most appealing to us, and ignores the rest (for the moment).

And which Planet is generating those beams of light for our **Sun** to follow?

Venus.

Because each beam of light represents something which we value, a path which we would want to actively pursue and explore in our life.

And value arises out of harmony... our inner harmony... as does self-knowledge and self-awareness... if our **Inner Venus** has managed to get everything neat and tidy inside our head, that is.

Mars gives us the strength to walk down this path, but **Venus** shines the light beam out, and so gives us a sense of direction.

In many ways, **Venus** and its system of personal values give us a structure for our life, creates a sense of individual uniqueness, and so is tied into our life-purpose and individual dharma.

My mother is into Western movies, but I am more into Sci-Fi, she likes gardening, I will cut the lawns, but that's about my limit. We all express our limited time, energy effort down value paths we want to explore.

You see, the thing is our life is short, and so our **Sun** cannot afford to expand outwards on all sides, in all directions, simultaneously. We just don't have enough time, not enough years in us to explore all possibilities.

So we must prioritise.

And how do we prioritize?

We focus on that which has real value for us. (And value is different to meaning, which is more of a **Jupiter** thing.)

So these lines of value radiate out across our Comfort Zone, lines illuminating what we value, what interests us, and our **Sun** follows a few of them out.

99% of the time, it's our values which truely motivate us into action.

And in this regard, in terms of paths of light and values, **Venus** can also work as much for **The Moon** as it does for **The Sun**.

Because our Comfort Zone is largely composed of what we value, and so **Venus**, once again, is what gives our Comfort Zone its coherence and structure, if it is organised well.

Now, there is one final interesting thing to mention, which concerns the 2 Meridians which are associated, connected, and plugged into **Venus**.

You see, in Traditional Astrology, a Planet is said to rule one or more Signs, these are Signs which have, for some reason, a strong affinity with that Planet.

And **Venus** is no exception to this.

In fact, **Venus**, along with **Mercury**, has 2 Signs attached to it, **Taurus** and **Libra**.

But because, in **Energy Astrology**, we can now translate Signs into Meridians, this allows us to say that the two Meridians most in resonance with the Throat Chakra and **Venus** are the Heart Protector Meridian and the Triple Warmer Meridian, which are both Fire Meridians.

And this is very interesting.

They are both Meridians which help protect **the Heart/The Sun** and Heart Meridian from external forces which are of a low vibe, and which would want to deplete, steal our energy or control us.

The Triple Warmer Meridian helps us to identify threat and non-threat, and the Heart Protector Meridian helps us to erect an energy boundary, around our Heart Space, against those energies and people who have been identified as a threat to our self-interests.

But, and this is the interesting thing, they are also the 2 Meridians which help us to organise our Inner World, our thoughts and emotional energy, and so create internal psychic boundaries and barriers against energies, within ourselves, which we don't like or want to own.

You see, there is one thing we can say about Evolution and Nature, why create something new when we can re-use something existing, something already created which can do the job just as well...

External boundaries become internal boundaries.

So if evolving Humans already had a psychic mechanism to protect them against harm on the outside, as they continued to evolve, and their Minds continued to expand and deepen, Nature decided to re-purpose said boundary mechanism to give them some protection against internal energies which they found troublesome, or which made them anxious.

So **Venus** is responsible for the order and harmony within our Mind, within our Comfort Zone, overall, and the Heart Protector Meridian and Triple Warmer Meridian are responsible for the internal boundaries which we create, and the enforcement of those boundaries, to maintain our sense of this safety and inner harmony, linking back to **Venus**, the ruler of both Signs.

Whether this is a good thing, that's debatable, and Humans tend to lock away energies which are not really harmful, but which we perceive to be harmful, or which we have been told are harmful by others, and this can include positive energies as well as negative, and if we do this too often it can cause us a whole heap of problems down the line.

Chapter 3-5: Jupiter & Saturn

Astrology is traditionally known as The Round Art.

And the reason for this is obvious when you look at any Astrological chart, such as this one, the Natal chart for **Marilyn Munroe.**

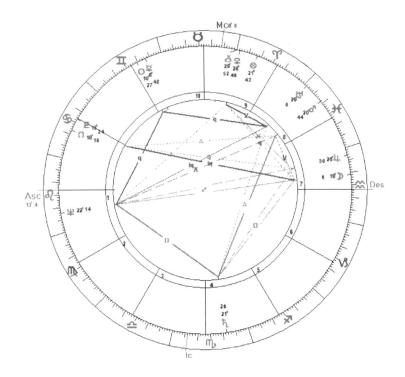

Marilyn Munroe's *Natal Chart*

And if you run your eye around the edge of this Astrological circle, you find all the Planets in the round.

But any Astrological chart is deceptive, because it looks as if all the Planets are going around the centre of the chart, all at the same distance from that centre.

And where is the centre exactly?

Well, we all know that the centre of the Solar System is **The Sun**... because all of the Planets revolve around our local star... **The Sun**... that's what Modern Science teaches us in school.

But on an Astrological chart, that is not the case, the centre of the Astrological chart is the **Earth** itself, with all the other Planets, plus **The Sun** and **The Moon**, revolving around the centre of the chart, as it is viewed from the perspective of the **Earth**.

Now, the first wrongness about this picture is that all the Planets in our Solar System orbit **The Sun** in elliptical orbits... and not in a circular orbit. Ditto **The Moon** orbiting around the **Earth**... also an elliptical orbit. In fact, most objects in outer space travel in an elliptical orbit.

But the other wrongness which an Astrological Chart suggests... which is just not true out in the Solar System... that all the Planets are the same distance from the centre.

Which is so not the case at all... and in order of the nearest to farthest Planet from **The Sun**... we have:

- **Mercury** – 57.91 million km
- **Venus** – 108.2 million km
- **Mars** – 227.9 million km
- **Jupiter** – 778.5 million km
- **Saturn** – 1.434 billion km
- **Uranus** – 2.871 billion km
- **Neptune** – 4.495 billion km
- **Pluto** – 5.906 billion km

Plus **The Moon's** distance from the **Earth**... 384,400 km.

And the reason why this is important... in terms of circles or ellipses... the further out a Planet is located from **The Sun**, the longer it will take to complete a single orbit around **The Sun**.

So if we come back to **Marilyn Munroe's** chart... it may look as if all the Planets are the same distance from the centre... but they are not…

And it may look as if all the Planets are travelling at the same speed around the centre…

But once again… they are not…

And these different distances from **The Sun** also mean that the time the Planets take to orbit around **The Sun** also differs greatly.

- **Mercury** – 88 days
- **Venus** –225 days
- **Earth** – 1 year or 365.265 days
- **Mars** – 687 days
- **Jupiter** – 12 years
- **Saturn** – 29 years
- **Chiron** – 50 years
- **Uranus** – 84 years
- **Neptune** – 165 years
- **Pluto** – 248 years

And this whole distance/speed/time thing allows us to organise the Planets into 1 of 4 Groups, depending on how long it takes for them to complete one orbit of **The Sun:**

The Luminaries: The Sun & The Moon… which takes 365.265 days for the **Earth** to orbit **The Sun**… and 28 days for **The Moon** to orbit the **Earth.**

The Personal Planets: Mercury, Venus and **Mars**… which take from 88 days to 2 years to orbit around **The Sun.**

The Social Planets: Jupiter & Saturn… which take from 12 to 29 years to orbit around **The Sun.**

The Transpersonal Planets: Uranus, Neptune and **Pluto**… which take 84 to 248 years to orbit around **The Sun**.

I tend to include **Chiron** with the **Transpersonal Planets**, as it's rotation takes 50.7 years.

As you can see, the further out you travel from our **Sun**, the greater the time periods for one rotation become... no real surprise there.

But where this becomes hugely important for Astrology... is when we gauge this all against the average Human lifespan.

For example, back in the Middle Ages in Europe, the average life expectancy for a male child born in the United Kingdom between 1276 and 1300 was 31.3 years.

Which means that they could have experienced a **Saturn Return**... just... but a **Chiron Return** was rare (50.7 years)... and a **Uranus Return** even rarer still (84 years).

In fact, when you think about it, **Saturn Returns** occurred around the time of the average person's death, and so probably **Saturn** had something to do with it... or at least got the blame... (no wonder **Saturn** got such a Bad Press in Medieval Astrology if people associated a **Saturn Return** with the time of someone's death).

A middle-class male in Victorian England could hope to do a little better... as their life expectancy was around 45 years... although a working-class male could only expect a lifetime of half that... so for both upper and lower-classes during Victorian England, their life expectancy still fell short of a **Chiron Return**.

If you are also into Past Lives, it is interesting to note that previous to the 20th Century, most incarnating Souls will not have experienced anything later then a **Saturn Return** for most of Human history... and were fortunate to even achieve that. For much of Human history, the populace was fortunate to reach their **Saturn Return**...

and anything else was a rarity.

In 1993, in the United Kingdom, the average life expectancy for a male had risen to 73 years... which now includes a **Chiron Return**... and more people were living on to experience a **Uranus Return** (although not everyone).

So as we are living longer, as individuals and a species, we are starting to experience different aspects of the Astrological energies on offer... especially in relation to **Chiron** and **Uranus**... plus a **2nd Saturn Return**... although no one has ever lived to experience a **Neptune** or **Plutonian Return**.

Which is something I always find fascinating... back in the Middle Ages, Astrologers saw **Saturn** as the Bad Guy of the Solar System. Who knows what they would have said about karma and fate if they had only been given a few powerful telescopes to see what was lurking out on the edges of our Solar System.

But the other fascinating thing about tracking the Planets in terms of how long they take to orbit **The Sun** is...

The 2 Social Planets... **Jupiter & Saturn**.

Because these two Planets are the first where the time gap involved with a single **Solar rotation** massively jumps... from 2 years (**Mars**) to 12 years (**Jupiter**)... and so they represent a shift into a completely different dimension of energy and focus.

You see, when people first get involved with Astrology, their focus is primarily upon themselves...

What does my Astrological chart mean for me... how can I get it to work for me... how can I change myself to get what I want in my life?

That was true for me... and pretty much everyone I have ever encountered to some degree (be honest now).

I have yet to meet someone who originally started to study Astrology because they wanted to Save the Planet... although who knows, there may be an Astrologer out there with lots of Planets in **Aquarius** for whom that was true.

99.99% of the time, people get involved with Astrology because it provides them with a fascinating window into Self... Themselves...

They want to understand and appreciate their own uniqueness... as well as understand what makes them tick... and discover if there are any hacks to increase their happiness and personal performance.

And I think that is the case throughout Human history...

I bet... back in the time of Mesopotamia... where the Astrologers of Ancient Babylon were focused on drawing up the Natal chart of the King to see what lay in store in his future... (because if you knew what would happen to the Ruler, that gave you a fairly good idea of what fate would befall the Kingdom he was ruling...)

I bet... back then... those Ancient Astrologers also drew up their own charts too... on the side... friends and family... and special commissions for rich people... just Human nature to do so.

Why just keep such wisdom for the King?

Although who knows now... back then, there may have been a special department of the Ancient Babylonian Police... tracking down and destroying rogue Astrological charts... ones drawn up for people who were not Royal in any way.

Fundamentally, people are, and always have been, fascinated with their own psyche... and like to hear and know about themselves...

and I can't see that changing any time soon.

That's one of the things that makes Astrology so appealing... it offers us a window within.

But the thing is... as we start to venture out beyond the inner Solar System... to the Social and Transpersonal Planets... our sense of uniqueness starts to fade... it has to...

For the simple reason that everyone born in the same year as ourselves will have **Jupiter** in roughly the same Sign... because it stays in that Sign for a year...

And everyone born in the same 2.4 year period (approximately) will have **Saturn** in roughly the same Sign too... because it stays in that Sign for 2.4 plus years...

So seeing that there are roughly 131.4 million people born each year (current estimate of World population growth in 2019, but set to go up)... if you were born now, that means there are 131.4 million people born in your year with the same **Jupiter Sign** as you... and that there are 315.36 million people alive who were born with the same **Saturn Sign** as you... give or take a few 100 thousand.

So... when you start to view it that way, the Social Planets start to chip away at our sense of being a unique individual... different... one-of-a-kind.

Because there is a minimum of 131 to 262 million other people walking around with the same Social Planets as you... actually, with an average Global lifespan of say 72 years... that gives us an average/approximate of 786 million people for Jupiter + 524 million people for **Saturn**... minimum.

But if we stand back and think... and factor in our metaphor of the Comfort Zone...

That's exactly what we want and need to happen...

We start to realise that when we come to **Jupiter** and **Saturn**... it's less about Me... and much more about We and Us...

We need **Jupiter** and **Saturn** to be Social Planets to have any chance of a successful Human life.

Let me now explain why that is so.

In traditional Astrology, the keywords which we would most commonly associate with Jupiter are probably... expansion, higher learning, life-meaning, philosophy and beliefs.

Simply put, the Sign in which **Jupiter** is located represents those beliefs and philosophy which give our life meaning and purpose.

But then the question arises... how does that relate across to our personal and psychological Comfort Zone?

Well... if we return to our basic understanding of Comfort Zones, they are composed of all the things which we own and identify with...

Our own personal likes, beliefs and skills... all on the inside.

Plus anything which we don't identify with... that we consider alien and unknown... well, that's all located outside of our Comfort Zone.

And that's kind of what allows us to fit in with our society and tribe... that we share common beliefs, ideas, values... a common culture... with the people around us... and we generally also agree on what we dislike and disown and definitely don't associate with.

This cultural Comfort Zone... that we share with others... is the glue which helps a large group of people to stick together and function as a Unit.

It's a bit like a shoal of fish swimming through the ocean… they tend to all turn together when swimming… for protection… they move and stick together.

A good example of this is the train scene from the movie *The Darkest Hour*, towards the end of the movie, where **Winston Churchill** escapes the British Parliament, and all the politicians who are trying to undermine him… and travels on the London Underground… connecting with members of the British public… asking them if they will fight on… and they tell him… Yes. He had connected with the real British Cultural Heart… and found it… strong and stable, and unafraid… and fully in support of him.

To be truly successful, a politician (at least in the democratic countries), needs to be able to sense this cultural Comfort Zone… sense what it is feeling and thinking… so they can articulate it through their policies.

Everyone is plugged into the cultural Comfort Zone of the country in which they are born… into its strengths and weaknesses… for both good and not… and often, we're struggling with that as much with that as we are with our personal and family stuff… although we don't register it as much.

And an interesting dynamic is how aligned, or not, an individual's Personal Planets are with this birth cultural Comfort Zone… with their Social Planets… whether they are aligned, or at odds… and so whether an individual moves abroad at some point in their life, seeking a different psychic atmosphere… or struggles against their home culture for their whole life… or is perfectly happy and at home.

But we are all influenced by the Comfort Zone of our tribe and country... the French have a different culture to the British... which is both different again to the Germans and Italians... Brazil... India... Australia... all different.

And that's OK... it makes the World are much more interesting and colourful place... (except around the times of political and cultural tension... and outright war...)

But for anyone who is born within any countries and cultures (i.e. all of us...) ... these sets of shared beliefs and ideas provide us with a set of guidelines to help us navigate through life (i.e. the people around us think and act in understandable and predictable ways, most of the time)... as well as a sense of belonging... plus a culture we can identify with... it boosts our sense of Self and helps to minimise our life-anxiety.

For example, if we go back in time 40,000 years, to what is now Siberia... if you and your tribe's survival depends on hunting Wholly Mammoths out on the tundra... then your chances of survival, and getting a much-needed kill, greatly increases if you all speak the same language, think in a similar way, believe the same things... and so can hunt together as an effective unit.

It is the same even now... and that's why military units train, over and over again... so that they get to know how everyone thinks and will act and respond... all grounded within a common culture and language.

And that's one of the keys to Humanities success on this planet... our ability to share a culture and communicate within it.

And when we fail... that tends to be because that common culture is non-existent... and/or communication has broken down.

And within any country's culture... people who are born with **Jupiter** and **Saturn** in the same Sign will be surrounded by many people who also think and act as they do... who share the same life-meaning, philosophy and beliefs... exactly because **Jupiter** or **Saturn** is in that same Sign.

And that provides any culture with some massive advantages...

For example... suppose there is an injustice in your country, and you want to change it.

Can you do it on your own?

Probably not... not when you are facing opposition from the power's that be... although we should never completely rule out the tenacity and inner strength of some individuals.

For most, the only chance you have to really change anything, especially in the wider social arena, is to connect up with other people... who share your outlook and beliefs... your sense of injustice... who see the world in the same way as you... and together you can campaign and press for the change you want to see.

Astrologers naturally assume that real, radical change is always down to **Uranus**... and this is true, up to a point...but the building of a social movement for change... that's much more **Jupiter's** area of expertise.

So the generation of **Jupiter** or **Saturn** you are born into means that you are surrounded by a number of socially like-minded individuals, who roughly think like you... who you can connect with... and hopefully move society forward in a new direction.

OK... that isn't always a total positive... because it also means they are struggling with the same issues as you are, and **Saturn** especially shows us the specific issues and limitations that a particular generation is dealing with.

But it does mean that you are not alone... even if you will never meet your whole **Jupiter** or **Saturn tribe** (there isn't a stadium in the World big enough to house you all)... in the social arena... on the World stage... you all have each other's backs.

Shared beliefs are important in many ways... because they focus and empower.

But only if you are aligned with them... and if not... they can also work against the individual.

For example, the majority of people now recognise that **Vincent van Gogh** was a genius painter...

But the truth is, during his life, he couldn't even give his paintings away... and his only sales came from other members of his family who really only wanted to ensure he was earning enough money to eat.

The majority of people alive back then just didn't see any beauty or value in his work...

He's someone who we now consider to have been ahead of his time...

Which means that the beliefs and values that were woven into his individual Comfort Zone... that allowed him to paint in the way he did... were alien, and totally at odds, with the cultural Comfort Zone he was born into... which dominated the minds and eyes of all the people around him.

And so the people of then couldn't see his genius... even though we can now.

He had to die, and the cultural Comfort Zone move on and evolve, for people to see and recognise his true worth and value... in all senses.

And that has been true, for many individuals, throughout Human history... their dominant cultural Comfort Zone couldn't see any value in what they were trying to do or achieve.

It was an eye of the beholder kind of thing... only the brain behind the eye had to be updated with a whole different way of seeing and understanding the World... (in contrast, **Picasso** was far luckier, and had overall an easier and more lucrative time)... and that updating only happens when the **Social Planets** move on and forwards.

It can happen both ways... an individual can be aligned with, and draw strength from their culture (like **Winston Churchill** in the early days of WW2)... or be at odds and out-of-sync with it (like **Vincent van Gogh**)... even though later generations may come to see their true value.

A similar thing happened with **Giordano Bruno** back in 16th Century Italy... where he was burned at the stack for saying things, which we now know to be the truth, but back then was total heresy against the teachings of the Catholic Church (i.e. stars are **Suns** with other planets)... and heresy is really another word to define material and information which lies totally outside the tribal Comfort Zone... and is therefore super-scary... and so the tribe needs to protect itself to continue its sense of social cohesion...

By finding some way to silence the individual.

However, fortunately for many... the much more common experience... is for the cultural Comfort Zone to move on, evolve and grow... transform and change... while the individual's who were born in earlier years remain the same... and so are left-behind.

For example, I was born in the early 1960s... and so my coming of age decade was really the 1980s...

And I often go on to YouTube, to listen to music from that decade... and often come across comments like... *"For music, the 80s was the best decade ever"* or *"I feel sorry for the young living now because back in the 80s we had the best music... today's music is rubbish."*

But then, I can remember, back to the 1980s, people who were born in the 1930s and 1940s saying that about our music... it was rubbish... and that their generation had all the best music back in the 30s and 40s.

I can also remember my Great-Uncle, who is long gone now, saying that he pitied me and my generation because after he was gone, he could see the World going downhill... fast.

But then every passing generation has probably thought that... that they had the best of times, and things now will never be as good again.

I think this passing of the generations thing must be hard-wired into our Universe... just something we have to accept.

The constant movement of the **Social Planets** in the sky... passing the batten of change from one generation to the next.

So now... summing up before we move on to focus on **Jupiter** and **Saturn** individually...

With **Jupiter** and **Saturn**, we must learn to look at them through two sets of eyes...

The 1st set of eyes... which sees these two Planets in relation to our own individual Natal chart...

And the 2nd set of eyes... which sees these two Planets in relation to how they impact our generation, our tribe, our culture… our society…

Plus, we also need to develop an understanding of how these two dimensions interrelate… how the individual relates to the social realm… and also how the social realm influences the individual…

Individual and social expansion…

Individual and social contraction…

Because as the poet **John Donne** once wrote… *No man is an island.*

Basically, when approaching the Social Planets… **Jupiter** & **Saturn** we need to develop a dual focus and approach.

JUPITER

As we said earlier, in traditional Astrology, the keywords which we would most commonly associate with **Jupiter** are probably... expansion, higher learning, life-meaning, philosophy and beliefs.

And in Energy Astrology, **Jupiter** is associated with the Base Chakra... which actually tracks back all the way to Yoga and Ayurvedic Astrology.

Which always seem a little odd initially... **Jupiter** = Base Chakra = Earth Plane?

What has the Earth Plane to do with expansion?

Until you realise that the only place that you can truly expand is on the Earth Plane.

Remember, our physical Universe is constantly expanding... galaxies flying apart, at tremendous speed... even if we can't sense this from our place on **Earth**. So expansion is hot-wired into our physical Universe.

And down here is where the Universe wants us to express all those positive, uplifting and empowering feelings we all dream about...

Which kind of undermines any attempt to escape and ascend this level of existence... because as Buddhism says... even the Gods in the highest heaven are envious of Man down on the Earth Plane... because, down here, we have a real opportunity to learn and grow.

If there is a life or Soul lesson you need to learn... then the best place to learn it is... on the Earth Plane.

It's like the character **James Halliday's** wisdom at the end of the **Speilberg** movie, *Ready Player One*... someone who created a virtual Universe known as the Oasis, which is used by the whole World... a Humanity which is choosing to escape into virtual reality to avoid the pain and poverty of their real World.

At the end of the movie, **Halliday's Avatar** remarks... *"I created the Oasis because I never felt at home in the real world... I was afraid for all my life... right up until the day I knew my life was ending... that was when I realised... that as terrifying and painful as reality can be... it's also the only place... you can get a decent meal."*

All the other planes of existence... emotional, mental, spiritual... although they do have their advantages... are too fluid... are always in constant motion... so nothing ever becomes set... and we cannot receive love and fulfilment back from our creations and experiences.

An artificial, virtual Avatar online cannot love you back in the same messy, inconvenient, unpredictable and utterly fulfilling way as a true Human Soul-Mate... and if you programmed the Avatar in advance... what are you going to learn that you haven't already set-up in advance?

The only place where things can be fixed and focused... which don't change instantly with a thought or emotion... but can also be unpredictable and new... experiences which can truly help you learn and grow... is on the Earth Plane.

Orin, the guide of **Sanaya Roman**, has called the Earth Plane... the plane of frozen thought... and the fact that it takes time to set-up, create and freeze events is seen as a good thing.

So if you want to build something... solid and permanent... and also learn and expand through the building process... acquiring new skills along the way...

Which you can then integrate into your Comfort Zone...

The only place you can do all that... is on the Earth Plane.

That is why **Jupiter** = Base Chakra = Expansion = Earth Plane.

Now, as we said earlier... through our natal **Jupiter**... we tie into energies which are trying to expand our individual Comfort Zone, as shown in the Comfort Zone diagram below...

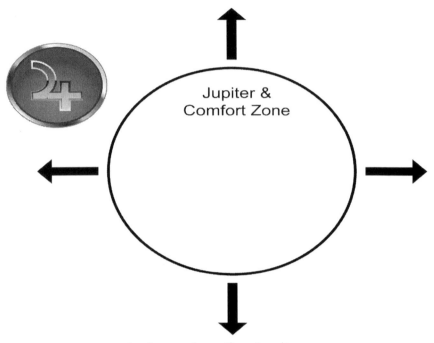

Jupiter and our Comfort Zone

But at the same time, **Jupiter** is a Social Planet (along with **Saturn**)... so it is trying to expand the Comfort Zone of our tribe, our group, our society, our culture.

Jupiter works on us as individuals... and also on the people around us...

Through us, **Jupiter** hopes to influence the collective... and through the collective, **Jupiter** also influences us, through the particular energies which it is trying to express through our particular Human generation... energies which are trying to change some aspect of our Human collective... our tribe... our country and culture.

Jupiter comes at us through either direction... individual and social.

Or to put it another way... **Jupiter** is working on the individual and social levels... at the same time.

Now... you can always tell when a debate is really about tribes and Comfort Zones by the amount of heightened emotional response the debate stirs up within people, and this is one of the big problems with tribal politics, and also with family dynamics... because very quickly a rational debate becomes very irrational and personal.

When you are part of a tribe, you feel safe and secure because the tribe is meant to protect you, and you theoretically share in the collective resources of that tribe.

However, when someone is attacking your tribe, they are also attacking your keep-anxiety-at-bay machine... and so it is not surprising that many people counter-attack with some ferousity, and often without thinking... because they are scared of losing their protection against inner anxiety.

Plus each tribe has its own set of beliefs, laws and customs, and to fit in, each individual needs to adhere to those beliefs, and follow the official line of behaviour... even if it goes against their own self-interests... and the calling of their heart. As long as you behave as the others believe you should you are allowed to remain a member of the tribe. But as soon as you step out of line... as soon as you question or dare to be different... then you will be thrown out and ostracized.

Which is a ticket to big-time anxiety...

To our primitive tribal ancestors, this was the same as passing a death sentence... one individual surviving in the wilderness, all alone, without the security and protection of the rest of the tribe... impossible. Ostracism not only got rid of the troublemaker, but it was a warning lesson to all the other members of the tribe to behave themselves and follow the tribal party line.

So to remain within a tribe, and the protection of the tribal Comfort Zone, there is a trade-off which needs to be made... safety/protection/ communal resources versus individual freedom and expression.

But there is another potential danger with tribal and family Comfort Zones.

Basically, the world around us doesn't stand still. Change is a constant.

As the Ancient Greek philosopher, **Heraclitus** once said... *"You can't step in the same river twice"*.

And this is as true for Human society as it is for any individual.

History is full of examples where a group of people have banded together, established their own collective Comfort Zone to protect themselves, and provide them with a sense of comfort and safety, created a shared set of beliefs and values that they all adhered to... and eventually, the rest of the world just bypassed them, and left them behind, stranded within their out-dated collective mindset.

The shared tribal identity provides a Comfort Zone for the members of that tribe, but unless the tribe is able to update their shared belief systems on a regular basis, to stay aligned with what is happening in the world around them... then the world has a nasty habit of eventually consigning that tribe to the dustbin of history.

Within the field of Astrology, that is the responsibility of **Jupiter**... working through individuals and groups... to expand our collective Comfort Zone so that we remain relevant to our World as it also changes around us.

The ancient Maya are a classic example of this. They had a very rigid social, political, and religious system, which bound the citizens of their city-states together, and seemed to be very effective for a number of centuries. But then, due to climate change, population growth and warfare, their city-states vanished under the jungle, as the populace deserted them.

Fundamentally, the Maya were unable to change their culture and lifestyle to adapt to changing circumstances.

It wasn't just climate change and constant warfare that destroyed their civilisation, but also their inability to step outside the constraints of their collective Comfort Zones, and change their society to one that was more aligned to their changing World... their entire civilization fell out of synch with the world around them... the world which supported them.

Anyone who questioned the political and social status quo... and suggested there was a better way of doing things perhaps... probably got quickly sacrificed at the top of the nearest stone pyramid.

Humanity as a whole faces the same kind of challenge as we speed headlong into the 21st Century... can we step out of our comfortable lives, and comfortable way of doing things... and face and accept the need to change... and fast?

Only time will tell.

There is a force within each Comfort Zone that fights to maintain the status quo, no matter what horrors lurk within. That is our inner **Saturn**... which we will focus on next...

But there is also a force within us which seeks to expand our Comfort Zone... especially on the cultural and collective level... and that is our inner **Jupiter**.

Fortunately, the more conscious we can become of these inner forces and process... the more we can make them work to our advantage.

That has always been the promise and gift of Astrology.

SATURN

In traditional Astrology, the keywords which we would most commonly associate with **Saturn** are probably... karma, time, life-lessons, foundations, teacher, inflexibility, and limitations.

In **Energy Astrology, Saturn** is associated with the Knee and Elbow Chakras.

Which takes us into the area of flexibility versus inflexibility... because **Saturn** is very much linked to areas where we are inflexible in our attitudes and beliefs... and where we are prepared to be flexible, change and let go of the old and out-dated... especially in relation to our thoughts and beliefs.

And to understand all that, and know what **Saturn** truly means to and for our Comfort Zone... we need to ask this important question...

Is it really a good idea to keep expanding all the time?

WARNING: Another Marvel movie reference coming up soon... and for **Saturn**, this one is literally huge.

OK, I know that the Universe, as a whole, is in a constant state of expansion... with Galaxies flying apart at tremendous speed, across countless billions and billions of light years.

But does that also hold equally as true for us, living on a much, much smaller scale, down on the **Earth**?

Definitely... not... as I shall attempt to explain with the following examples...

In Nature, there are these things called Seasons.

Winter follows Autumn, Autumn follows Summer, Summer follows Spring... and Spring follows Winter.

It's been going on for millions of years and has been very successful.

And this pattern is, hopefully, repeated wherever you go on our Planet... and it is a cycle of expansion and then contraction... flowering, fading, and then rebirth.

Which is the thing which is the most important to understand... and which our ancient ancestors understood well.

So they flowed with the seasons as best they could.

No matter how much we dislike Winter, where we happen to live on the **Earth**, how cold and bleak it may feel... it is essential to the process.

It is a time when the **Earth** energies sink down into the ground, re-charge themselves, and then re-appear in Spring.

If there were no Winter or Winter is cut short for any reason, then you get a weak Spring and a poor harvest in late Summer / Autumn.

Without the period of Winter, there would be no period of re-charge, and so no new energies to kick-start the annual process once again.

Every season within the annual cycle is equally important, and it is foolishness to think otherwise.

Now, let's track this ancient wisdom against the current modern 20th/21st Century business model... the Old Paradigm approach to business.

Do we see a cycle of expansion and contraction... expansion and re-charge?

No... we absolutely do not.

What we see instead is the demand for... 20% ... 25% ... 30% growth each year, every year, for the rest of eternity!

Which is totally impossible... and so in the World economy, we have something called the Boom-Bust Cycle, where the economy continues to expand relentlessly until it suddenly crashes, and is forced to lie fallow during a period of recession... and governments all crave a return to the good times because their popularity is largely based upon telling people they have never had it so good.

Roman Emperors used to bribe the populace with bread and circuses... the modern Western democracies do it with the promise of economic growth and success... vote for us and you will be better off financially... you will be able to buy your way to happiness!

Plus medium, large and multi-national businesses, they are all driven forwards, relentlessly, by their pursuit of profit and constant expansion... grow or die... until some event occurs which shows up the whole enterprise to be unsustainable, or having no real foundations, and so the whole thing collapses into a heap, in need of restructuring, or bankrupt and beyond salvaging.

And usually, this event of doom can be traced back to an act of arrogance, or hubris... where the Senior Management didn't listen to wise counsel, thought they could buck the trend, allowed their egos to run away from them.

For want of a nail, the shoe was lost.
For want of a shoe, the horse was lost.

Usually, these large companies are run by Alpha Males who don't switch off, ever, even when they do take a break... because it is the only way to keep their egos pumped-up.

You see, what really distorts things is the thinking of these Alpha Men at the top (sometimes women, but most often men).

Their view of themselves that they're so rich and powerful that they don't need to worry about the little things or details...

But as we shall soon see... **Saturn** is all about getting the little things right and solid first time out... the building of a firm and secure foundation...

If you don't do that, then the Old Man of the Solar System isn't going to cut you any slack... it's karmic payback time... every time.

And as the Ancient Greeks used to say, those who the Gods want to punish, they first make mad... although in this context of modern Big Business, mad = blind and deaf to every voice but their own ego.

In our modern age, that could also be re-written as... those companies who the Gods want to punish, they first get a bunch of total egomaniacs elected to the Board of Directors (in fact, all it takes is one or two... and the Titanic has suddenly changed course, and is heading straight for the iceberg because the Captain has decided there is no money in shipping, and so they are now in the ice capture and refining business).

OK, I am going to be fair here… and usually a Middle / Senior Manager is under pressure to deliver from their Director, who is under pressure from their Parent / Holding company, who is under pressure from their Shareholders, who are really large Pension companies, who are under pressure to perform so they can deliver a good return to their Customers… etc… etc… a whole, system where the Groups above are pilling down the pressure on the people below… and the people down the bottom are utterly crushed by the weight of financial expectation.

That's a lot of places and levels where the small details can be missed… overlooked… forgotten… or just plain ignored… mistakes and flaws which **Saturn** can later uncover and magnify.

And I mean this quite literally. I have seen this time and time again… at the start of the financial year, the Managing Director gets up, tells the workforce that the company needs to achieve 30% growth that year, but not to worry, because we are all in this together… But then, 8 months later, when they have 4 months to go before the end of the financial year when sales are low to non-existent, and things are looking dire, the Managing Director and the Financial Director get together and decide to boost the accounts by… getting rid of 10% of the workforce (redundancy in the UK, severance in the US)… thus making up the shortfall in the growth (because if they do it 4 months before the end of the financial year, that gives them 4 months to smooth everything over, and hit their yearly target).

Hey, everyone is a winner… Well, no, the people who have been let go aren't too happy about it… but the Managing Director and Financial Director have hit their profit targets, and so have earned their nice big bonus, and can afford that loft conversion or the family holiday in Tahiti, or to send Freddie off for his year studying in the Sorbonne.

… OK, am I being too cynical here?

No, I have seen this scenario played out too many times... this is what happens.

Because the pressure is always on *for constant expansion*... **Jupiter** on steroids... squeezing until the pips cry out in pain, and then throwing a few on the fire, the ones who are surplus to requirements... all so that the people at the top can reap the rewards (and the promised benefits never seem to trickle down to the people at the bottom, who did all the hard work and were at risk of losing their jobs).

Basically, from an Astrological point of view, these people are expecting **Jupiter** to work for them... 24/7... 12 months of the year... year after year... until they retire early... and then some.

They're expecting Summer to last all year round...

They expect the expansion to be constant and never-ending...

They're asking for and expecting the impossible... and in their hubris, they taking short-cuts, making mistakes... weakening the foundation of their whole enterprise.

OK, putting morality to one side, and just looking at it from the point of view of business structure and dynamics... you can probably do this once or twice and get away with it. But the constant pressure to continually make 20% each year... year after year after year... with no let-up, especially when your market isn't as healthy as you would like, puts incredible strain on any business... and is usually the thing which kills them off in the end (although we could argue that this is healthy... the winning factor in capitalism... competitive natural selection etc).

But here is the interesting thing... here are the words that you never hear uttered in the boardrooms of the Big Business World... *"Why don't we have a period of consolidation?"*

The commercial equivalent of Winter... a period where things are allowed to go fallow for a short period and the organisation can re-charge before the next period of expansion.

It doesn't happen. Because the pressure for constant expansion from above is too great.

And what Director is going to stick their neck out and say... *"I think we need to go slow for a while"*.

In the Old Paradigm Business set-up, these things just don't get said, they would be considered a sign of weakness.

And yet, those phrases which are most beloved by Directors and Senior Managers... thinking outside the box... blue sky thinking... they are most likely to occur during Autumn/Winter when someone has a chance to relax and stand-back... then during the hectic times of Spring and Summer.

And I can guarantee you, they seldom occur during times of stress and anxiety... during the *"We are all in this together"* periods.

Let me explain with an example.

I heard this story from a friend of mine, who used to work for a company which had front-office products, and back-office systems (production, customer management systems, accounts, stuff like that).

Now, the company was based on a product set that had been created about 20 years ago, fit the market perfectly, and had continually generated the profits since, but now dominated that particular market, and so this left very little room for growth and new development within that product set... and every attempt to come up with new products, which were just as successful, had largely failed... even though the expectation from above (and there were several levels of above), was that this company was capable of generating 20% growth every year as it had done for the past 20 years.

So the pressure was on, each year, to deliver a minimum 20% growth in profits... and for the last 2 years, there was an annual laying off of people to close the gap so the Directors could achieve their financial targets.

Now... one year, using blue sky thinking perhaps, a senior manager pointed out that... those back-office production and accountancy systems are so old, and so inefficient, that if we spent some time and resources updating and upgrading them, the increase in productivity, the savings through greater efficiency, would help to boost the companies financial health... in fact, the company would probably save more money that way then all the money it might make through releasing that years weak new products.

So she pitched the idea to anyone who would listen... and was totally ignored.

Why?

Well, maybe it was because she was a woman... maybe because all the Directors and salesmen and account managers had their annual bonuses tied to developing/selling the annual new products... making the thought of sorting out back-office systems appear very unattractive. Maybe they just didn't understand what she was talking about, because they were so focused on delivering to the External Customer, they had no real understanding about how their business actually worked internally.

Who knows?

Anyway, she was ignored... the company tried to hit the 20% target with the latest batch of new products... failed dismally... and so another wave of people lost their jobs so that the magic numbers (which might have been plucked out of the air for all we knew) could be achieved.

Now... I am not arguing that it is wrong to earn money (personally, I love having money... it allows me to do cool stuff)... and I am not arguing that business expansion is wrong either... and I am not pitching to be a Communist either...

But what I am strongly suggesting is that the Western, macho, aggressive approach of Constant Business Expansion leads, eventually, to more problems then it solves... and to more pain for more people... especially the little people down the bottom... who are actually doing the lion share of the work.

Unfortunately, it is the people at the top of these organisations, the ones making the decisions, who need to change their thinking to avoid the pain... but all too often they are totally isolated from the pain and can walk away from the consequences of their actions, with their bonus cheque safely tucked in their shirt pocket.

But now... how does all this relate to **Saturn**?

Well... take a look at our Comfort Zone diagram for **Saturn** below...

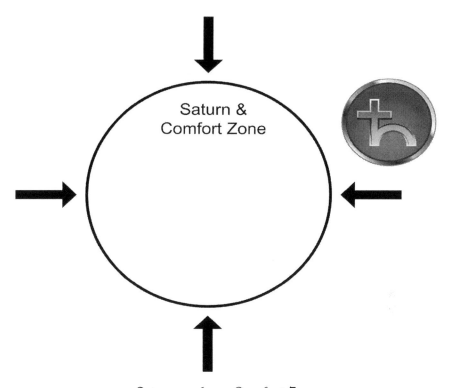

Saturn and our Comfort Zone

Well, if we take a look at this diagram, we can see that **Saturn**, as a force, is one which tries to contain... hold... maybe even push in.

So if **Jupiter** is all about expansion... in contrast, **Saturn** is all about contraction and containment... and the two forces work very much together... especially if an individual knows how to use them well and wisely.

WARNING: Another Marvel movie reference coming up... very soon.

Basically, the message of **Saturn** to **Jupiter**... or anyone alive who happens to be listening...

"Look I don't mind your plans for expansion and growth... but I want you to do it from a firm and stable foundation... so if you do that... if you cross the Is and dot the Ts... everything will work out fine... But if you don't... if you try to run before you can walk... if you move too fast too soon... if you set things up too quickly, with flaws and mistakes all the way... if you try to take dodgy shortcuts... and have shaky foundations... then when I put the pressure on... things are going to fall apart... and you are going to wish you had done things in the right way from the start."

You know that old nursery rhyme...

For want of a nail, the shoe was lost.
For want of a shoe, the horse was lost.
For want of a horse, the rider was lost.
For want of a rider, the battle was lost.
For want of a battle, the kingdom was lost.
And all for the want of a horseshoe nail.

The essence of this nursery rhyme is so **Saturn**...

If you're too focused on all the Big Picture stuff, too obsessed with your dream, that you forget to check all the small details upon which your vision is built... all the little nails which need to be in place for your vision to be firm and secure... then **Saturn** will come along and crucify you, using the same suspect nails... in some way or other.

Many people assume that the containing force of **Saturn** is trying to stop them from having what they want in life... that **Saturn** is a Planet which says No! far too often... which is blocking their progress in life... undermining all their hopes and dreams.

But that's not really true.

Because **Saturn** is all about giving people what they want... but at the right time... when things are stable and built on firm foundations...

so there will be no comeback at a later date...

So if you do the work... and you build it right... then **Saturn** will let **Jupiter** through... and will let things start to grow and expand...

For **Saturn**... if you build it right, they will come...

But if you don't build right or well-enough... then **Saturn** will either block the whole enterprise... or stand back, allow **Jupiter** to expand things, at which point the whole enterprise falls flat on its face, because the flaws and mistakes start to come to the surface and distort the expansion... and you are left wondering what went wrong.

You see... if we return to our Comfort Zone diagram again... there is a subtle dance between **Jupiter** and **Saturn**... between expansion and contraction...

Or maybe that should be apparent contraction...

Yep, here it is... the BIG IDEA... with thanks to the late **Stan Lee** and all the other people at Marvel...

Anyone who has seen the Marvel Movie *Ant-Man*... and the follow-up movie *Ant-Man & The Wasp*... you'll know all about the Quantum Realm below us...

Based on the idea that just as there is an infinity of space above us... there is also an infinity of space below and within us...

Infinitely small spaces which exist between molecules, atoms, protons, and electrons... and everything else which exists down there... in the infinite smallness of space...

Which leads me to consider... maybe **Saturn** isn't always about contracting...

Maybe sometimes **Saturn** is also about *expanding small*...

Maybe **Saturn** is also about expanding into the smallness of energy of any situation or project... testing it... and finding what is there... and discerning whether something was built right or wrong.

I know, I know... a strange idea, perhaps... but stay with me here...

I mean, **Saturn** is all about foundations... and if an engineer or surveyor is identifying whether foundations are strong enough, whether they were built right and stable, for any house built on those foundations... they don't take along a radio telescope...

They're not Astrophysicists studying the Planets and Stars up above...

They take along a microscope... or similar equipment for analysing the microscopic world... because they need to look down and within... they need to look small to find where any faults and weakness are.

And really, it's the same here...

Back in Medieval times, **Saturn** was also known as the Old Devil... well, like they say, the Devil is always in the details.

Just as **Saturn** looks within us... into our personality... **expands small**... to discover where our own faults and weaknesses are located... and then tests them... so that we can fix ourselves, and hopefully grow, become stronger, and then expand in the right way.

Saturn expands small to examine whether the details of any situation where set-up right...

And in the Business examples, I touched upon earlier, they were never set-up right, to begin with... because the Big Bosses in charge where too interested in their Big Vision plans, that they lost sight of what was important, didn't pay attention to the small details, or cared about the little people, and so eventually tripped up on their own egos when **Saturn** eventually paid them a visit...

OK, in this section I have been drawing on the world of Big Business as examples... but the truth of **Saturn** expanding small can be found in any Human interaction and endeavour if you care to look and explore.

That's what **Saturn** is doing when it is testing whether something... some event or situation... was built right...

It's not necessarily contracting... but **expanding small**... getting down and deep into the details... to locate the cracks and weaknesses... to try and make things better if it can... although while it is doing this, it can look like things are on hold for a while... at a standstill... even contracting...

A great example of this is in the book *The Breakthrough Experience*, written by **Dr John Demartini**... which teaches you to approach your issues, life-lessons... the difficult experiences in your life... in a non-dual way...

He tells the story of how he was once working with two New York investment bankers, who had just lost out on a major deal... which would have earned them many millions... and so set them up for life...

Only someone in their firm had blocked the deal going through at the last minute...

And both bankers were red-hot furious with this person...

So **Demartini** was working with them both... trying to get them to move beyond their anger and resentment...

So he asked them...

"OK... what is the potential positive in this situation?"

Their reply... *"Easy... we would have been mega-rich... set-up for the rest of our lives... with second homes in the Carribean..."*

"Next... so what is the potential negative in this situation?"

And this floored the two bankers for a while... and they had to think about it...

But then... one of them finally said...

"Well... I suppose our deal was sailing over the line in terms of legality... and if the financial authorities in the U.S. had found out about it... they might have taken us to court... and we might have ended up in jail... Yep, instead of earning millions... we could have both ended up in jail."

And they both went silent at that point...

And Demartini then said to them... *"So on the one side... this individual blocked a deal going through which might have made you super-rich... But on the other side... they also blocked a deal that was probably highly illegal... and would have ended up in you both going to jail... So how do you feel about this man now... a man who helped prevent you both from doing serious jail time?"*

And their eventual replay...

"Well... now that we see it that way... totally grateful... he saved us from our ourselves... because all we could think about was the money... and we probably cut corners in our negotiations... which would have come back to bite us... badly... Wow... that guy saved our butts... and all we have done is be furious at him... but he saved us..."

And at that point... their anger towards the guy totally transformed... into gratitude... and they even went and thanked him.

And that... I believe... highlights the pivot point in learning a life-lesson... which brings us back to **Saturn** again...

Jupiter is there to help us expand... and **Saturn** is there too, hopefully, to save us from ourselves... which ties into the whole life-lesson thing again with regards to **Saturn**.

Remember, the message of **Saturn** for us all... no exceptions:

"Look I don't mind your plans for expansion and growth... but I want you to do it from a firm and stable foundation... so if you do that... if you cross the Is and dot the Ts... everything will work out fine... But if you don't... if you try to run before you can walk... if you move too fast too soon... if you set things up too quickly, with flaws and mistakes all the way... if you try to take dodgy shortcuts... and have shaky foundations... then when I put the pressure on... things are going to fall apart... and you are going to wish you had done things in the right way from the start."

So it's always best to try and set things up right at the start... best we can... whether in personal development, business, education, or relationships...

The Universe all around us is expanding... and it wants us to expand with it...

But we have got to do it in the right way...

That's the real lesson of **Saturn**...

Energy Astrology

And if you want to find the flaws and weaknesses ahead of time...
better learn to surf **Saturn**.

Chapter 3-6: Chiron

To understand the Planetoid **Chiron**, from an **Energy Astrology** perspective, we need to think less Planetoid, and more Black Hole.

As the diagram below shows, **Chiron** can appear anywhere inside our Comfort Zone, or just outside the Zone, or even crossing over the boundary of our Comfort Zone, but it is a psychological space *where our Mind and Consciousness does not want to venture*, because, for some reason, entering that space is too painful for us, and, early on in life, our only defence against all the immense hurt and pain, connected with this psychological location, is to try and forget about this Black Hole in our psyche.

CHIRON

OK, it's not really a Black Hole, but in an Astrological Chart, **Chiron** does act like a Black Hole in many ways, pulling in the light of our Consciousness, while we fight to pull away from its influence and inherent pain.

And that's how we struggle on in life until we know how to counteract its effects.

In the whole of our Astrological Pantheon of Planets, **Chiron** is probably the hardest one to understand, approach, and deal with.

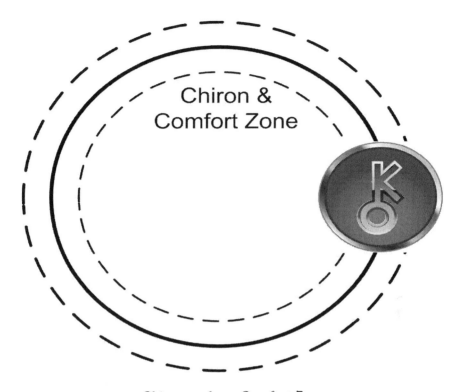

Chiron and our Comfort Zone

Chiron and our Comfort Zone

And the reason for this is because it represents the one place in our Subtle Anatomy where ***it is just not possible to protect ourselves***, and where any attempt at creating an effective boundary or shield is an actual impossibility... where even bringing something inside our Comfort Zone doesn't help... in fact, it just makes our life harder and more painful (and trying to keep it outside doesn't help either).

This is the painful psychological space associated with the Planetoid **Chiron** in our Astrological natal chart, and it is a place where it is impossible for us to create or erect any kind of psychological barrier against the great pain which exists on the other side of the Black Hole.

To explain where this no boundary space is located in our Subtle Anatomy, and why it is not possible to protect ourselves there, I need to take you on a little trip, not only into the field of Astrology but also back into the mythology of ancient Greece.

In Greek mythology, **Chiron** was a centaur, a creature half-man and half-horse. Amongst the Centaurs, he was quite unique. The majority of Centaurs were little better than beasts, dominated by their animal nature. But **Chiron** was not only in control of his animal side, but he was learned and wise and had even been taught the healing arts by the God **Apollo** himself. He, therefore, acted as counselor and tutor to all the Greek heroes, who would spend time with him before they embarked on their great individual quests. He was the most civilized, and civilizing, of all the Centaurs, and had learned to contain and control his animal passions.

According to the ancient Greeks, Humanity owes a great deal to **Chiron**.

Which leads me to assume that, before any individual goes off on a dangerous quest, and they want to succeed, they will need to locate and spend time with their inner **Chiron**. This, of course, is a paradox. In the real world, individuals don't experience their **Chiron return** until their 49th or 50th year. However, the Ancient Greek heroes were all much younger men, and probably never got to see their 40s, let alone live to the age of 50. But, if we step back, and look for a more metaphorical meaning, for any quest to succeed we need first to have made peace with our own inner **Chiron**, we need to have gained a certain degree of emotional integration for our life quest to succeed.

One particularly fateful day **Chiron** was visited by **Hercules**, who in many ways was the most popular Hero in the Greek Pantheon... a sort of act now, think later sort of guy... although with more emphasis on the acting, and much less on the thinking it through side.

Hercules had just slain **the Hydra**, a fierce and terrifying beast, whose blood was deadly to any mortal creature who came into physical contact with it. Being a practical sort, **Hercules** had made his own set of poison arrows from dipping them into the **Hydra's blood**. Unfortunately, **Hercules** also had a reputation for being clumsy, and so while staying in **Chiron's cave**, he accidentally scratched **Chiron's flank** with one of these deadly, poisoned arrows.

Now **Chiron** was an immortal creature, and so could not die, however, the blood of **the Hydra** was deadly poison... and so **Chiron** was caught in a place betwixt life and death. He couldn't die but was trapped in a state of perpetual pain and suffering, and the irony was, although he was the world's greatest healer, thanks to **Apollo**, he could do nothing to heal himself, or relieve the excruciating pain, or drain out the **Hydra's blood** from his system. He was a healer, unable to heal himself. He continued in this state of unending pain until **Zeus**, King of the Gods, took pity on him and arranged a life-swap with **Prometheus the Titan**. **Chiron** was allowed to die, and was transformed into a constellation of stars, in return for **Prometheus** being set free from his perpetual torment of being chained to a rock, and having his liver torn out afresh each day by an eagle, all because he had stolen fire from the Gods and given it to mortal men (... but that's another story entirely).

I think the fact that what happened is down to **Hercules**... who was a clumsy sort of Hero... also adds something to the meaning of **Chiron**... that the great pain wasn't intentional, that it almost arises due to an accident.

Now... In Western Astrology, the Planetoid **Chiron**, which roughly lies between the planets **Saturn** and **Uranus**, makes an orbit of our **Sun** every 49 to 50 years, so around this age people experience their **Chiron return** (i.e. **Chiron** returns to the same spot on your Astrological natal chart as on the day you were born).

Drawing on the Greek myth, in the Western Astrology system, **Chiron** is associated with the wounded healer, and the concept that within our psyche there is a place where we have experienced, and still continue to experience unimaginable and unending pain, mental, emotional and/or physical suffering. It is also believed that there is nothing that we or others can ever do to end or heal this pain. It is only through the application of compassion, acceptance and forgiveness that we can learn to possibly channel this pain towards a more constructive end.

Although, the myth does suggest that **Chiron's pain** can be brought to an end through the intervention of a transpersonal force or power – i.e. literally being taken by God and placed in amongst the stars. But what are compassion, love and forgiveness if not transpersonal powers?

And often the healing isn't just about compassion, acceptance and forgiveness, but about self-compassion, self-acceptance and self-forgiveness, which sometimes are harder to achieve, but often the real healing juice we need.

If we cannot learn to heal ourselves, then at least we can use what our **Inner Chiron** has taught us to heal others. But this possibility of being able to heal others comes at quite a high price to the individual self. Many New Age Astrology books put too much emphasis upon the healing side of **Chiron**, while downplaying the excruciating pain part, and suggest the gift of healing is something you can casually acquire just through wishing it to be, or through completing a few courses on New Age healing.

From my own experience, based on several years struggling with the **Chiron process**, I can honestly say that it just doesn't work that way. You must literally be prepared to face your pain, and try to heal and learn from it, while also understanding that your own personal healing is impossible, that you are engaged in a fool's quest, and only then, if you can continue to walk on, knowing that nothing you learn will ever save you, will you be given the power to heal others. It's a rite of passage without any chance of gaining any personal reward.

It's a Grail Quest kind of process, only when you totally surrender and give-up in a positive way, will you be given what you seek and most need.

My father struggled with Parkinson's Disease until his transition in late 2017. There was no magic cure, only drugs which could delay the progress of the illness. In this context, healing wasn't about suddenly being able to throw away his sticks and walk unaided... it was about being able to still continue, even in the face of adversity. As **Victor Frankl** once said, even when everything else has been taken away from a Man, he still has the ability to choose how he responds to the circumstances he finds himself in... even on his deathbed. That is his greatest freedom, and that is also where true victory often lies.

The modern astrologer **Liz Greene** describes the reality of **Chiron** in a way I have found to be particularly useful:

*"With **Chiron**, there is a sense of something unfair hurting or humiliating us, something that we didn't merit... There is an irredeemable flaw. Something has crippled us, and because of that injury we must take a different path in life, one which often we feel we would not have chosen if we had been left "intact"... Many of you who keep pets will know that an animal in extreme pain will bite, kick, or claw anyone who comes near, even if one is trying to help."* (**Liz Greene**, *Barriers & Boundaries: The Horoscope and the Defences of the Personality, Centre for Psychological Astrology Press, 1998*)

As **Greene** suggests, when experiencing the pain and suffering of **Chiron**, the beloved family pet turns into a savage beast, which bites the owner's hand, even when the owner is only trying to help or provide comfort... because the animal is in so much pain, it defends itself without thinking.

The idea of **Chiron** when applied to the Astrological natal chart is that every individual has someplace in their psyche where they are the same as this poor, suffering animal, where they will lash out at anyone who comes near, or who tries to help them. When this pain zone is triggered, an individual's automatic, unconscious defences take over.

This is one of the things that people need to understand about **Chiron**... the pain is *intolerable*, and eats away at our rational mind, our ability to put things into perspective, to look on the positive side, all the things that normally help us to deal with our pain and suffering... and, as **Greene** rightly points out, during a **Chiron transit** people are often heard to say *"This is so unfair... what have I ever done to deserve this!"*

The difference between **Saturn** and **Chiron** is that with **Saturn**, you can at least build tangible defences to hold back the pain or develop a strategy to relieve it. But with **Chiron**, the defences are less tangible, and more a case of misdirection. If you can never build an effective boundary to keep out the pain of your **Chiron**, then your next best defence is to disguise it so that it isn't constantly in your view/awareness.

Which is why, in our Comfort Zone metaphor, I describe **Chiron** as a Black Hole, lurking somewhere in our psyche... a place where our Consciousness does not want to go... and we have disguised it in some way so that it is no longer visible to our everyday Mind... literally out of sight, out of Mind.

This space can be inside our Comfort Zone, or lurking just outside, connected to someplace we really need or want to go for our self-development, but which is blocked off to us, or can even cross over the boundary line of our Comfort Zone. All of the above is possible with Chiron.

However, during your **Chiron Return**, or a heavy **Chiron transit**, someone or something pulls back the magic curtain of illusion behind which you have hidden your **Inner Chiron**, allowing you to see and experience the pain once again, and that pain, triggered by some external circumstance, perhaps, comes flooding back.

In terms of **Energy Astrology**, I have found that **Chiron** energetically resonates with the Thymus Chakra, which is above the Heart Chakra, and is physically located in the centre of our upper chest. It is also associated with our ability to love and accept ourselves.

The Thymus Gland/Chakra is also believed to be the master controller for our 12 Meridians, and so has a great deal of influence on the flow of Chi through our Meridian system. And so if we block or suppress it, there is bound to be some kind of distortion in our energy system.

According to **Liz Greene**, the negative personal feelings and emotions normally associated with **Chiron** are:

• Intolerable Pain & Suffering

• Humiliation

However, I would like to add the following two to this list:

• The Feeling of Being Unloved (and so cut-off and disconnected)

• Rage

When someone is undergoing a heavy **Chiron transit**, alongside the pain, there is a feeling of being totally cut-off, and being unloved and unlovable. You feel totally alone, and you also feel that no one is going to come and help you. Ever.

In fact, there is no one who could possibly help you. You feel separated, adrift and alone.

And it feels so unfair... because you can't understand why any of this is your fault. It can feel like the whole Universe is ganging up on you for no apparent reason, and your life has been completely overturned.

In addition, rage is a feeling which often overtakes someone who is undergoing a **Chiron return** or difficult transit. Rage is defined as an extreme form of anger, where the individual loses control of their senses and becomes an uncontrollable blind rage. Lashing out without thinking. Just like a wounded animal.

This is one of the reasons why I believe **The Incredible Hulk** is one of the fan favourites of all the Marvel Heroes... because many people can identify with **the Hulk**... because we all have a large Green Rage Monster in us somewhere, thanks to **Chiron**.

In Western Astrology, **Chiron** has not been assigned rulership to any of the 12 Astrological signs, although there was an attempt by the Astrologer **Barbara Hand Clow** to assign **Chiron** to the rulership of Virgo. Personally, because of their shared connection to rage, I believe **Chiron** has more resonance to Capricorn than any other Astrological Sign, although I don't believe it rules any of them.

Why? Because **Chiron** is capable of channelling the negative energies associated with any of the 12 Astrological Signs... and so doesn't belong to any single Astrological Sign... and this is where it starts to get really interesting... because the Sign in which **Chiron** is located in our chart also shows us the energies to which we are totally vulnerable, the negative energies against which we are totally defenceless.

Here the feeling associated with our **Chiron sign** is the trigger
for our feelings of humiliation, of being unloved, of spiritual
disconnect, of rage and intolerable pain. But it is more than just that
(…if that wasn't bad enough). Our **Chiron sign** also indicates where
we are totally open and defenceless to a particular type of Glamour.

Glamours are basically accumulated clouds of emotional energy,
especially negative emotional energy, which can attach to people,
places and groups, and influence their behaviour. Whenever
someone experiences an emotion internally, they also radiate that
emotional energy externally, and that energy tends to merge with
other similar energies to create vast Glamour clouds.

So with Glamours, you are basically dealing with the collective pain
of Humanity on some level… all the fear, all the shame, all the guilt,
all the anxiety… which Humanity has been able to generate, now
and since the dawn of our species.

If you think of Glamours as a kind of emotional toxic pollution, then
you won't be far wrong.

And just like a cloud of toxic smog can affect people's health… so a
toxic Glamour can also affect people's emotions… especially those
who are super-sensitive to it.

And thanks to **Chiron**, every individual is super-sensitive to one
particular type of Glamour… is plugged into one type of World
suffering.

OK… Glamours can be destroyed and eliminated… but that
takes focus and effort… and just as the majority of Humanity is
not currently involved, or much concerned, with cleaning up
the planet… there aren't too many people tackling the Glamour
problem either (… and maybe there is a strong connection between
the two).

So... if **Chiron**, and the Thymus Chakra, is a place in our Subtle Anatomy where we cannot erect any kind of barrier or boundary, then our **Chiron Sign** shows us which particular type of Glamour we have no defence against, as is detailed in the table below:

- **Aries Chiron** = Glamour of Fear
- **Taurus Chiron** = Glamour of Despair
- **Gemini Chiron** = Glamour of Unhappiness
- **Cancer Chiron** = Glamour of Hunger & Emptiness
- **Leo Chiron** = Glamour of Anger
- **Virgo Chiron** = Glamour of Guilt
- **Libra Chiron** = Glamour of Regret
- **Scorpio Chiron** = Glamour of Frustration
- **Sagittarius Chiron** = Glamour of Anxiety
- **Capricorn Chiron** = Glamour of Rage
- **Aquarius Chiron** = Glamour of Arrogance
- **Pisces Chiron** = Glamour of Sadness

For example, someone with:

• **Chiron in Pisces** is totally open to and has no defence against the Glamour of Sadness.

• **Chiron in Scorpio** is totally open to and has no defence against the Glamour of Frustration.

• **Chiron in Leo** is totally open to and has no defence against the Glamour of Anger.

In each of these cases, the individual is completely open to that Glamour, and literally to all the pain and suffering in the World ever experienced on that particular wavelength of Consciousness. For example, for someone with **Chiron in Pisces**, it isn't just a case of their having to deal with their family sadness, or the sadness from a past life, or the sadness passed down along their ancestral line, or the sadness of the group of people they choose to associate with.

No. A person is literally plugged in to all the sadness in the World, and as a child, there is nothing they can do to prevent it... except learn to misdirect their consciousness.

A Chiron transit can feel like this...

With **Chiron** and Glamours, the individual is literally standing alone in front of a massive tsunami, all the collective pain, coming their way.

This is why **Liz Greene** is right when she says that it feels so unfair. What possible sin or karma would require someone to be literally crucified on a cross made from all the World's sadness, or anger, or guilt, or fear? They have done nothing to deserve this?

But in reality, it has nothing to do with sin or a mistake made in a past life, and it has everything to do with a design flaw in our Subtle

Anatomy (and that is also there for a good reason).

Plus, we also have to remember, that alongside our individual **Chiron**, the **Chiron** in the sky is also transiting around the Solar System. passing through all the 12 Astrological Signs, stirring things up for Humanity and us as a whole.

Which may be a good thing, even when it hurts like Hell while we are going through the process.

Because **Chiron** literally reaches the parts of our individual and collective psyche which the other Planets cannot reach.

Let me explain that with this analogy.

The Glass of Water Analogy below comes from **Bruce Frantzis Kumer**, who got it from his final Taoist Master **Liu Hung Chieh** (although I have amended the metaphor slightly to better fit in with a therapy context, it is still a brilliant analogy either way). The story upon which this analogy is based is to be found in **Kumer's** book *Relaxing Into Your Being: The Water Method of Taoist Meditation*, page 105.

The basics of the analogy are as follows:

Take a clear glass, fill it with water, pour some sand into the glass, and then leave the sand to slowly settle to the bottom of the glass. As it does so, the water becomes clear.

Take a spoon, stir up the water, and observe how the sand is also stirred up by the motion of the water, making the clear water clouded again.

Let the water stand, and observe how the sand slowly settles to the bottom of the glass once again.

Well, what does that show us?

Well, the glass is Us as an individual, our personality, and the clear water is our Consciousness.

The sand is all our psychic material and debris, our beliefs, fears, and/or karma, which is clouding, disguising, or hiding our true Consciousness, making it murky.

Normally, we don't see this stuff, because we go through life in such a way that our Consciousness is stable, and the karmic sand stays still at the bottom of our container.

But we can't live our lives that way 24/7, 52 weeks of the year, for the whole of our life, because eventually life comes along with a big spoon and stirs things up, stirs us up.

Maybe we are made redundant, maybe our one and only Soul-mate leaves us, maybe a parent or child dies suddenly and unexpectedly, maybe we are living in a war-zone, or at a time of economic or political turbulence.

And when that happens our Consciousness is stirred up, and all the material at the bottom of our container is automatically disturbed and shaken, and so starts to cloud our Consciousness, and suddenly everything becomes murky and unclear. We can't see where we are going, we don't know who we are anymore, we may not even be in control of our lives, which can be very scary indeed, and instead, we feel we are at the mercy of unknown desires, thoughts and feelings, crashing against us like some monster psychic tsunami.

We feel that our safe life is at an end, we don't know what is happening, we are in pain, and we don't know what to do to get it to stop, and we can't even see a way forward anymore.

Now, at this point, we usually find that time is a great healer, in that, once the stirring stops, the debris settles down in our Unconscious Mind, just as the sand will eventually settle down to the bottom of the glass, and the water becomes clear once again.

It just takes time and patience...

Which means that over time, eventually our experience settles, and clear Consciousness returns, just like the sand in a glass of water.

This is sometimes why conventional talk counselling works, not that the therapist has done anything much, except listen, but over time things have just settled down by themselves, and the client has achieved a degree of clarity, which the therapist can then take credit for.

But the problem is that, after things have settled down again, the sand is still down there at the bottom of the glass, and so can still be stirred up again by some future event or shift. And remember, this is all the psychic material which you don't want to face, so you are probably glad that it has gone away for a while at least, out of sight, out of mind. You feel much better, and that's what counts, even though nothing much got healed or resolved along the way.

For true healing to occur, then you must tackle the question of how to get rid of the sand at the bottom of the glass.

Well, let's go back to the Glass of Water Analogy.

Take the glass with the sand, hold it underneath a tap, and turn the tap on fast.

Water pours from the tap, rushing down into the glass, and at first, the rushing water stirs up the sand, making the glass cloudy again.

But as more and more water pours into the glass, it starts to pour out over the sides of the glass, taking some of the sand with it,

As more water pours into the glass, so the process continues, over time, more and more sand is carried away by the overflowing water, making the water still within the glass become clearer and clearer.

If you were to turn off the tap now and let the water stand for a while, you would see that even if there is still some sand left still in the glass, it is far less dark and unclear then before.

Well, this is what also happens when someone goes in for energy healing, whether for therapeutic, personal or spiritual development.

The energy stirs you up, and things may look worse for a while.

But if you stick with it, if you can be still and patient in the midst of all the inner chaos, then eventually the flowing energy starts to carry all your psychic debris away.

And so you become clearer and clearer.

Initially, all you could see was the sand clouding the water, but as the sand is gradually washed away, you start to become more aware of the clear water in which the sand is suspended, and when this starts to happen, there is much less negative psychic material which can knock you off centre.

The same is true for personal growth.

First, you are only conscious of your issues, your limitations, what is wrong with your life, and what isn't working inside your head.

But as your Consciousness clears, as you become less and less identified with the psychic sand swirling around, you start to look beyond this, and realize that there is a new clarity within your Mind, or better still a clarity behind your Mind, that you are more than your issues, more than your Mind and personality.

As time passes, you start to become more conscious of your Consciousness.

So how does that all relate to **Chiron**?

Well… **Chiron** is the one Planetoid that can really reach down and stir up the bottom of the psychic glass, both in terms of the individual and also in terms of the collective, all the material that you were hoping to avoid.

And also like the 3 Transpersonals (**Uranus**, **Neptune**, **Pluto**), as we shall soon discover, it can seriously test the integrity of our Comfort Zone, and its relationship to the World around us, make us re-assess who and what we are.

Basically, **Chiron** makes us look at things we just don't want to look at because they hurt too much, because they are too painful for us to contemplate, and for Soul Healing, that is a must (even if it hurts like Hell).

From my own experience with **Chiron**, my own life has been put back on course after each encounter, so I was more aligned to my real Soul purpose for this lifetime.

OK, it wasn't the direction I originally intended to take in life, but now, looking back, I was put on the most right and fulfilling direction for my highest reason for coming and being here.

And so I am grateful it happened.

Although at the time, it hurt like Hell and felt so unfair, and whether I would have done it if had known what lay ahead, debatable.

Chiron is the Planetoid which makes us look at that which we don't want to look at, which we are trying to hide from so that we can

Volume 1 - Introduction

change and transform.

So when I consider the Black Hole that is **Chiron**, and all that we have discussed above, the following poem from the Sufi poet **Rumi** comes to mind:

A chickpea leaps almost over the rim of the pot where it's being boiled.

'Why are you doing this to me?'

The cook knocks him down with the ladle.

'Don't you try to jump out. You think I'm torturing you. I'm giving you flavor, so you can mix with spices and rice and be the lovely vitality of a human being. Remember when you drank rain in the garden. That was for this.'

(Translated: *Coleman Banks*)

For anyone who has ever been through it, and successfully come out the other side transformed... the **Chiron** healing journey is kind of like that.

Final Thought... if all the above sounds ultra negative and gloomy... there is also a positive and amazing side to **Chiron**... but it only arises after you have faced and willingly embraced the apparent negative... and so will have to be for another time and place.

OK... clue... when **Chiron** is healed and set amongst the stars... **Prometheus** is set free.

Page 385

Chapter 3-7: Uranus, Neptune & Pluto

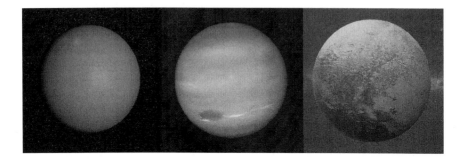

The 3 Transpersonal Planets - Uranus, Neptune & Pluto

There is an ancient Indian teaching story about a young man who goes into the forest to study with **Lord Shiva**, to become part of his ashram, in search of enlightenment.

One day, **Lord Shiva** turns to the young man, saying "*Could you please fetch me a cup of freshwater.*"

So the young man leaves the forest, heads for the nearest village, and knocks on the door of the first hut he finds.

A beautiful, young woman opens the door.

The young man asks her if he could have a cup of freshwater, to which she says agrees, and goes and brings him a cup filled with cool, freshwater.

But then she says to him:

"It's such a long trip back into the forest and your ashram, and night will soon be falling. Why not stay the night, take food with my family and me, and then start on your return trip in the morning."

Which is exactly what he did, enjoying the food prepared by her family, and a comfortable, warm bed for the night.

But then, in the morning there was another reason for him to stay longer, and in the afternoon, another reason arose to stay, and in the evening, he decides to stay over one more night.

Then, before he knows it, he has fallen in love with the young woman, and they are soon married.

They settle down in the village, start to farm their own land, and very soon they have children, and then grandchildren and their long life together is both prosperous and happy.

Over many years, the young man matures and grows old.

And one day, 60 years later, as he sits outside his hut, contemplating all he has achieved, and how good life has been to him, a huge tsunami wave roars up through the valley, destroying all in its path.

It destroys his crops, it destroys his properties, it destroys their village, and it kills all the members of his family, all before his very eyes.

And in the final moment, before the great tsunami wave crashes down and kills him, the old man looks up and sees that on top of the tsunami wave, riding it, is **Lord Shiva**, who looks down at the elderly man with great sadness, and says, *"I am still waiting for my* *cup of freshwater."*

Now, as with many ancient teaching stories, this one has multiple meanings.

The meaning which arises first is that we all have a life-purpose, something which we have come here to do, with limited time to achieve it, and it so easy to get sidetracked, to get blown off course.

So in the final moments of their life, many people must think, *"No! That's what I wanted and needed to do in this lifetime, and I didn't get around to it!"*

But the other meaning which is most apparent here is that this story highlights the process surrounding the **3 Transpersonal Planets**, especially concerning our psychological Comfort Zone.

No matter how well prepared we are, no matter how secure we believe our Comfort Zone has been built around us, how firm the foundations of our life, there is no way we can stand firm against all that the Universe can throw at us.

There is always the unknown, the unexpected, waiting around the corner of life to ambush us.

And the thing is, our Comfort Zone is only intended to keep the anxiety at bay and provide us with a set of skills to hopefully cope with some of the bad things if they do occur.

But it cannot stop ALL the possible bad things from happening.

Nothing ever can, because:

- Your Comfort Zone may contain the skills you need to survive an economic downturn, but it won't prevent it from occurring, and it won't stop you suffering some loss.

- Your Comfort Zone may contain the skills you need to survive an earthquake, knowing what to do to protect yourself and your family best, but it won't prevent it, and it won't stop you suffering some loss, and it won't guarantee that you and your family will survive.

Your Comfort Zone would also not be of any use if our Sun were to turn Super-Nova and burn up the Earth, it would not be able to protect you in any way. OK, maybe next year, someone invents a spacecraft that can travel faster than light, and allow you to escape to another Solar System, that would be a way of escaping. But right now, there is no spaceship, no other options exist, and so your Comfort Zone would be of no effective use.

Our Comfort Zone exists to help us to navigate through life, and hold back the anxiety connected with the thought of bad things happening to us, especially if and when we venture outside of our Comfort Zone.

But the thing with the **3 Transpersonal Plants**... **Uranus, Neptune** and **Pluto**... they all represent different forces which exist outside our Comfort Zone, forces which can literally blow our Comfort Zone up and out of the water, completely, and over which we have no influence or control.

The **3 Transpersonal Planets** represent external, Universal forces against which our Ego and Comfort Zone can erect no credible defence.

Our Comfort Zone is literally blown apart whenever we seriously encounter any of the **3 Transpersonal Planets** headon.

OK, each of these 3 Planets works in different ways, blows us apart in different ways, but the outcome is the same. Our Comfort Zone is either shaken to its foundation, or torn down, and can no longer serve us and function in the way that it once did.

Now, in a Universe which many Spiritual Masters say is friendly, why would the Universe want to do that to us?

Why would the Universe want to give birth to us, raise us and support us and then want to blow us up?

It makes no sense.

Well, actually it does make perfect sense, but we do need to radically change our perspective in order to understand what is happening. We have to look at the situation, what is really going on, from the perspective of the Universe.

Let's rewind a few sentences, back to:

Our Comfort Zone is either shaken to its foundation, or torn down, and can no longer serve us and function in the way that it once did.

The key phrase there is can no longer serve us and function in the way that it once did.

The Enlightened Master **Meister Eckhart** once said that:

"The eye with which I see God is the same eye with which God sees me."

Or put another way, the Universe is learning and growing through each of us, when we learn and grow. Our Consciousness is the same Consciousness as the Universe, all around us, so there is no separation.

So when our individual Consciousness expands, so does the Universal Consciousness, win-win.

However, a problem arises when you also factor in the Human Mind,

Personality, and Ego.

I once had some dealings with a Big Financier, a Man who worked for a Financial Institution in the City of London, and he was rich, powerful, successful, and also totally miserable.

You see, when you talked to him about his life and early dreams, when you looked at his Astrological chart, and when you listened to his early life story, it soon became apparent that he never wanted to be a Banker, instead, he wanted to be an Artist.

But the trouble was, under pressure from his family, especially his father, he chose the safe route of money and security and not the route of happiness and purpose. So his inner misery arose from the fact that he was not following the passion and calling of his Heart, and that is a void which no amount of external success, money and physical stuff can ever fill. And shouting out at the Universe *"Look... I am doing this to please my Father!"* that doesn't cut it either. Either you are following the Call of your Heart, or you are not.

But from the perspective of the Universe," *Wait, we gave birth to you to learn about Art, not Finance. We have other people incarnate who are meant to focus in on that? You're not following your true life-purpose, and all the situations, the relationships which were meant to happen in your life, aren't happening, because you are going in totally the wrong direction? You didn't marry the person you agreed to, you didn't even meet them, and you didn't give birth to the children you were meant to. Those people have had to live totally different lives as a consequence of your actions and choices. Your life is totally not what was planned out. There are repercussions and ripples, all over the place, all in response to you going in a different life-direction."*

According to **Eckhart**, The eye with which I see God is the same eye with which God sees me.

But when that eye is the wrong place, seeing the wrong picture, experiencing the wrong things, not what God was expecting, it's a BIG problem.

It's kind of like NASA sending up a space probe, destined and designed for Mars, which decides to go to Venus instead. Not a good idea, especially when it is Planet for which the probe (i.e. you) were not designed.

I know another man who went into the British Army, under pressure from his family tradition, when what he really wanted was to be a Doctor. But in his family, for the last four generations, all the sons had gone into the Army, and so he thought he would be letting the side down not to follow in the family tradition, even when it wasn't the true calling of his heart.

And what I always find fascinating, how we continue to tie ourselves up in knots, and can't see it, even when a viable solution presents itself, such as:

"Now that you have all this money, literally in the Bank, why not leave Banking, and start studying Art, why can't you become a painter now. Plus your father is dead now, what's to stop you?"

"Why can't you become an Army Doctor, isn't that possible? Wouldn't that be the best of both worlds?"

But often, we limit ourselves and sabotage ourselves on so many different levels. We're just not aware that it is happening. We're not able to think outside the box we have trapped ourselves in.

One of the saddest things anyone can say, *"No, sorry, it's too late to change now."*

When you hear that you know that someone's Comfort Zone has turned into their cage and prison.

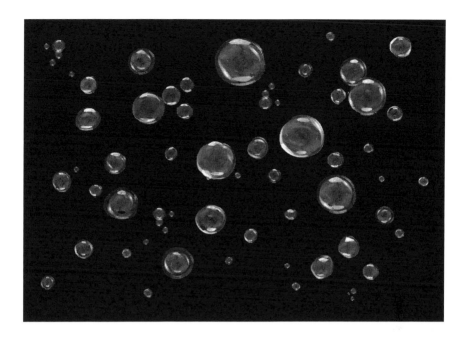

A Universe of Floating Bubbles

A good way of getting your mind around all this is if we take our Comfort Zone, and turn it 3D, into a sphere.

And then imagine a Universe full of floating Soap Bubbles.

So imagine that each Bubble is an individual Human Comfort Zone, floating through their life, floating through the Universe.

In this analogy, the whole Human Race is 7 to 8 billion Soap Bubbles, floating and moving in this Universal space + interacting and relating, some bumping up against each other and sticking together, others colliding, and then shooting off in different directions.

And you can also have Bubbles inside Bubbles, inside other Bubbles, which is the equivalent of a Human Comfort Zone inside the Family Comfort Zone inside the National Comfort Zone. Our individual Bubble can be located inside a whole host of different larger Bubbles, just as we can be connected to, and held within, a whole host of different Comfort Zones. - a kind of multi-dimensional series of Venn diagrams perhaps.

But here's the interesting twist, and remember, we're coming at this from the Soul perspective.

In this Universal Space, if the Bubble is in resonance with the energies around it, then it will rise up, and if not, if it is not in resonance with the energies around it, it will start to sink.

And rising up equates to happy and fulfilled, and sinking down equates to unhappy and miserable.

In the Lightbody tradition, this rising or falling is known Self-Exciting.

So if our Bubble is rising, then this means that our Comfort Zone, all that we believe and identify with is roughly in resonance with the energies which surround us. We are lifted and buoyant, which is another way to describe being in the Flow.

So this is the equivalent of someone who wants to be a Doctor, finally making it to medical school, completing their studies, and following the calling of their Heart.

(In Energy Astrology, this ability to be in resonance with the energies all around us, and to be light and buoyant, is linked to Taurus and our Triple Warmer Meridian.)

But if we are sinking down, becoming more miserable and unhappy, then this means that our Comfort Zone is definitely not in resonance with the surrounding energies, and we are no longer in the general

Flow of life.

Now, returning to our earlier example of the Financial Man, the City Banker, that was a person who had definitely fallen out of the Flow and was unhappy and miserable, despite all the money and prestige.

OK, during his life, he had managed to acquire skills and resources, stepping out of his Comfort Zone enough to achieve a successful life, so from the perspective of the External World he looked rich and highly successful.

All that can definitely happen; it is possible. On one level, it is possible to step out of your Comfort Zone to get what you need and be successful but totally fail on another level, because the general direction of your life is no longer aligned with your Heart or true life-purpose.

From the perspective of the Energy Universe, this man was a failure and was sinking down, fast, which was fuelling his inner sense of misery, Heart pain, and desperation, because his unfulfilled life-purpose was not in harmony with the Energy Universe.

And when you step back to think about it, our Universe is more energy then it is solid matter, so energy and Flow always decides true success and fulfilment in the end.

OK, many people cling on to their misery, in the same way that someone desperately clings to a life-raft. But in the end, misery never saved anyone.

OK, from my observations, when someone decides not to follow their Heart passion and life-purpose, then the Universe starts to re-write the life around them, re-write their life-script. So it's not that they will never find happiness or love, and the Universe does try to make the best of the new direction they are taking. After all, each individual has free will and can choose to head off in a different life-direction.

But there is a heavy cost to going against your Heart purpose, a price that will need to be paid down the line. And no one can ever avoid it.

It's as if all the missed chances, the relationships that never happened, the opportunities that were never taken up and followed, all the seeds and skills that never had a chance to flower, eventually start to weigh down an individual's heart. And there is no rewind button on life, all of us have to live with the consequences of our choices.

Now, the answer to the problem of sinking is fairly easy. Change the contents of your Comfort Zone to bring it back into resonance with the surrounding energies, so you get back into the rising up Flow. And it is never too late to do that. Even right at the end of their life, some people do shift and seriously change within, I have seen it, and so know it possible.

Yes, it is the answer, but obviously, it's often easier said than done.

Remember, all the new ideas which we would need to bring us back into the Flow, back into resonance and the rising, are located outside of our existing Comfort Zone, and so will mean we will have to go outside of our Comfort Zone, into some level of anxiety, in order to get these new ideas, own them, and then integrate them back into ourselves, to bring us back into resonance.

And like I said, that's often easier said than done, plus there is also the whole *How exactly do you do that?* to consider.

But the other problem is, sometimes, an individual is just not capable of doing that. They are so tied up inside themselves, so conflicted, tied down within, that they block themselves repeatedly. They either don't want to change or cannot change. Or don't believe they can change.

They stop themselves, worried about what their father might think, even when their father died twenty-five years ago, and so prevent themselves again... and again... from living the life they are meant to be living.

So what does the Universe do then, when someone is not aligned with their Heart? Does it give up on that individual?

To be honest, sometimes it does give up, the Universe can only set-up so many chances or fresh starts in a single lifetime, and we all run out of time in the end.

Eventually, even the Universe gives up, saying *"OK, we're throwing in the towel on this current incarnation, press the reincarnation button, let's see if we can do better next time around."*

Or, while there is still time, does it send in the Big Boys... the **3 Transpersonal Planets**... **Uranus**, **Neptune** or **Pluto**... to try to rectify things, to try and save the individual and the situation?

Remember, the Universe was expecting to learn something through the metaphorical eyes of that individual, and so will try to get things back on track, because it's got a lot invested in each of us. Otherwise, that individual and life was a No Show from the Universe's perspective.

Basically, it's like when you invest money in a company, and they are struggling, and they ask for your help in turning the situation around. If you say Yes, there is no guarantee that things will work out, but if you say No, then there is a strong chance that you will lose your money. So Yes, you do what you can to help.

The Universe isn't prepared to give up on anyone until it has no other choice, or our allotted time has run out.

And remember, we are all interconnected, we're all part of a vast and infinite web of relationships. So if we turn things around, then we create a better chance for all those who we came here to help and support.

Sometimes, in Modern Medicine, a person can be healed by taking pills. But other times, more drastic action is required, like full-on surgery, to try and save the patient.

And sometimes, if a broken leg has healed badly, then a surgeon will break it all over again, reset it, so it can heal again in the right way.

And the **3 Transpersonal Planets** can, therefore, be seen as the 3 Surgeons of Astrology.

They go to work when there is no other alternative for that individual, or for the Family, Tribe, or Nation, because rigidity and stuckness can occur at so many different levels of the Human Equation.

When someone or something has a Comfort Zone which is so rigid that they cannot change themselves, and are in desperate need, although they may not know it, or is resisting, then the **3 Transpersonal Planets** often come in and break apart that which needs to change, the rigid Comfort Zone, in the hope that the breaking apart will open that individual to change and new ideas, that they will change for the better, and re-align with the true life-purpose.

Hopefully.

But we have to be honest here, and as we shall see, the phrase you can't make an omelette without breaking eggs comes to mind here.

The **3 Transpersonal Planets**... **Uranus, Neptune**, or **Pluto**... will probably require you to re-assess your life and let go of something, some area which is not required, no longer needed.

And this is most likely an area which you value highly and will want to hold on to, desperately.

And the phrase *kicking and screaming* also come to mind here because that is what a lot of what people do when they are undergoing a serious Transpersonal transit.

Uranus, **Neptune**, or **Pluto** can put people through different kinds of Hell, but this experience of Hell only exists because an individual is resisting in some way, desperately holding on to that which is no longer needed, or which they need to let go, and this resistance has been going on for a long while.

The story of **Buddha's boat** comes to mind here.

Gautama the Buddha often told the story of a man who was on a journey, has to cross a river, is fortunate to find a boat along the riverbank, and so uses the boat to cross the river.

And then the man is so grateful for the boat and so scared that he will have to cross another river at some point in the future, that he starts to drag the boat along after him.

Which is such a tiresome and exhausting thing to do.

According to **Buddha**, leave the boat where it is, and if you find you need to cross another river in the future, look for another boat when you need it.

But this is something you see in life, people dragging along physical/emotional/mental "boats". Hoarding objects, over-complicating their life with ideas, thoughts and beliefs they have outgrown, and should have discarded long before, but they just can't.

Note: Maybe boat-dragging should be an Olympic sport because we all do it to some degree.

The **3 Transpersonal Planets** are the Universe's way to get us to see sense in these areas; however, many people resist and resist some more, continue to fight to carry their boat.

But the **3 Transpersonal Planets** will always win out in the end, because they have size, weight and time on their side, and will eventually wear us down, even to nothing if necessary.

The people who tend to fair the best with the **3 Transpersonal Planets** are the ones who give up and let go earlier in the process, sooner rather than later, because they don't become totally exhausted.

But that is rare because, most often, the area of life which the **3 Transpersonal Planets** want us to reassess and let go is so valuable to us that we fight, resist and struggle for as long as we can.

We fail to see how much better our life would be if we let go of our particular boat, and so desperately continue to hold on, dragging it along behind us.

Plus, as we discussed with **Jupiter** and **Saturn** earlier, each of the **3 Transpersonal Planets** take a long time to complete a single rotation around the Sun:

- **Uranus** – 84 years
- **Neptune** – 165 years
- **Pluto** – 248 years

That means that everyone born in roughly a seven year period will have **Uranus** in the same sign, although with an elliptical orbit, some Signs get more of the cosmic love than others.

For **Neptune**, it is roughly 13.75 years average, and with **Pluto**, it is roughly 20.6 years average (but with variations between Signs because of the elliptical orbit).

So if **Jupiter** and **Saturn** are the Social Planets Mark I, then the **3 Transpersonal Planets** are also Social Mark II... but on steroids.

And just as the **3 Transpersonal Planets** require an individual to look at some area of their life and Comfort Zone which isn't working, and let it go, the very same thing is happening to Groups, Communities, Nations, and the whole World of Humanity. And you can often detect this Global process at work by asking the question *"Where in the World is Humanity resisting the need for change?"*

Usually, these places of Global resistant are not that hard to find.

And if you think about it, it's only **Uranus**, **Neptune**, and **Pluto** that can often keep the pressure on Humanity for long enough to ensure that real change does happen.

All the Inner Planets are moving too fast; they don't stay around for long enough.

It's only the **3 Transpersonal Planets** which can keep up the pressure for longest.

Final thought, a few years ago now, the Director of a well known Cancer Clinic + Hospice in the United States was retiring, and someone asked him:

"With all your long decades of experience in this field, what is the difference between those people who get better, and those who don't?"

He thought about it for a while and then replied.

"Well, this is a simplification, and everyone is different, but if I had to put the general difference into words. Those who don't get better are often desperately clinging on to their old life, and want it back, exactly as it was, even after all they have gone through. While those who do improve do tend to be the ones who embrace the journey and accept the need for change in their life, and so come out the other side transformed in some way. Now, that is not to say that there aren't people who do embrace the need to change, do change, but who go on to die eventually, which is sad. But in some way, their end is more peaceful, more orientated, and they go with less guilt and regret. I would say that is the real difference I have witnessed, time and again, over the years. The people who do better tend to be those who are open to having a different kind of life, are open to being transformed by the hard experience in a positive way. Who eventually embrace the new direction on offer."

I have also found this to be true in my own life.

They often say that whatever doesn't kill us makes us stronger.

And they also say that the Universe never gives us anything that we cannot handle.

But for that to be true, we have to believe, deep within, that we have the strength to handle the hard situation which faces us. Platitudes won't do. We have to find some steel in our Soul to seriously tango with either **Uranus**, **Neptune** or **Pluto** (and sometimes they gang up on us, and we are dealing with two or three at the same time… or we have them plugged into our **Natal Sun** or **Moon** in some way, and have to live and walk with them, walking close beside us, each moment of our life).

We have to embrace the new situation, which is trying to make us stronger, but which also feels like it is ripping us apart.

With the **3 Transpersonal Planets**, we have to not only step outside of our Comfort Zone, we have to be prepared to see it ripped apart in front of our very eyes, just like the old man watched as the tsunami wave destroyed all that he had built over a lifetime of effort in our teaching story at the start, so that we can find ourselves rebuilt anew in the very next Universal breath.

Or as the Hospice Director suggests... we have to totally embrace the transformation which we didn't consciously ask for because we thought our old life was OK, and didn't intend to change it.

And if you can find within yourself the strength to undergo such an extreme transformation, then you will know the true gift of the **Transpersonal Planets**.

But as we said earlier, each of the **3 Transpersonal Planets** works in a different way to rebuild our Comfort Zone. So now, let's explore those differences, starting with...

URANUS

In **Energy Astrology**, **Uranus** is associated with our Brow Chakra, the Ajna Centre, otherwise known as our Third Eye. Which means that **Uranus** is associated with light, vision, our ability to see, or remain blind, and also lightning.

When **Uranus** is active, for a brief moment, we can see, just like lightning flashing across the sky, *but do we like what we see? Do we even understand what we are seeing?*

Seeing is not always the same as understanding.

Well, when **Uranus** starts to play with our individual Comfort Zone, it's as if there is a flash of lightning, and we can suddenly see out beyond our psychological barriers, out into the darkness, truly see what is there.

Imagine a family of early Humans, clustered around the safety and warmth of their tribal fire, on a dark Moonless and stormy night, unsure of what is lurking out there in the darkness around them. Suddenly there is a burst of lightning in the sky above them, the landscape is ablaze with bright electric light, and they can see exactly what is out there in the darkness.

When Uranus is active, for a brief moment we can see, just like lightning flashing across the sky... but do we like what we see?

Well, that is also us to a large degree, and the **Uranian gift** is a temporary deeper and stronger vision - the ability to see what is really out there, what is all around us.

OK, the nature of our tribal fire has changed, we have replaced glowing embers with gas or electricity, but we all stand between the light and the darkness, between the known and the big and Universal unknown.

And so we are all scared about what might be lying in wait for us in the darkness beneath our warm and comfy bed, no matter how young or old we are.

And when **Uranus** comes along, we are given a brief moment of deeper seeing... a brief moment of lightning flashing across our

Energy Astrology

consciousness.

And that's often when the problems start.

We may see something we like or desperately need and want, but which we can never really have or achieve, and that continues to pick at our inner wounds and emptiness.

We may see something which we actively dislike, or have tried to reject our whole life, or which shocks and horrifies us, and so we engage in a never-ending quest to destroy it, or just run away, terrified.

We may see something which totally challenges our view of the World and how it works. Like a **St Paul** on the road to Damascus moment, that led him to cease persecuting Christians and become a follower of **Jesus**, and help found the early Christian Church, spreading the new message across the Roman Empire.

This sudden moment of **Uranian seeing** is so powerful and illuminating that it literally overturns our whole World view in some way, and so we can never be the same again. Because we now know, and cannot go back to a state of unknowing.

And it is then down to the strength and integrity of our Ego and Comfort Zone to decide what happens next, how well we have been built within.

Like when lightning strikes a house, as shown in the diagram below, when **Uranus** hits our Comfort Zone, it can be channelled safely into the ground, via a copper lightning conductor of some kind, or it is not safely conducted and causes the building to burst into flames.

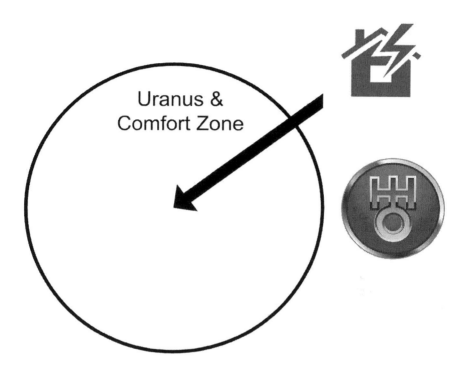

Uranus & Comfort Zone... the illuminating lightning strike.

Remember, from a scientific perspective; fire is created when the lightning cannot easily flow and when there is some kind of strong resistance in the material through which it is passing. And the same is true with our Human psychology. The problems occur when we resist the energies on offer from the Universe.

And the same is also true of our psychological Comfort Zone and our Ego.

Some people take their illumination, their plugging into a Higher Vision, as a sign that they are the Messiah, and so start out on an individual crusade of some kind.

Some people are completely scared by their moment of illumination and what they are shown. It cracks them within, and they start to descend into what is often called madness.

Although, as many modern psychologists now say, madness is often an inability to function correctly in the world, to no longer fit in with those around you.

And that is something which can definitely happen when **Uranus** strikes, and someone can no longer see the world as the rest of their family, friends and society does. They no longer speak the same language, or perceive the world in the same way; hence communication becomes difficult.

If after that inner change, they are considered dangerous to their society, they may even be locked up.

But there are a whole number of different possibilities in and around a visitation from **Uranus**.

Some people *break down*, while others *break up*, and are able to channel their illumination positively and creatively, into the arts or scientific discovery, or the drive to change the world for the better.

But the crucial thing to understand, when the lightning strikes, that individual cannot remain the same, they have no choice, their life is changed by what they have seen, and they cannot go back.

They are stuck with their vision, and they have to find a way to either live with and integrate it, or not, in which case it burns painfully within their mind from that point onwards until it is earthed in some way. Which path is chosen, integration, rejection, or distortion, that's down to the individual involved, but it's all the same to **Uranus**, which in the end is really just a Transpersonal vision passing through us.

NEPTUNE

In **Energy Astrology**, **Neptune** is associated with our Crown Chakra, our Sahasrara, otherwise known as our Thousand Petalled Lotus. It is our gateway out into the Universal energies, and from where the Universal energies can most easily flow into us.

Which means that **Neptune** is associated with Enlightenment, Cosmic Consciousness, Non-Attachment, Spirituality, Unconditional Love and Bliss.

When **Neptune** starts to play with our individual Comfort Zone seriously, it's as if we are overwhelmed by Water in some way.

But the thing which we need to understand about Water, it can come at us in several different ways, and in several different forms, as can **Neptune**.

Water can come at us in the form of a massive tsunami wave, the form where it is at its most destructive and overpowering.

But Water can also destroy as gentle waves on the beach, as in the picture below, which is more deceptive, gradually eroding away the coastline, one grain of sand at a time. But we Humans just can't see the change which is occurring, because it is happening out of sight of our normal sense range, and on a timescale, we don't really appreciate.

Neptune erodes our Comfort Zone, just like the ocean gradually erodes the seashore.

So why would you ever want to resist gentle waves breaking on the seashore?

OK, Water may take longer than Fire, Earthquakes or Lightning, but it gets the job done in the end.

It is estimated the average life span of a seawall is 50–100 years and the average for a groyne (i.e. a rigid hydraulic structure built out from an ocean shore) is 30–40 years. Which in terms of the average Human life seems a lot, but in terms of the Earth is nothing. And what is also interesting, a Man could visit these structures every day of his life and be totally blind to the erosion which is occurring, slowly, all around him. Maybe after ten years or twenty years, he might be able to notice the changes, but it would take time to see what is really occurring all around him.

And that defines one of the differences between **Neptune** and the other **2 Transpersonal Planets**, **Uranus** and **Pluto**, in that **Neptune** is transforming us, even when we don't realise it is happening, literally it is working on us *beneath the waves*.

When we are hit by **Uranus** and **Pluto**, we know it. But with **Neptune**, it can be a lot more subtle, like waves breaking gently on the beach, and so we don't realise what is going on, not until it is too late, and the damage to our world view is done.

Like **Neptune**, Water can be subtle, deceptive, but gets the job done in the end. But also, like **Neptune**, Water can also come in the forms of violent flash floods, tidal waves and tsunamis, rapid and sudden, and it can also contain within it strong currents and tides which can pull us under.

So to really understand **Neptune**, it is necessary first to understand how Water works, and this understanding then opens doors to the other **Neptunian qualities**.

Well, Water erodes, it breaks things down, and once things are broken down, then the elements can mix, interact, form and reform.

Water mixes and merges to create new forms on the chemical level.

And that allowed life to take hold on this planet, turned the Earth from a barren rock in space, to the Blue and Green wonderland it is now, allowed Evolution to start and continue, got those Amino acids going, and the rest is planetary history.

Without Water, life would not have been possible, because Water is the Universal solvent.

Eroding the rocks, releasing minerals, allowing those elements to mix and combine was essential.

Because once those amino-acids were in place, then life could start... first as single-celled organisms... and then those cells combined... specialized... then they evolved into fish... who eventually crawled out on to dry land... becoming insects taking the water with them sealed in their bodies/eggs... later amphibians... became reptiles... big scary dinosaurs... (Watch out for the Asteroid!!!... Ouch)... mammals replaced the dinosaurs... a few dinosaurs became birds... and about 3 million years ago, one big Ape started walking upright... Us!

You and Me!

If you stand back and consider, the Earth's packed a lot into the last 1 billion years.

And none of that would have been possible if Water wasn't a Universal solvent, breaking things down, and mixing things up.

And that's also what **Neptune** does, it is the Cosmic Solvent.

It breaks down the walls of our Comfort Zone, either suddenly and violently, or more slowly and gently over time, and the barrier between the inside of our Comfort Zone, and the outside, slowly starts to disappear.

And what **Neptune** is most known for bringing in is Unconditional Love, Beauty, and Bliss.

So what would be wrong and unsettling about those higher energies and qualities?

Well...

If you think about it, the essential quality of Unconditional Love is that there is nothing or no one who is unworthy of being loved, Unconditional Love means just that... Unconditional.

Which means that Unconditional Love is a subtle form of Cosmic Solvent, and it is most often trying to break down the illusory barrier we Humans erect, within and around us, and so bring things together.

Now, don't get me wrong, often, in living an Earth-plane existence, some of those illusions are necessary, they work and are effective on certain levels, and for certain situations, and they help us to survive down here. But as we start to evolve our consciousness, and reach higher, some of what served us well down here, needs to slip away and be replaced by new kinds of thinking.

No matter what blocks and barriers we may be put up to stop the flow of energy, Unconditional Love is able to break them down, erode them, flow around, over, and under them, eventually the unworthy are touched by Unconditional Love, raised up, made worthy and whole again. They are permitted to see themselves as the Universe sees them.

And when you bring in Bliss and Peace, the inner transformation, started by Unconditional Love just grows and intensifies. Bliss starts to reorientate our personality self, and Peace, according to **David R Hawkins**, has the power to erase our sense of being separate from the Universe, which then dissolves our Ego.

No wonder our Ego is wary of letting **Neptune** in, its the start of its own, eventual demise.

Love reclaims... it re-builds... it makes new.

But that is an ideal and once again we need to talk basic Human here.

Because if you turn up at someone's door, and offer to forgive them for all their sins, and love them unconditionally, and so allow them to love themselves totally, and all for free.

Chances are they will reject you because they believe themselves to be unworthy, or have done something in the past which is unforgivable, or see a catch, what are you really trying to sell them, and so deny themselves of such a blessing.

Although, that is the exact sales pitch which many established religions have been making for the last 2000 years, and they haven't done too badly with that marketing approach. They got millions and millions of followers out of it.

So when you think about it…

Neptune is outside of our Comfort Zone, with all the Unconditional Love and Forgiveness we could ever want or need, and it slowly, over time, finds a way to erode through the defences of our Comfort Zone, finding a way inside, but then, when it is finally inside, what happens?

99% of the time, the Unconditional Love and Forgiveness are totally rejected because the individual at the centre of the Comfort Zone believes that they are unloved, unloveable, unworthy, and beyond any kind of forgiveness. They are guilty, shamed, damned, and unforgivable. Forever. With no hope of release or reprieve.

A lot of this programming probably exists on the Unconscious level, so the individual is largely unaware of it, but no matter, it is still active, and so dictates the course of their life.

And for the 1% who do accept the Unconditional Love on the doorstep, if they don't do the inner work to upgrade their own psychological Comfort Zone, they can easily become addicted, and dependent on what they see as the source of this Love, which they believe is out there, and not within their own Heart.

But for the vast majority, the 99%, they believe that God has given up on them, removed them from prayer speed-dial.

So they totally freak out at the sheer thought of being forgiven and loved, that their life could be any other way.

Now, how weird is that?

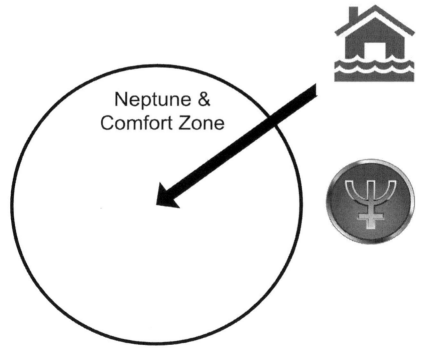

Neptune and our Comfort Zone

But that's what **Neptune** is trying to achieve for us, and also the reason why people resist. **Neptune** is trying to lift us up, while most people are struggling and resisting, trying to stay on the same level, or sink down lower.

But there is another problem when **Neptune** calls... psychic projection.

Most Humans aren't very good at dealing with Transpersonal energies, staying non-attached around vibrations such as Unconditional Love and Bliss.

We much prefer to give it a form, to personalise it, to project it out on some situation, or preferably on another Human Being. We find that easier to approach and deal with.

"Wow... you are all loving... you are totally beautiful... and spiritual... and you are all-forgiving... everything I have been searching for... So please love and forgive me! ... I can't do it myself... I am so full of guilt and shame, how can I love myself? ... I totally need you to do it for me!"

Around 2500 years ago, **Buddha** said *"If you meet the Buddha on the road, kill him"*... and also... *"Be a light unto yourself."*

Buddha is the ultimate Do-It-Yourself Master.

But your average Human isn't comfortable doing that, many of us don't seem to know-how.

So **Buddha** has been worshipped, had big statues created of him, built on mountain tops, or carved into stone cliffs, covered in gold leaf, all because the default Human setting is to project out Transpersonal energies.

And this projection thing has been going on for a long, long time.

If you consider Ancient Greek mythology, **Narcissus** fell in love with his own reflection, and **Pasiphae**, the wife of **King Minos**, fell in love with a beautiful Snow White Bull and so gave birth to the **Minotaur** (which was then disowned and locked up in a Cretan labyrinth, a negative projection, cast out).

One of the common things running through Humanity, we're psychic projection machines, there's no getting away from that, and that is as true on the Cultural and Collective level as it is on the Individual. It may indeed be one of the defining characteristics of being Human, and if you're still breathing and projecting out, then you must be alive.

But it is down to the health and integrity of an individual's Comfort Zone as to whether we project our **Transpersonal Neptune** out in a healthy and positive way, on someone who will help us, or on someone who is as cracked and warped as we are, and will eventually take advantage of us and the whole situation.

"Hey, as your most spiritual and otherworldy Guru, you wouldn't happen to have some spare cash I could borrow... What? You have just sold your house, and all your worldly possessions, so that you could be with me permanently in the Ashram, forever? Well, if you insist... leave the cheque over there... and you are now my most favourite sannyasins of the week. Although, what happens next, when I need to hit you up for more cash, and you haven't got any... Don't worry, trust, and I am sure the Universe will provide... Have you got any rich and elderly relatives about to die soon?"

I have a theory that **Neptune** is the most dangerous of all the Transpersonal projections, because it is so subtle and deceptive, and so hard for most people to handle, or see coming.

And because it is about Unconditional Love, which is something which, at our core, we all want, need, and long for, while we consider ourselves to be unworthy of the love which the Universe offers us so freely, then we will continue to project it out.

On to anyone who happens to be standing around, nearby, and who also happens to fit any particular psychic projection profile we may have lying around inside our head, i.e. the tall, dark, handsome stranger syndrome.

And that's not always a good recipe for a long, fulfiling and loving relationship.

And it can't be until we learn the real lesson of **Neptune**, which is, when dealing with love, of any kind or level, you first need to learn to love yourself. You need to establish a love foundation within yourself, only always, no exceptions permitted.

You need to be able to let the love flow through you... unconditionally.

PLUTO

In **Energy Astrology**, **Pluto** is associated with our Soma Chakra, located just above the Brow Chakra.

Pluto shakes the ground from underfoot, either like a volcano or an earthquake.

So if you have built your Comfort Zone wrong, then the Universe sends along **Pluto**, to create some kind of earthquake, whether internal or external, which reduces our Comfort Zone to rubble, making you start over again, making you rebuild your sense of Self.

In the hope, you will re-build yourself right next time.

Or maybe, your **Pluto** comes at you as some kind of volcanic eruption, wiping your Comfort Zone slate clean with a layer of red hot lava, covering and burying the old you, ensuring that you have to start over again, after things have cooled down.

OK, all these forces and metaphors which are associated with **Pluto** are violent and destructive, and no sane individual would even want to be caught up in them.

I also have a theory that people tend to experience **Neptune** as a violent tsunami when there is **Pluto** also involved somewhere in the mix… turning the **Neptunian waters** violent and destructive.

Something else which is interesting, the order of the **3 Transpersonal Planets**, in terms of nearest and furthest from the Sun, gives us:

1. **Uranus**
2. **Neptune**
3. **Pluto**

Pluto shakes the ground from underfoot, either like a volcano or an earthquake.

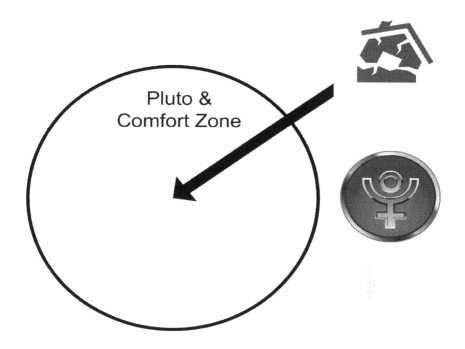

Pluto and our Comfort Zone

But the order in terms of our Chakras, lower and higher, is instead:

- Brow Chakra – **Uranus**
- Soma Chakra – **Pluto**
- Crown Chakra – **Neptune**

Which means that Pluto sits in between **Uranus** and **Neptune** in terms of our energy anatomy.

Is there any significance to this?

Well, to be honest, I think there is.

Energy Astrology

From my own experience and observations, if the Crown Chakra is where we tap into the Universal energies, and the Brow Chakra is where we start to step those energies down and into individual expression and form in some way.

Then the Soma Chakra is where we are select, from the Universal energies, the energies which we are choosing to express through our individuality, in our specific lifetime.

Put another way, the Soma Chakra holds the life-script of our specific lifetime, what we have come here to do and achieve:

Yes to being a father of 4 kids, and running our own business. No to climbing Mount Everest, or becoming President of the United States.

And maybe this is why **Pluto** activates when people get seriously off-track in their life, the Soma Chakra is trying to pull them back towards the purpose of their life, to remind them what they came here to achieve, although maybe that is true for any of the **3 Transpersonal Planets**.

Or, put another way, the Soma Chakra is also sometimes referred to as our Karma Chakra, and each one of us probably has a thousand plus past lives which we could draw upon, and pull into this lifetime… bucket loads of karma which we need to address, sort through, and resolve, much more than can ever be tackled in a single lifetime.

To try and access them all, resolve them all, would be too much even to consider, let alone try and do, so the Soma Chakra acts as a filter, allowing us to pull down only the karma and energies which are safe and appropriate for us to access and live out.

So the Soma Chakra/**Pluto** has the task of holding back all the karma which will not, and cannot, be dealt with in our single individual lifetime, while bringing through that which is appropriate, plus opening us to new karmic opportnities if situations change, and the opportunity for new growth suddenly occurs..

So instead of tackling the whole of our personal Underworld, Hades and Tartarus combined, we are much more selective about what we take on.

And not all of this unexpressed karma is necessarily bad, sometimes the good karma has to be held back as well, for some higher, cosmic reason.

It is also said that the Soma Chakra can emit a liquid... known as Soma, surprisingly... which when flowing through our energy body, presents us from accumulating new karma, as well as helping us release old karmic patterns and vibrations from the past.

OK, serious confession time, in my own Astrological Natal Chart I have **Sun conjunct Pluto**, which in the first part of my life was a total pain until I achieved an understanding of how **Pluto** works. And now, I am able to work with **Pluto**, and not try to resist the inevitable, although no way can I ever say I am in control.

That's not to say that I am always enjoying the cosmic ride I am on, but I do now realise that I am not in control, so I can let go of desperately trying to grab and turn the steering wheel, and focus instead on what I can actually control, which is my own inner transformation.

So after all this time, the way I describe **Pluto**?

Well, you know those TV shows you get, programmes about house renovation, where people buy an old and derelict house, plan to do it up over time, and also plan to live in the house while they are doing the necessary renovation work? Usually, it's a newly married couple, trying to keep costs to a minimum.

Well, when the programme goes back after six months, to see how they got on, the general response is:

"It was a total nightmare; it was like living in a building site. OK, we got one room finished early on, our bedroom, but it was like that room was our kitchen, bathroom, bedroom, and living room, all in one, and overall, everything around us else was in a state of chaos, for months and months, and there were no other rooms we could escape into. No escape from the dirt and mess; it got everywhere. Just like living in a building site. Not a pleasant experience at all."

Well, from my own experience, **Pluto** in your chart is a bit like that, especially if it is plugged into **The Sun** or **Moon**, or the other Personal Planets to some extent.

It's like living in a building site, where the site is your own personality.

Pluto is continually tearing down parts of your personality so that it can rebuild you better (**Pluto's words**).

The Universe is trying to renovate you, trying to re-build you.

From my experience, if you have **Sun conjunct Pluto**, then throughout your life it is continually tearing down and updating your sense of Self, and if you have **Moon conjunct Pluto**, then throughout your life it is continually tearing down and upgrading your Comfort Zone. Plus **Mercury** (your ability to communicate), **Venus** (your self-worth), **Mars** (your ability to empower, motivate, and defend yourself), all being torn down and rebuilt.

And, to a large degree, your happiness in life is tied into your ability to accept that fact, and sit back and enjoy the ride to the best of your ability.

Now, admittedly, this is worst for **The Moon**, because our **Moon** and its Sign is meant to be your Comfort Zone, the inner space into which you go to escape from the anxiety of your life. But when **Pluto** is closely attached to your Comfort Zone, it has literally been given the keys to your home and can wander in and out as it pleases, so there really isn't much escape from that anxiety when **Pluto** is at home in your living room.

Hades really is stalking the home where you live.

And this is particularly stressful when you are a small child and adults tell you not to be afraid of the Boogeyman, and that he doesn't exist. But you know different, you know he does, because **Pluto** is permanently lurking in all your supposedly safe spaces, and he's definitely not soft and cuddly. Someone with **Moon conjunct Pluto** (aka **Hades Moon**) is raised in an atmosphere of constant anxiety, for whatever reason, along with the feeling that their Comfort Zone and place of safety is continually under threat, or is being torn down for whatever reason. For much of their childhood, unfortunately, they don't feel they have a safe space they can go to.

But now, here was the real turning point for me, when I realised that **Pluto** wasn't always the bad guy of Astrology.

True, every couple of years I am torn apart and put back together in a different way (ala **Jerry Cornelius** from the **Michael Moorcock** novels.), which is kind of like a **Dr Who** regeneration.

Yes, it can be stressful, and often the life and circumstances around me change markedly, and there is a regular brush with the unknown. But if I go with the process, rather then fight it, things do tend to turn out OK.

Doors close, but new doors also open, and the flow continues.

And the thing is, my life definitely isn't boring, and with **Pluto** upgrading me at regular intervals, it means I am living several different lives within the single lifetime.

But there is another side to this **Plutonian regeneration**, which ties back to the Ancient Greek Myths.

Because we tend to put a lot of emphasis on the tearing downside of **Pluto's work**, but there is also the other side, the rebuilding and regeneration of the psyche.

Take one of the archetypes of **Pluto**, for example... the volcano.

The green jungle starting to reclaim the slopes of an active volcano.

Living on the side of a volcano can be dangerous, especially if it is active because it could erupt at any time, and kill off you and your family, and your whole village, and the neighbouring villages, basically, anyone for a radius of several miles.

And you would think that at the first signs of trouble, people would evacuate. But there are so many tremors which don't result in anything bad happening, people start to take them for granted, they become an accepted part of life, and so people no longer run when they should, and then it is the BIG ONE, at which point they have probably left it too late.

Which also ties in with **Pluto**, because usually, in my experience, there are also similar life-tremors, ahead of the main event, but we tend to ignore them, and so we ignore the warning signs ahead of the full-blown eruption.

So why do it, why live on the slopes of an active volcano?

Because the soil is super-rich and fertile, and it is easy to grow your crops. In between the eruptions, which may not happen for hundreds of years, and never in your lifetime, life is really good, and that's why people choose to live there.

And that also ties in with **Pluto** from an **Energy Astrology** perspective.

As well as being the God of the Underworld, **Hades** was also the God of Riches and Hidden Treasures.

And just as a volcano can bring up from the Earth minerals and nutrients which feed the soil, leading to better crops, and supporting a richer harvest.

With a psychic eruption, as well as flatten the old, **the Astrological Pluto** can also bring up new riches and treasures from deep within us, talents and skills and ideas which have been long buried inside us perhaps, but which once back on the surface, lead us to have a happier and more fertile life.

Maybe these are qualities and skills which we once suppressed, perhaps they just laid dormant inside, and we never knew they were even there.

That's why, whenever I have been made redundant (severance in the U.S.), which has always been a very **Plutonian experience** for me, I have always allowed myself time to recuperate and rejuvenate, allow the old parts of myself to fade, and the new parts to come to the surface and become integrated and established.

And then I have always found that when that process is complete, as if by magic, the new stage and direction for my life suddenly appears, and I can head off on the next stage of my life adventure, until **Pluto** decides it is time to uncover a new and different Me.

And so life is never boring.

But all that is possible now because I take the time and have faith in the **Plutonian process**.

But not everyone does.

I knew someone who was also having a full-on **Plutonian transit**, and who was made suddenly made redundant. Now, for the past 5 years, he had gone around telling everyone that he needed some personal downtime, time and space to sort out his head, and the funny thing was, his redundancy from work gave him the time and money to do just that, take a few months out, take time to re-think his life, just as he said he wanted.

It could have been an opportunity to reassess his life. He certainly got exactly what he had been asking for.

His response to his redundancy was sheer panic, and a desperate attempt to get himself back into work asap.

When I pointed out that he had been given exactly what he wanted, and had been asking for, the chance to sort himself out, and others pointed that out to him as well, it wasn't just me, he ignored all of us and blindly went for the first job which came along.

Which turned out to be a total disaster, and he was fired from that job after a few months, leaving him in a far worse situation then if he had relaxed and followed the **Plutonian process of rebirth**.

Now, I am not saying that taking time out from work, or relationships, or whatever, is always the right thing to do, and a lot will depend on personal circumstances, and with 7 to 8 billion Humans on the planet, personal circumstances can be so very, very different, so you do have to listen to your own intuition to a large extent, get the opinions of those you trust.

And also, be practical, most of the time, I feel the **3 Transpersonal Planets** are OK with practical as a way forward with your life.

But what I can say, from personal experience, when **Pluto** is active in your life:

There will be a tearing down stage, and the more you can let go of the old, outworn, and no longer needed, the easier that stage is.

And there will be a rebuilding stage, and the more you can be open to new ideas and opportunities, the easier that stage is too. You may even discover sides to your personality, which you never knew existed, so it can be a bit of an adventure.

When you look back at your recent past, you may uncover hints and clues, signs to the way things were eventually going to go, but which you ignored at the time, perhaps because they didn't make sense to you, or made you feel uncomfortable. But thinking about them now, re-considering those clues now will help you figure out the new path your life needs to take going forward.

You see from my own experience, even at the hardest times, I found that the Universe wasn't being mean and nasty to me, it sincerely wanted me to change and grow.

OK, there are people out there who have definitely suffered a lot worse than me, but I don't believe that life is really all about giving the highest award to the person who has suffered the most. If that was the case, those who have suffered violent abuse or been tortured in prison, they would always win.

Basically, your life is your life is your life, and you must live it the best you can.

There is no race, and you are not in competition with anyone else.

If there is a competition, it is to be the best person that you can be, and the Universe is rooting for you, and is also fascinated to see how things turn out for you in the end.

Draw wisdom and inspiration from the lives of others, but always apply it to your own individual life circumstances.

And finally, love is the glue which holds everything together, binds us all together, including all elements of your own psyche. Love always heals, and Unconditional Love even more so.

In the end, there is no map for your life apart from the one which you choose to create for yourself. Astrology can provide you with massive clues about direction and focus, but in the end, they are all meaningless if you choose not to listen, or you listen and interpret them in the wrong way.

PAGE FOUR:
WORKING WITH ENERGY
ASTROLOGY

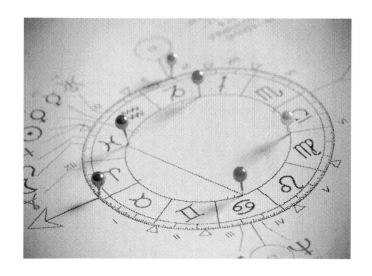

Chapter 4-1: Fitting It All Together

Above is an image of kid's building blocks... all different colours and shapes... which can be re-arranged in a vast variety of different shapes and patterns...

A bit like how a patchwork quilt is created from many pieces of different cloth and fabric... thus creating a vast array of different patterns and colours.

And the same is so very true of Astrology... whether **Traditional** or **Energy Astrology**.

Any Astrological Chart is composed of a fixed number of elements, which includes:

- 11 Planetary energies (with the option to include Asteroids if you want to increase this number)
- 12 Astrological Sign energies
- 12 House energies
- Plus there are a number of other Astrological energies (Nodes, Angles, Arabic Parts etc.) that also play their part in any Chart

Each of these can be seen as a different coloured block or piece of cloth.

But then how those fixed number of elements are re-arranged... fitted together... to create an almost infinite number of different patterns and permutations... that's what makes Astrology such a fascinating art.

If you just take your own Natal Chart as an example. If you limit it to just the main 11 Planets, then the exact moment of your birth, the exact same placement of those 11 Planets in the 12 Signs, and in relation to each other, will not be exactly repeated for another 22,000 years and a bit.

The thing is we are all the same... because the energies flowing through us are the same... the same Archetypal energies... the same 10 Planets... the same 12 Signs...

But how each of us is *expressing* those energies is so very, very different... because the position on the Chart is different... 22,000 years different.

However... there are several things we must understand at this stage in the discussion.

The Astrologer **Sue Lilly** likens an Astrological Natal Chart to being dealt a hand of cards in a game of poker.

So part of your success in life is due to the cards you are dealt...

But the other part of the success *is how you choose to play those cards.*

And someone with a weak hand at poker can still win because they know how to play the hand well and to their advantage.

Which also involves an individual having the skill to read the other players in the game... bluff when needed... strike home their advantage when required...

So no one should ever feel trapped by the cards they have been dealt...

A master poker player has been known to win even with a weak hand...

And likewise, no one should ever feel trapped by the Astrological Chart they are born with... because in any Astrological Chart... there are strengths and there are weaknesses... and it's always a matter of how well someone plays the hand they are dealt...

(And for the moment, I am putting aside the common belief that you, as your Soul, choose to explore these energies **before** you were born... that you wanted to be you... and you choose it all for a reason...)

For example (and I love this story)...

One of the things I have found in life, sometimes great and practical wisdom can come from the most unexpected places and people.

For example... there is a small book called *Zen in the Martial Arts* by **Joe Hyams**.

I bought it back in the mid-1980s... and since then have come across copies of it in several 2nd hand bookstores over the years (... as if the original owner didn't really understand what they had in their hands... and so gave it away).

And yet... it is packed full and solid with chapters containing golden gems of practical wisdom.

And because **Joe Hyams** had the great good fortune of knowing and being trained by the great martial arts star and master **Bruce Lee**... there are many chapters containing the wisdom which **Bruce Lee** gathered through his own life... and passed on to this students...

And some of his insights into life, I have found to be very useful.

For example...

You see, **Bruce Lee** had one leg shorter than the other... which might have been a problem with his becoming a great martial arts master...

Until he realised that his apparent disability gave him a distinct advantage when it came to certain kicks/martial arts moves... basically, it gave him greater momentum on take off...

And so focusing on those moves, the ones he was strong in, and not on the ones where he was at a disadvantage because of his shorter leg, made him one of the greatest martial arts masters of his generation.

He decided to turn his apparent weakness into his greatest asset... and everything he achieved in his unfortunately short life, all his success in the martial arts gym and in front of the film cameras, was based on that original decision.

Because... it's all a matter of perspective really...

Advantage... Disadvantage...

Often, a matter of perspective...

But another story... another example... drawn from my own life...

I was once in a room, with a Director of a Company, who was raging about the fact that his employees were under-performing in his eyes...

And the more I listened to him, the more I realised that the core of his complaint was:

"Why can't my staff be more like me... go-getting... dynamic... hungry. for success?"

Now, the first thing to be said... and we can take this as one of the core themes of Astrology...

No one is ever exactly like anyone else... because everyone has a different arrangement of the Celestial energies...

But, looking even deeper...

Because each Astrological Chart has strengths and weaknesses woven into it...

It shows each person who has ever been born... themselves on a Good Day... and themselves on a Bad Day...

What I was trying to tell this Director, who most definitely wasn't listening because he didn't want to hear...

"People only seriously change if they go in for some kind of therapy and counselling, and successfully work with their inner process...

Otherwise, people are usually set in their ways, in their behaviour, in how they respond to the world around them. In which case... they have Good Days and Bad Days... depending on their personality make-up... a spectrum of possibilities... and so a Managers job is to persuade people to have more Good Days then Bad Days... operate more up the positive end of their personality spectrum... and less down the bottom."

And that is another way of looking at an Astrological Chart, really...

It is a snapshot which shows us our Personality Spectrum...

Shows us our potential... both on a Good Day and a Bad Day...

The positive and negative energies we are playing with and expressing...

So it is our job, as individuals, to try and spend more time down the positive part of our Personality Spectrum... and less time down the negative end...

Plus it is more fun down the positive end... and people tend to respond to us more favourably...

Like that ancient Native American teaching story...

A young man asks the tribal Shaman... *"I have two wolves within me... one an angry wolf... the other full of love... which one will dominate my life?" And the Shaman replies... "The one you choose to feed."*

Yeah, it's a bit like that.

But the other thing... the other massive piece of wisdom embedded in the Astrological approach...

No one ever gets to be Superman... whether the **Nietsche** or **D.C. Comic** kind.

Success and happiness comes... on all levels... through being and accepting who you are...

We begin and end in the same place... who we were born to be...

To quote the wise **Freya**, mother of **Thor** in the Marvel Universe, who was raised by witches, and so sees with more then Human eyes...

"Everyone fails at who they are supposed to be... the measure of a person... is how well they succeed at being who they are."

And that is the BIG problem... a HUGE problem... often made worse by social media pressure...

The feeling that we are not good enough... we are lacking... that with sustained effort we can change ourselves into something other... something better... something different... bigger... stronger... hopefully, more attractive...

But your personality self is not the same as going to University and studying to be an accountant, or physicist, or biologist...

You can't change your Natal Chart...

You can accept it... you can work with it...

You can strive to have more Good Days than Bad Days...

But you can't change your Natal Chart...

Now... true... if you are **Mars in Cancer**... then you can step into **Mars in Aries** for a while... **Energy Astrology**... the practical kind, using **Audio Essences** say... allows you to do that...

Enjoy that energy for a time... use it...

But being able to do that is **NOT THE SAME** as disconnecting from your core Mars in Cancer energy... which is... and always will be hard-wired into you...

And it is the same for any energy found in your Natal Chartrt...

It's who you are... and so you will always have to return there... no matter how hard you fight and struggle against the flow of your true nature...

It's a bit like someone born and raised and living in Chicago... OK, they can go for a 2-week vacation in Florida... but they will always have to return to their home, the Windy City, the place of their birth... their friends, family and job... where they are based...

So even though you can work and express other Astrological energies (which is what transits are partially about, and which Energy Astrology AEs allow you to do)...

You still need to learn to accept and get comfortable with the energies of your Astrological Natal Chart...

Because they are who you will always come back to...

Your success in life depends on that...

Because you can never be truly fulfilled... on different levels... ***if you are pretending to be someone else...***

And also... trying to change yourself into something other...

You can waste a whole lifetime trying to do that...

DaBen, the guide of the spiritual teacher **Duane Packer**, has advised that the purpose of a lifetime is to BE the person who you came here to be... and trying to be anyone else... that can lead to a lot of wasted time and effort...

Which requires an acceptance of who you are... and a willingness to engage and express the uniqueness of your personality and energy essence...

And there is a story which I love from the **John Cleese** book, *Families & How To Survive Them*... which he co-authored with the psychiatrist **Robin Skyner**...

At the end of World War 2, a young gay man in the British military has been seriously struggling with depression and his sexual identity...

And so he goes to see the Regimental psychiatrist, to ask him if he could undergo some kind of conversion therapy... to burn-out his homosexual feelings... and turn him into acceptable heterosexual...

And psychiatrists reply:

"Well... from what I have read... those techniques don't always work... and they require years and decades of painful effort and struggle... My advice would be... accept who you are... find someone like yourself... find a quiet corner of the world, were you won't be bothered... settle down together... and try and have a happy life."

Which is exactly what he did... found someone... settled down... and they had a happy life together...

One can never understate the amazing self-transformation which comes... when you stop trying to be different to who you really are within... and accept and become the person you were

meant to be...

Stop living the life-script which others have written for you, which totally contradicts the one which has been written deep down in your own Heart...

Stop striving to be some kind of Superman...

And accept who you are... fully and completely... or as much as you can at that time... actively working towards full acceptance...

And allow yourself to become who you were meant to be...

The person you were meant to be ... on your Best Day...

And so... another useful metaphor...

The Ocean... The Clouds... The Land...

Water erases from the Ocean... via evaporation... and rises up into the sky...

That's like the Astrological Archetypal energies which create us...

Which sets our personality in motion at the moment of our birth...

Now... when the water vapour rises up into the sky, it forms into clouds, some white, some dark and grey, and each one a different size and shape...

That's like how we are each created by the same Astrological energies, to be individual and different and unique...

The same basic energies (like the coloured blocks... like the quilt patches) re-arranged within in so many different ways...

And then the clouds float overland... eventually it starts to rain... sometimes over fertile fields and sometimes over deserts...

That's how each of us, as individuals, are not only unique and different...

But we are born into different circumstances... different families... different cultures... different nations...

So it is also how our core and unique energies interact with the people and situations around us...

Sometimes the energies... inner and outer... are in harmony... and life feels good...

And sometimes the energies are in total conflict... and life is hard and a hardship...

Although it is only us who can ever kill ourselves at core, others may be able to harm our physical body, but only we have the inner ability to harm our expressed Soul...

But whatever... it's always a dance of energies...

And as they say... into each life a little rain must fall...

The question is... will it drown us... or lead to new growth and new life as the barren soil starts to reawaken?

Now... There is a long-standing tradition in Astrology, especially when someone is teaching it.

"Sorry, but we haven't got time to go through each Planet, in each Sign, and in each House... haven't got time to compile an Astrological cookbook."

And the same is true here.

And that's what we will be doing in each of the Energy Astrology books in our series... the coming Volumes... ones which focus on each of the Planets... and other Astrological energies...

The intention behind this Book is to lay down the foundations of Energy Astrology, the building blocks, and it is in the subsequent Volumes of this Series that we will be exploring the different Planet / Sign combinations.

Because we can dive in much deeper with each of the Planets, and other Astrological Formations.

But, hopefully, by now, we have covered the basics, the elements of the Energy Astrology foundation, so that we can see how it can be brought together...

And you can see it's potential... how it can help you to live more down the Good Day part of your personality spectrum.

Chapter 1: What's Next?

After completing this book, people may want to explore the **Audio Essences** which support the practical exploration of **Energy Astrology** and their own unique natal chart. They can do this in a number of ways:

- Via the free and accessible **Audio Essences** available on our **How To Club** YouTube Channel
- Via our website **www.audio-meditation.com**, where we offer a range of personal development **Audio Essences** for people to purchase, download, work with and keep
- Via our dedicated **Energy Astrology** website... **www.energy-astrology.com**... were the full range of the **Energy Astrology Audio Essences** are being put out into the publish domain... for people to also purchase, download, work with and keep

In addition to this book, **Volume 1 - Introduction**, subsequent books will focus in on specific areas of our Inner and Outer Solar

System, with a Volume devoted to each Planet, along with further Volumes exploring other Astrological elements and approaches.

When complete, this **Energy Astrology** book series will provide people with a new and comprehensive approach to Astrology, one which supports both the intellectual and feeling approaches to the Round Art. The full range of books in the **Energy Astrology** series, which will come Online during the period 2020 and 2021, is as follows:

- Volume 1: Energy Astrology – Introduction
- Volume 2: Energy Astrology – The Sun
- Volume 3: Energy Astrology – The Moon
- Volume 4: Energy Astrology – Mercury
- Volume 5: Energy Astrology – Venus
- Volume 6: Energy Astrology – Mars
- Volume 7: Energy Astrology – Jupiter
- Volume 8: Energy Astrology – Saturn
- Volume 9: Energy Astrology – Chiron
- Volume 10: Energy Astrology – Uranus
- Volume 11: Energy Astrology – Neptune
- Volume 12: Energy Astrology – Pluto
- Volume 13: Energy Astrology – The Aspects
- Volume 14: Energy Astrology – The Nodes
- Volume 15: Energy Astrology – The MC & IC
- Volume 16: Energy Astrology – The 3 Transpersonal Planets
- Volume 17: Energy Astrology – Chart Interpretation
- Volume 18: Energy Astrology – Practical Energy Astrology
- Volume 19: Energy Astrology – The 4 Elements
- Volume 20: Energy Astrology – Yin & Yang
- Volume 21: Energy Astrology – The 3 Modalities
- Volume 22: Energy Astrology – Practical Crystal Techniques
- Volume 23: Energy Astrology – Elemental Archetypes

Note: It is unlikely that the books in this series will be published in numerical order, but they will be published as and when complete.

Chapter 4-1: Crystal Antidotes for Energy Astrology

The concept and approach for the 1st Crystal Antidote originally came from an idea spark from **Dorothy Roeder's** book *Crystal Co-Creators*, where she has a whole section of crystal combinations for different issues/focuses.

In fact, the 1st Crystal Antidote (shown above) was Fear (Amethyst, Kunzite, Tanzanite)... which is shown in the photograph above... and comes from the lists in her book.

It inspired me to experiment, and so I came up with my own Crystal

Antidotes[1]... and the ones listed below tie into **Energy Astrology**, becaus they link to the major issues of Meridians/Signs and Chakras/Planets.

I probably have now identified over 300 different Crystal Antidotes, for a wide range of different issues, focuses and uses... and the majority have all gone through a proving process which involves:

- Work with **Sue Lilly** or **Sue Keeping**, two very experieced U.K. Kinseiologists, to ensure that the Crystal Antidotes indeed do what they say
- Work with my clients over time to see if they come up in a session (i.e. the **Jane Ann Dow** approach)
- Work with my students to see if they also find them useful... and they show up for *their* clients

Crystal Antidotes are usually 3 crystals, although a few contain 2 or 4 crystal combinations... but all the crystals are different... and the Crystal Antidote is a merging of their vibrations... in to a single, overall vibration.

The best way to think of Crystal Antidotes is like a string quartet. A solo violin can make music... but that violin brought together with a 2nd violin, a cello, and a viola can produce a whole range of different kinds/shapes of music.

A crystal on its own can produce a vibration that you need... but if you don't have that crystal, then a number of the *right* crystals brought together in combination can also produce the same vibration.

In essence, that is the Crystal Antidote approach.

---

1   The name *Crystal Antidote* is not the name which **Dorothy Roeder** uses, but a name which I came up with, with the help of **Sue Lilly**.

And there are some distinct advantages with Crystal Antidotes... and my students often report that time and again CAs come up for clients in a session.

Basically, a Crystal Antidote takes a negative/limiting energy and *transforms* it into a positive/enhancing energy, and are great for people who feel blocked, or who want to manifest a better path in their life. I have also discovered Crystal Qualities which allow people to step into and experience positive energy... but those are for another day, another book.

Crystal Antidotes are great for working with personal issues, and often tie into an individual's personal astrological chart, so can provide very effective and targeted relief.

Crystal Antidotes Disadvantages:

The primary advantages with Crystal Antidotes is as follows:

* *You have to buy/acquire 3 stones instead of just one.*

And... basically... that's it as far as disadvantages go... and you will see if you get involved with CAs, what I have done is as far as the 3 crystals go... tried to go for ones which are easy to obtain and relatively inexpensive (where ever possible).

Crystal Antidotes Advantages:

The primary advantages with Crystal Antidotes is as follows:

* *It may be easier to acquire the 3 stones needed for a CA then the rare and expensive crystal talked about in a Crystal Bible say. The 3 crystals may be cheaper, in total, then the expensive single crystal that the books say you need.*

- *If you a crystal therapist, and a CA comes up with a client, then you can be pretty certain that issue has arisen to be dealt with... although how you tell the client about the issue is another thing.*

- *Crystal Antidotes can be applied in a number of different ways... are suitable for different people and situations.*

- *Crystal Antidotes can be a very pleasant experience... as the energies are gently released and transformed... and there is no need to re-live or re-engage with the limiting emotion.*

I have found that Crystal Sellers love CAs as well... because instead of selling 1 crystal, they end up selling 3... and they can quote the author as saying this CA is good for this issue... and this is how you should use them too. The name of the CA tells you what it is for... which means that CAs are very, very practical.

How to Apply a Crystal Antidote:

There are a number of ways... but the 3 ways which I prefer, and which are perhaps the easiest:

Method 1: Place the 3 crystals for that Antidote together in your pocket... (or if you are a female student of **Judy Hall**... safely tucked together inside your bra)... although, as per the Note below; if you are using 2 different Antidotes simultaneously, which it may be appropriate to do, they need to be stored in different pockets (or on opposite sides of your bra), so the body doesn't get confused when reading the two energy signatures. Putting them altoegther in the same picket only creates a mash-up of the different vibrations, which the body finds confusing, and cannot read. It would be like trying to swipe two different barcodes, at the same time, and expect the computer to understand the difference.

Method 2: Place the Crystal Antidote on the Solar Plexus Chakra (all together, in a small cloth bag perhaps, or wrapped in tissue paper, with 1 Clear Quartz point above the head pointing up, and 1 Smoky Quartz point below the feet pointing down, which is a basic **Sue & Simon Lilly** layout, creating a flow of energy along the body's centreline.

Method 3: Place around the body, in a Seal of Solomon (aka. Star of David) shape... with 6 crystals, 2 of each of the ones used in the CA, located on opposite sides of the body. With Method 3, you also have the option of inter-locking 2 different CAs, with one as the *below* triangle, and the other as the *above* triangle. This way the body reads the 2 Antidotes as different and distinct... and this is a very useful approach wihen applying crystals to Energy Astrology, as we shall see.

Note: I often come across people who have 7 crystals stuffed in a pocket... "*This stone is for grounding... this stone is for self-love... this stone is for prosperity...* " that kind of thing. Now I am not saying this approach is necessarily wrong, but when viewed from the perspective of Crystal Antidotes... each stone will have its own unique vibration, but those 7 stones will also be producing a *combined vibration...* and you won't know what that combined vibration is, or whether it is 100% beneficial for you. A far more sensible approach... either dowse or muscle test to find out whether carrying those 7 crystals around in the same pocket is a good and positive thing... and also for how long you need to do it.

CRYSTAL ANTIDOTES FOR MERIDIANS & ASTROLOGICAL SIGNS

Unhappiness Crystal Antidote - Liver - Gemini:

- Amazonite
- Emerald
- Light Blue Emerald

Rage Crystal Antidote - Gallbladder - Capricorn:

- Moss Agate
- Pietersite
- Red Jasper

Anger - Heart Meridian - Leo:

- Red Carnelian
- Moonstone
- Dark Blue Sapphire

Sadness - Small Intestine Meridian - Pisces:

- Aragonite or Bronzite
- Pyrite
- Sodalite

Regret - Heart Protector Meridian - Libra:

- Blue Kyanite
- Labradorite
- Sunstone

Hopelessness - Triple Warmer Meridian - Taurus:

- Larimar
- Sunstone
- Yellow Topaz

Worry & Anxiety - Spleen Meridian - Sagittarius:

- Amethyst
- Orange Citrine
- Turquoise

Emptiness - Stomach Meridian - Cancer:

- Amethyst
- Aquamarine
- Golden Tiger's Eye

Intolerance - Lung Meridian - Aquarius:

- Green Aventurine
- Heliodor
- Blue Topaz

Guilt - Large Intestine Meridian - Virgo:

- Orange Citrine
- Charoite
- Malachite

Fear - Kidney Meridian - Aries:

- Amethyst
- Kunzite
- Tanzanite

Frustration - Bladder Meridian - Scorpio:

- Red Jasper
- Yellow Topaz
- Turquoise

CRYSTAL ANTIDOTES FOR CHAKRAS & ASTROLOGICAL PLANETS

Rejection Crystal Antidote - Heart Chakra - The Sun:

- Moss Agate
- Dark Blue Apatite
- Pyrite

Guilt Crystal Antidote - Sacral Chakra - The Moon:

- Charoite
- Malachite
- Orange Citrine

Deceit Crystal Antidote - Hand & Feet Chakras - Mercury:

- Lepidolite
- Malachite
- Morganite

Lies Crystal Antidote - Throat Chakra - Venus:

- Green Aventurine
- Rhodonite
- Turquoise

Shame Crystal Antidote - Solar Plexus Chakra - Mars:

- Yellow Apatite
- Lapis Lazulli
- Clear Quartz

Worry & Anxiety Crystal Antidote - Base Chakra - Jupiter:

- Amethyst
- Orange Citrine
- Turquoise

Inflexibility Crystal Antidote - Elbow & Knee Chakras - Saturn:

- Bloodstone
- Pyrite
- Turquoise

Unloved Crystal Antidote - Thymus Chakra - Chiron:

- Pietersite
- Sugilite
- Sunstone

Deception Crystal Antidote - Brow Chakra - Uranus:

- Labradorite
- Sunstone
- Yellow Topaz

Attachment Crystal Antidote - Crown Chakra - Neptune:

- Yellow Amblygonite
- Labradorite
- Rhodocrocite

Survival Crystal Antidote - Soma Chakra - Pluto:

* Bloodstone
* Golden Tiger's Eye
* Turquoise

The why behind each of the Planetary Crystal Antidotes we will be exloring in each of the subsequent Energy Astrology Volumes relating to that Planet.

WORKING WITH CRYSTAL ANTIDOTES FOR ENERGY ASTROLOGY

A Crystal Antidote (is usually) composed of 3 different crystals.

The traditionl Seal of Solomon crystal layout is composed of 6 crystals... either the same or different.

This means it is possible to put... to fit... 2 Crystal Antidotes within a Seal of Solomon.

But, if we standback, and consider things from a traditional Astrological perspective, then we are dealing with a Planet in a Sign.

For example:

* **Mars in Libra**
* **Jupiter in Aries**
* **Moon in Virgo**
* **Pluto in Aquarius**

But for Energy Astrology, each of the above can also be aproached via their respective linked issues, such as:

- Shame and Regret (Mars in Libra)
- Worry & Anxiety and Fear (Jupiter in Aries)
- Guilt and Guilt (Moon in Virgo)
- Survival and Intolerance (Pluto in Aquarius)

Which means, you can adapt the Seal of Solomon shape to reflect this... for that particular Planet / Sign relationship... any Astrological possibility... (and the diagram below shows this)... with each of the two interlocking triangles being made up of a particular Crystal Antidote.

So for the above 4 examples...

For **Mars in Libra**... the Shame CA is the upper triangle, and the Regret CA is the lower CA.

For **Jupiter in Aries**... the Worry & Anxiety CA is the upper triangle, and the Fear CA is the lower triangle.

For **Moon in Virgo**... the Guilt CA is the upper triangle... and *also* the lower triangle.

For **Pluto in Aquarius**... the Survival CA is the upper triangle, and the Intolerance triangle is the lower CA.

I tend to put the Planet CA as the upper triangle, and the Sign CA as the lower trianagle... but there is no real reason to say you can't have them the other way around.

If we remember back to our initial discussions on Planets and Signs... when the energy flows through a Meridian you experience the positive energy for that Meridian... and it supports the positive expression for any attached Planet... but when the energy becomes blocked in some way, and cannot flow through the Meridian, then it goes into negative expression, and so pulls the Planet down with it into a negative expression.

So all of the CAs given above help to transform negative energy, a lack of flow... thus allowing energy to flow through the Meridian again... thus supporting the Planet into an expression of its own positive energies.

Note 1: The Crystal Qualities associated with positive energies of each Meridian and Planet will be included in a future Volume in the Energy Astrology series.

Note 2: If you are someone who is unfamiliar to working with crystals... or can't source what you need... then we are putting out a range of Energy Astrology Audio Essences, which will be available on our **www.audio-meditation.com** and **www.energy-astrology. com** websites, to help you work with these energies that way.

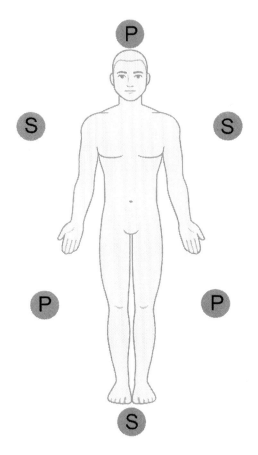

Planet-Sign Seal of Solomon Crystal Layout

If You Have Enjoyed This Book:

If you have enjoyed reading this book, then why not take a moment to give it a favourable review on Amazon or other retail websites, explaining what you found most helpful and beneficial, and why you would recommend it to others.

Any positive feedback you can provide is much appreciated, and helps support small independent publishers, such as myself, who rely on positive feedback and recommendations to get our work out to the world.

And if you have found any of the information in this book helpful, highlighting it becomes your way of passing it on to other people in similar circumstances (which is what good friends and neighbours do).

In addition, why not befriend Samarpan Alchemy on Facebook, and leave a positive recommendation there, along with any successes you may have had using these processes and techniques.

Thank you & Best Wishes!

Brian Parsons
January 2020

About the Author:

Brian was drawn to his spiritual path from early childhood, enjoying his first experience of real meditation at the age of nine, and since then he has explored a number of different meditation and personal development systems. When teaching, he is therefore able to draw upon a wide and diverse knowledge base to help his students achieve their true potential.

He has extensive experience as an energy worker, and is a trained crystal therapist with the Institute of Crystal & Gem Therapists in the U.K. He is currently an I.C.G.T. Fellow, as well as one of their tutors and internal course moderators. He is qualified in Health Kinesiology, and over the years has studied a range of different therapies and energy systems.

Brian awakened his own light body, using the techniques created by Sanaya Roman and Duane Packer and their guides Orin and Daben, in the early 1990s, and has completed many of their graduate courses to develop and enhance his skills since then. To date, he has completed the LuminEssence courses which allow him to teach the following: *Awakening Your Light Body*, *Radiance (Self-Exciting and Filling in the Frequencies)*, and *Light Body Consciousness*. He is one of the few people in the U.K. authorised by LuminEssence Productions to teach other light body teachers.

Since the early 2000s, Brian has been developing his own series of Light Body Graduate courses, along with *Energy Astrology*, a personal development course unique to Samarpan Alchemy, and which allows an individual to directly experience the energies of their natal chart.

He is deeply committed to providing students with a path of humour, commitment, integrity and trust. In return, he hopes to attract students who are prepared to make a strong and serious commitment to their own personal growth.

Brian also has a number of formal qualifications in both business and teacher training, and so is able draw upon a wide range of experience in the 'external' world to help fuel his teaching and therapy practice. His formal qualifications include a B.A. (Hons), an M.A., an M.B.A (International), and a Diploma in Teaching and Lifelong Studies.

Here is what one of his former students has written about Brian:

> *Brian Parsons is quite genuinely one of the most inspired and inspiring teachers I have come across! As a student I found myself hanging on to his every word because each word was important, no word was wasted, each informed, encouraged and inspired. His thoroughness in preparation meant that each session was packed with information and totally supported with excellent paperwork. Brian teaches so that you understand, every piece of information is digestible, meaningful and if you don't understand the first time he will patiently explain until you do. His enthusiasm raises the vibration of the group so that wonderful and unexpected openings occur.*

Christine May

Brian can be contacted through his websites, He currently lives in Devon.

Chapter 4.7: Bibliography

Robin Antepara, **Aspects: A New Approach to Understanding the Planetary Relationships**, Llewellyn Publications, December 2006.

Stephen Arroyo, **Exploring Jupiter: Astrological Key to Progress, Prosperity and Potential**, CRCS Publications, February 1995.

Gwyneth Bryan, **Houses: A Contemporary Guide**, Llewellyn Publications, August 2006.

Barbara Hand Clow, **Chiron: Rainbow Bridge Between Inner & Outer Planets**, Llewellyn Publications, 2005.

Mihaly Csikzentmihalyi, **Flow: The Psychology of Happiness**, Rider, 2002.

Darby Costello, **The Astrological Moon**, Centre for Psychological Psychology, January 1996.

Darby Costello, **Earth & Air**, Raven Dream Press, August 2018.

Darby Costello, **Water & Fire**, Raven Dream Press, January 2019.

Dr John F. Demartini, **The Breakthrough Experience: A Revolutionary New Approach to Personal Transformation**, Hay House, 2002.

Hazel Dixon-Cooper, **Harness Astrology's Bad Boy: A Handbook for Conquering Pluto's Tumultuous Transits**, Beyond Words Publishing, July 2015.

Reinhold Ebertein, **The Combination of Stellar Influences, American Federation of Astrology**, December 2004.

Freda Edis, **The God Between: A Study of Astrological Mercury**, Penguin Arkhana, 1995.

Adam Gainsberg, **Chiron: The Wisdom of a Deeply Open Heart**, Soulsign, September 2006.

Liz Greene, Lynn Bell, Darby Costello, Melanie Reinhart, **The Mars Quartet: Four Seminars on the Astrology of the Red Planet**, Centre for Psychological Psychology, December 2001.

Liz Greene & Howard Sasportas, **Dynamics of the Unconscious - Seminars in Psychological Astrology - Volume 1**, Red Wheel/Weiser, November 1990.

Liz Greene & Howard Sasportas, **Dynamics of the Unconscious - Seminars in Psychological Astrology - Volume 2**, Red Wheel/Weiser, November 1988.

Liz Greene & Howard Sasportas, **The Luminaries: Psychology of the Sun & Moon**, Red Wheel/Weiser, May 1992.

Liz Greene & Howard Sasportas, **Inner Planets: Building Blocks of Personal Reality**, Red Wheel/Weiser, January 1993.

Liz Greene, **Barriers & Boundaries: The Horoscope and Defenses of the Personality**, January 1996.

Liz Greene, **Saturn: A New Look At An Old Devil**, Weiser Books, August 2011.

Liz Greene, **The Dark of the Soul: Psychopathology in the Horoscope**, Centre for Psychological Psychology, February 2015.

Liz Greene, **The Horoscope in Manifestation: Psychology & Prediction**, Centre for Psychological Psychology, January 2016.

Liz Greene, **Astrological Neptune & The Quest for Redemption**, Red Wheel/Weiser, December 2000.

Liz Greene, **The Outer Planets & Their Cycles: The Astrology of the Collective**, Centre for Psychological Psychology, July 2005.

Liz Greene, **The Art of Stealing Fire: Uranus in the Horoscope**, Centre for Psychological Psychology, September 2004.

Liz Greene, **Apollo's Chariot: The Meaning of the Astrological Sun**, Centre for Psychological Psychology, October 2014.

Steven Forrest, **The Book of Astrology: Finding Wisdom in Darkness with Astrology**, Seven Paws Press, December 2012.

Charles Harvey, **Anima Mundi: The Astrology of the Individual and the Collective**, Centre for Psychological Psychology, February 2012.

Valerie Hunt, **The Invisible Mind: Science of the Human Vibrations of Consciousness**, Malibu Publishing Co., 1996.

Anodea Judith, **Eastern Body, Western Mind, Psychology and the Chakra System as a Path to Self**, Celestial Arts, 2004.

Alice Loffreddo, **Healing the Karmic Wounds: Chiron & Pluto**, Inkwater Press, April 2018.

Martin Lass, **Chiron: Healing Body & Soul**, Llewellyn Publications, October 2005.

Simon Lilly, **The Crystal Healing Guide**, Thorsons, February 2017.

Sue Lilly, **Healing with Astrology**, Capall Bann Publishing, January 2002.

A.T.Mann, **The Round Art: Astrology of Time & Space**, Paper Tiger, 1979.

A.T.Mann, **The Divine Life: Astrology & Reincarnation**, Vega, September 2002.

Clare Martin, **Mapping the Psyche: An Introduction to Psychological Astrology - Volume 1 - The Planets & Zodiac Signs**, The Wessex Astrologer, February 2016.

Clare Martin, **Mapping the Psyche: An Introduction to Psychological Astrology - Volume 2 - The Planetary Aspects and the Houses of the Horoscope**, The Wessex Astrologer, February 2016.

Clare Martin, **Mapping the Psyche: An Introduction to Psychological Astrology - Volume 3 - Kairos, the Astrology of Time**, The Wessex Astrologer, February 2016.

Damo Mitchell, **The Four Dragons and Clearing the Meridians and Awakening the Spine in Nei Gong (Daoist Nei Gong)**, Jessica

Energy Astrology

Kingsley Publishers, 2014.

Brian Parsons, **Energy Boundaries How to Protect & Affirm Your Personal Space, Volume** 1, Samarpan Alchemy Publishing, 2018.

Brian Parsons, **Energy Boundaries How to Protect & Affirm Your Personal Space, Volume 2**, Samarpan Alchemy Publishing, 2018.

Melanie Reinhart, **Chiron &The Healing Journey**, Starwalker Press, February 2010.

Melanie Reinhart, **Saturn, Chiron & The Centaurs**, Starwalker Press, June 2011.

Melanie Reinhart, **Incarnation: The Four Angles & The Moon's Nodes**, Starwalker Press, September 2014.

Dorothy Roeder, **Crystal Co-Creators**, Light Technology Publishing, 1995.

Howard Sasportas, **The Gods of Change: Crisis & The Transits of Uranus, Neptune & Pluto**, The Wessex Astrologer, June 2007.

Howard Sasportas, **The Twelve Houses: Exploring the Houses of the Horoscope**, Flare Publications, August 2007.

Howard Sasportas, **Direction and Destiny in the Birth Chart**, Centre for Psychological Psychology, January 2002.

Jan Spiller, **Astrology for the Soul**, Dell Publishing, October 1997.

Erin Sullivan, **Venus & Jupiter**, Centre for Psychological Psychology, January 1996.

Richard Tarnas, **Cosmos & Psyche: Intimations of a New World View**, Plume, January 2008.

Bill Tierney, **Dynamics of Aspect Analysis**, CRCS Publications, October 1983.

Bill Tierney, **The Twelve Faces of Saturn: Your Guardian Angel Planet**, Llewellyn Publications, April 1998.

Bill Tierney, **Alive & Well with Uranus: Transits of Self-Awakening**, Llewellyn Publications, January 2000.

Bill Tierney, **Alive & Well with Neptune: Transits of the Heart & Soul**, Llewellyn Publications January 2000.

Bill Tierney, **Alive & Well with Pluto: Transits of Power & Renewal**, Llewellyn Publications, January 2000.

Sue Tompkins, **Aspects in Astrology: A Guide to Understanding Planetary Relationships in the Horoscope**, Destiny Books, January 2004.

Sue Tompkins, **The Contemporary Astrologers Handbook**, Flare Publications, May 2007.

Jeffrey Wolf Green, **Pluto: The Evolutionary Journey of the Soul - Volume 1**, The Wessex Astrologer, May 2011.

Jeffrey Wolf Green, **Uranus: Freedom from the Known**, CreateSpace Publishing, June 2016.

Jeffrey Wolf Green, **Pluto: Volume 2: The Soul's Evolution Through Relationships**, The Wessex Astrologer, July 2009.

Jeffrey Wolf Green, **Neptune: Whispers from Eternity**, CreateSpace Publishing, June 2016.

* * * * * * * * * *

Printed in Great Britain
by Amazon